Embodied Hope

Embodied Hope

— *A Homiletical Theology Reflection* —

Veronice Miles

CASCADE *Books* • Eugene, Oregon

EMBODIED HOPE
A Homiletical Theology Reflection

Copyright © 2021 Veronice Miles. All rights reserved. Except for brief quotations in critical publications or reviews, no part of this book may be reproduced in any manner without prior written permission from the publisher. Write: Permissions, Wipf and Stock Publishers, 199 W. 8th Ave., Suite 3, Eugene, OR 97401.

Cascade Books
An Imprint of Wipf and Stock Publishers
199 W. 8th Ave., Suite 3
Eugene, OR 97401

www.wipfandstock.com

PAPERBACK ISBN: 978-1-5326-9986-3
HARDCOVER ISBN: 978-1-5326-9987-0
EBOOK ISBN: 978-1-5326-9988-7

Cataloguing-in-Publication data:

Names: Miles, Veronice, author.

Title: Embodied hope : a homiletical theology reflection / Veronice Miles.

Description: Eugene, OR: Cascade Books, 2021. | Includes bibliographical references and index.

Identifiers: ISBN 978-1-5326-9986-3 (paperback). | ISBN 978-1-5326-9987-0 (hardcover). | ISBN 978-1-5326-9988-7 (ebook).

Subjects: LCSH: Preaching. | African American preaching. | Womanist theology. | Hope—Religious aspects—Christianity. | Despair—Religious aspects—Christianity. | Pastoral theology.

Classification: BV4221 M4 2021 (print). | BV4221 (ebook).

12/22/21

Scripture quotations are from New Revised Standard Version Bible: Catholic Edition, copyright © 1989, 1993 National Council of the Churches of Christ in the United States of America. Used by permission. All rights reserved worldwide.

Scripture quotations marked (NKJV) are taken from the New King James Version®. Copyright © 1982 by Thomas Nelson. Used by permission. All rights reserved.

To My Parents, The Reverend William Arthur Miles
and Mrs. Ollie Louise Miles Johnson

and

My Stepfather, Mr. Orlando Johnson
Your legacies continue to nurture my sense of well-being!
With Love and Gratitude

Contents

Acknowledgments | ix

Introduction: Is There a Word from the Lord? | 1
1 Toward an Embodied Theology of Hope | 14
2 Culturally Induced Despair Revealed | 33
3 Disclosing the Dangers of Culturally Induced Despair | 60
4 The Anticipatory Language of Hope | 110
5 The Disruptive and Energizing Power of Proclamation | 136
6 The Courageously Audacious Practice of Hope | 172
Epilogue: Contemplating Embodied Hope | 219

Appendix: A Critical Analysis for Preaching | 223
Bibliography | 227
Index | 241

Acknowledgments

THIS BOOK WOULD NOT be possible without the support and encouragement of a broad range of mentors, colleagues, friends, and kin who journeyed with me throughout the process. I owe gratitude to the faculty, administration, and board of the Wesley Theological Seminary for granting me sabbatical time and a course reduction in the subsequent semester to work on major portions of this project. President David McCallister-Wilson, Dean Phil Wingeier-Rayo, preaching colleagues Lucy L. Hogan and William "Bobby" McClain, each of you were significant sources of support as I brought this project to completion; thank you. Immense appreciation to my writing partner, colleague, and friend Renee K. Harrison for your consummate support throughout the process of developing this book. Your wisdom, insightful feedback, willingness to listen to me think through various aspects of the writing, and gentle challenges helped me sharpen and give form to the embodied theology of Hope and reflection on preaching I offer in this writing. Your current work on the contribution of enslaved laborers to the construction of Washington, DC serves as a poignant reminder of the necessity of new theologies of Hope. Thank you, Renee; we anticipate your upcoming publication.

The language "labor of love" describes well the process of writing this book. This book began as series of questions during my graduate studies about the source from which Hope arises and what it might take to activate Hope in a more substantive and robust manner. In a graduate school paper, I explored the life of Sojourner Truth with the intent of completing a psychological profile that would reveal the source of her audacious declaration, "Ain't I a woman too?" I soon realized the tools of psychological analysis were ill-equipped for such a task, as Sojourner's capacity to live with Hope came from reservoirs deeper than thought, emotion, or praxis. Sojourner taught me the value of hearing and reflecting upon stories and honoring their capacity to invite deep reflection upon our own stories and the quality of our relationship with God, self, and others. My appreciation goes out to Sojourner and to the two groups of contemporary women who entrusted me with your stories during the seminal years of my investigation of Hope. Your powerful ruminations created fertile ground for theological and praxiological reflection and reimagination. May Love, Faith, and Hope abide with each of you.

From my earliest musings about Hope, Brian J. Mahan journeyed with me, adeptly reading and commenting on every aspect of my then inchoate writing about Hope. Brian, you challenged me toward deeper theological reflection, bolder reimagination, and broader engagement with thinkers, some of whom I might have otherwise omitted. Mentor, colleague, and friend, thank you. To Teresa Fry Brown, who affirmed my voice in preaching, nurtured my confidence to stand in prohibited spaces, and continually exemplifies what it means to embody excellence in teaching and preaching, thank you for your wisdom, insight, and mentoring presence. Diane M. Stewart, thank you for introducing me to womanist theology and thought—I fell in love. Thomas Long, deep appreciation for your wisdom, insight, and advocacy throughout my time in theological education. Thank you for providing me the space to write and think as I gave form to this project. Gail O'Day, you left us too soon, but your wisdom lingers still. Katherine Turpin, Jill Crainshaw, and Diane Lipsett, thank you for reading and responding to earlier iterations of this work.

Colleagues in my broader connection have supported and encouraged me throughout this process. I offer appreciation to the Academy of Homiletics and its Black Caucus and Executive Committee, the Fund for Theological Exploration, the Wabash Center for Teaching and Learning in Theology and Religion, and the Engle Institute of the Princeton Theological Seminary. Frank Thomas, thank you for your gentle yet direct nudge in 2019 for me to secure a publisher and complete this work. Words of appreciation go to the numerous scholars and practitioners who have mentored me directly and from afar, especially womanist and Black feminist scholars whose work contribute significantly to my own. Over the years, many have afforded me opportunities to preach, teach, lecture, conduct workshops, and participate in other forms of pastoral ministry—you keep me grounded. The classroom is also one of those grounding spaces. To my students from Wesley Theological Seminary, Wake Forest University School of Divinity, and Candler School of Theology, thank you for the opportunity to teach and learn with you.

Family and friends, you have provided bread for the journey throughout the process of writing this book. I stand proudly in the legacy of my parents, Rev. W. A. Miles and Mrs. Ollie L. Miles Johnson—everyday God-fearing, working-class folk from Georgia and Florida whose faith moved mountains. Memories of you continue to nurture my sense of well-being in every way imaginable. I also honor my stepfather, Orlando Johnson, who nurtured the Miles children after my father's death. My brother Arthur, the elder of our family, has been a constant source of encouragement and support for which I am immensely grateful. My siblings, nieces, nephews, great-nieces and -nephews, godchildren, and close friends are too numerous to name, so please accept a collective thank-you for your biased and unwavering support of me and the work I do. I say again, you provided bread for the journey, literally and metaphorically, and I could not have asked for a richer and more loving community of support. To the ancestors, I give thanks.

Thanks be to God for all that God has done and for the ways the Spirit continues to work in and through me and numerous other travelers on the journey toward a more loving, just, and life-affirming existence for all creation.

INTRODUCTION

Is There a Word from the Lord?

(Jeremiah 37:17a)

On Sunday, July 10, 2016, congregations across the nation gathered for worship asking, *"Is there some word from the Lord?"* News of the latest fatalities in a series of tragic shootings in our nation had filled the airwaves throughout the week, and people wanted to hear some word of assurance that God is still speaking, still present, still active in our world today. On July 5, 2016, two White police officers fatally shot Alton Sterling, a thirty-seven-year-old Black man in Baton Rouge, Louisiana. This shooting added fuel to an already smoldering fire of distrust between law enforcement and African American communities. Sparked by the not-guilty verdict in the case against George Zimmerman, who shot and killed Trayvon Martin in 2012, and by the police shooting and subsequent death of Michael Brown on April 9, 2014, in Ferguson, Missouri, many African Americans questioned law enforcement's commitment to securing justice on their behalf. The fire of distrust flared when on July 6, 2016, police shot and killed Philando Castile, a thirty-two-year-old Black man, during a traffic stop in Falcon Heights, Minnesota, as his girlfriend and their four-year-old daughter, passengers in the car, watched in horror. Immediately after the officer fired, Castile's girlfriend, Diamond Reynolds, began streaming the shooting live on Facebook, leaving all who viewed it to ingest and decipher what they were witnessing and experiencing.[1]

Numerous people expressed frustration and disbelief on social media. Thousands took to the streets across the nation in protest, emphatically denouncing and lamenting acts of arbitrary violence against Black-bodied individuals in America. The rallying cry "Black lives matter" rang from urban centers and small towns alike, not in devaluation of other lives, but

1. Domonoske, "Minnesota Gov."

as an affirmation of Black people's inherent value as human beings and as American citizens. National and international news outlets covered the stories, unveiling what was then the latest chapter in the tragic national saga of police and other violence against Black Americans, to which no end seemed apparent. Then, as if these two killings were not heart-wrenching enough, the following evening, a peaceful Black Lives Matter march in Dallas, Texas, became the scene of gunfire. Micah Xavier Johnson, a Black Army veteran who expressed anger about police shootings of Black men, opened fire on Dallas police, killing five officers and wounding seven other officers and two civilians. People across the nation were stunned.

The anguish and grief that engulfed the nation on July 10, 2016, was also palpable as people crowded into the sanctuary of our local congregation, the United Metropolitan Missionary Baptist Church in Winston Salem, North Carolina. We, like the nation at-large, were perplexed and brokenhearted by the shootings, violence, and senseless death. All of which compounded our fear that the cords intended to bind us together had been irreparably damaged. Tragedy, loss, and grief had become all too common, and relief was nowhere in sight. Even as we held in our hearts the tragedies of the previous week, we could not forget the 2015 slaying at Mother Emmanuel African Methodist Episcopal (AME) Church in downtown Charleston. The shooter, Dillon Roof, killed nine congregants after joining them in Bible study, including the Reverend Dr. Clementa Pickney, a South Carolina legislator and the congregation's pastor. We were perplexed by the 2016 shootings at the Inland Regional Center in San Bernardino, California, and the terrible massacre at Pulse Nightclub in Orlando, Florida.[2] We were heartbroken over the police shooting of twelve-year-old Tamir Rice in 2014, and stunned at Sandra Bland's apparent suicide while in jail following a traffic stop in 2015.[3] Eric Garner's cry, "I can't breathe," arrested us in 2014, only to ring out again in 2020 when George Floyd uttered the same words as he died at the hands of a police officer who knelt on his neck for 9 minutes and 29 seconds.[4] We would surely have wailed a preemptive lament as we gathered for Sunday worship that day in July 2016 if we could have anticipated the senseless murder of Botham Jean in 2018, and the killings of Ahmaud Aubery, George Floyd, and Breonna Taylor in 2020—all unarmed and all killed by off-duty and on-duty police officers or White vigilantes.[5] Despite our best

---

2. Ellis et al., "Orlando shooting"; Ahmed and Ellis, "Mass Shooting."

3. Izadi and Holley, "Video Shows Cleveland Officer"; Montgomery, "The Death of Sandra Bland."

4. Lowery, "'I Can't Breathe'"; Bogel-Burroughs, "8 Minutes, 46 Seconds."

5. Allyn, "Ex-Dallas Officer"; Fausset, "Two Weapons"; Haines, "Breonna Taylor."

INTRODUCTION: IS THERE A WORD FROM THE LORD?

efforts to approach life as *normal*, these tragic events and more stagger us in magnitude and frequency. They create *a troubling in our souls* too deep for utterance and too painful to ignore.

But there was more than grief and bewilderment in our congregation on July 10, 2016. Many who gathered on that day came expecting, anticipating, desiring a word from the Lord. Words of assurance that the growing malaise in our nation—the maladies that prevent us from seeing the *Godness* in each other—would not utterly consume us. Like the metaphorical mother Rachel in Jer 31:15, whose inconsolable tears and bitter lamentation for her "children who were no more" resounded throughout Ramah, we were in mourning. And, as Rachel called upon God to restore her people, we too came to worship longing for and seeking God's restorative presence in this death-dealing moment. We gathered for worship—mothers and fathers, youths and elders, students and educators, law enforcement and community activists, administrators, professionals, retirees, faithful believers, seekers, congregational regulars, and guests—not to be placated by churchly platitudes, but to discern a faithful response to the tragic circumstances encompassing our lives.

As we clergy began the processional down the long aisle of the church, we knew we could not allow tragedy and death to speak the final word. We also knew the fearful presence of evil would not permit easy answers to the unsettling questions people were asking about God's presence among us and about how believers might faithfully respond at times such as the present. This moment required a meaningful and exacting word, a Hope-filled prophetic utterance that could meet us where we were but not leave us where it found us. With eyes fixed upon the black-robed-clergy processional making its way to the pulpit, the gathered community awaited words of Hope to heal our wounded souls. Their anticipatory gaze exerted a claim upon our lives, issued a call we could not ignore. For they demanded of us, clergy women and men, a faithful response to the tragedy, loss, and grief so palpably present among us. And that was our challenge, to discern a word that could break through the dissonance of this tragic moment, awaken hearts to the voice of Hope, and equip us to discern a faithful response.

As we took one step and then another, our silent prayers echoed the prayer we voiced just minutes before in the pastor's office as we prepared for morning worship: "God grant us the wisdom and strength we need to assure this community of your power, faithfulness, and redemptive presence, even in the deepest tragedies of our world. Lord have mercy upon us, we pray. In the name of Jesus, the Christ. Amen."[6] The praise team was just concluding the

---

6. Loosely recalled.

morning devotional as we ascended the steps to the pulpit. Standing there in God's presence and before the gathered community, we humbly awaited some word from the Lord. Is there a word from the Lord for times such as these, or will tragedy, loss, and grief overwhelm the claims of the gospel? How do we proclaim Hope when life is, in the words of hymn-writer Thomas A. Dorsey, "Like a ship that's tossed and driven, battered by an angry sea"?[7] Where do we find the courage to keep proclaiming, "the Lord will make a way somehow" when *somehow* seems improbable and so far away?

This book is addressed to all pastors, and, ultimately, to all who find themselves in this place. All who are called upon to proclaim the Hope of the gospel in the face of challenges that negate the possibility of God's *somehow* and threaten to plunge us into the depths of despair. This book is for faithful proclaimers who are tired, weary, and worn but stand to proclaim Hope even as the deceptive voice of despair threatens to overshadow, or worse, annul the claims of the gospel. Eventually, of course, this includes all of us—all who occupy space or stand in solidarity with communities for whom personal tragedy, loss, and grief are no strangers. It includes all those who worry that the ever-widening divide in our nation arising from our varying and at times divergent interests, identities, and commitments may never find resolution. This book is written for all who ache for a word that can embolden people of faith to live with Hope and embrace the promise of the gospel.

Faithful proclaimers lean into these challenges. We share Emilie Townes's conviction in *Embracing the Spirit: Womanist Perspectives on Hope, Salvation and Transformation*: "I am convinced that evil and suffering should never be our last and only word about the nature of humanity and the ways in which the divine works in our lives."[8] The presence of evil and suffering is not determinative for our potential as human beings. We are the *imago Dei* (image of God), created to live as an expression of divine presence in the earth. And, despite the despairing realities of life or the threat they pose for our ability to remember who we are and of what we consist, God continually fills us with Hope, so that we, with all creation, might be whole again.

It is my desire that this book contribute to a growing interdisciplinary conversation about the necessity of Hope and its implications for our shared existence.[9] I am particularly interested in the power and poten-

---

7. Dorsey, "The Lord Will Make a Way Somehow."

8. Townes, "Introduction," xi.

9. See Crawford, *Hope in the Holler*; Parker, *Trouble Don't Last Always*; Moltmann, *Theology of Hope*; Alves, *A Theology of Human Hope*; Long, *Preaching from Memory to Hope*; Powery, *Dem Dry Bones*; Thomas Aquinas, *Summa Theologiæ*; Williams, *Sisters*

tial of preaching to awaken individuals and communities to the voice of Hope and nurture Hope-filled action even in the most chaotic of times. My disciplinary foci in homiletics and religious education; my identity as womanist scholar, teacher, and preacher in church and academy; and my formation in the teachings and preaching of the Black church coalesce to fuel my interest in exploring Christian theologies of Hope and their praxiological implications. My interests in the practice of preaching and its significance for our ability to live with Hope also invite me to reimagine the theological language with which we speak about Hope and to think reflectively about the starting point for this homiletical reflection. I add my voice to the growing list of womanist scholars in homiletics whose theological and praxiological reflections enrich the homiletical discourse, including Teresa Fry Brown, Donna Allen, Kimberly Johnson, and Lisa L. Thompson.[10] Their scholarship embodies N. Lynn Westfield's description of womanist epistemology as "grounded in the notion that change, reframing, re-thinking, re-imagining, re-naming, re-structuring, re-conceiving—birthing anew, is not only possible but also necessary."[11] The conversation to which I invite us embodies homiletical, theological, and praxiological reimaging regarding the contextual and theological starting points for an embodied theology of Hope, for preaching's role in amplifying the voice of Hope, and for the practices such proclamation cultivates.

The formative experiences I name above enable me to approach Hope from the perspective of individuals and communities who have too long experienced violence, suffering, oppression, and other forms of dehumanization as a daily reality in their lives. I am not the first to approach Hope from this starting point or to consider the necessity of Christian praxis for our ability to live with Hope. Scholars of and practitioners in religious education, educational theory, theology, and philosophy enrich our reflections on praxis, including Patricia Hill Collins, Paulo Freire, Maria Harris, Katherine Turpin, Michael Warren, Paul Ricœur, and an array of theorists and practitioners in various other disciplines.[12] Voices in the conversation about theological starting points include womanist scholars A. Elaine Crawford, Evelyn Parker,

---

in the Wilderness; Townes, Breaking the Fine Rain of Death; Townes. ed., Embracing the Spirit; Brueggemann Hope in History; Brueggemann, The Prophetic Imagination; Giroux, On Critical Pedagogy; Moss, Blue Note Preaching; Griffen, The Fierce Urgency.

10. Brown, God Don't Like Ugly; Brown, Weary Throats and New Songs; Allen, Toward a Womanist Homiletic; Thompson, Ingenuity.

11. Westfield, "Toward a Womanist Approach," 134.

12. Collins, Black Feminist Thought; Cone, God of the Oppressed; Harris, Teaching and Religious Imagination, Turpin, Branded; Warren, Seeing through the Media; Ricœur, History and Truth.

Emilie Townes, and Delores Williams; liberationist scholars Rubem Alves, James Cone, and Gustavo Gutiérrez; and biblical scholar Walter Brueggemann; among others. These scholars rescue Hope from the theological eschaton as its primary home and invite expressions of Hope that seek divine and human responses to the despairing realities of the present even as we live toward the future. They remind us that attentiveness to Hope's resonance in the midst of the despairing realities of life is an ontological necessity. It is necessary for life, for survival, for emancipation, and for a just and life-affirming future for ourselves and generations to come. Thus, as we await Christ's ultimate return, we are also called to embrace purposeful, Hope-filled action that can lead to a qualitatively better state of existence in the meantime. Other important voices in the larger discourse include those of Thomas Aquinas, Jürgen Moltmann, Thomas Long, and others whose reflections on Hope accentuate God's enduring faithfulness. These scholars call upon Christian people to live in anticipation of Christ's return and in expectation of the ultimate fulfilment of God's promises. They remind us the God who has been faithful in the past remains faithful even now.

So, why another theological reflection on Hope? I enter this conversation with three important questions in mind. The first involves the theological language with which we speak about Hope. In his seminal work *Theology of Hope*, Moltmann turned theology on its head by claiming that eschatology is not the doctrine of things to come but rather the doctrine of Christian Hope. Specifically, he writes, "Eschatology means the doctrine of Christian hope, which embraces both the object hoped for and also the hope inspired by it."[13] He continues, "For Christian faith lives from the raising of the crucified Christ, and strains after the promises of the universal future of Christ. Eschatology is the passionate suffering and passionate longing kindled by the Messiah."[14] I do not disagree with Moltmann's basic contention that Christians anticipate and await the return of Christ. I am concerned, however, that the long delay of the parousia has in many cases rendered Christian people numb to Hope's presence within. And as I will claim in Chapter 4, because the gospel is the archetypal reservoir from which Hope's anticipatory language flows, the delay alongside preoccupation with the *things of this world* (read: money, position, power, privilege) have rendered far too many Christian people of faith listless regarding the praxiological implications and the ethic to which the gospel invites us. Preoccupation makes it difficult for us to sense the voice of Hope within, calling us not to the end of all things but to patterns of perceiving,

13. Moltmann, *Theology of Hope*, 17.
14. Moltmann, *Theology of Hope*, 17.

thinking, imagining, and behaving that make possible a more loving, just, and God-infused existence in the present. I am concerned that we have set our sights so intently upon the eschatological return of Christ, that we are straining so ardently toward the end, that we risk forfeiting the opportunity to live with Hope in the present by embracing the ethic to which Jesus's gospel proclamation calls us. What is needful, I propose, are new or renewed ways of speaking and thinking about Hope.

I ground this exploration in an embodied theology of Hope. This theological understanding affirms Hope as an expression of God's presence within each of us by virtue of our inherent identity as *imago Dei*. It also affirms humanity's capacity to live responsive to Hope's assurance and call by imagining and living in anticipation of a new reality, which biblical writers characterize as the kin(g)dom of God or kin(g)dom of heaven. M. Shawn Copeland's embodied theology significantly informs my understanding of embodiment and Hope as subjects of theological reflection.[15] The designation *embodied Hope*, therefore, denotes Hope's enduring presence within each of us. It is a conceptual metaphor for *that which creates within human persons yearning for wholeness and well-being, the always-speaking voice of God's Spirit assuring us of God's presence, power, and fidelity and calling us toward loving, just, and restorative action*. Embodied Hope is also anticipatory in nature. It acknowledges that the world as we know it is not yet what it should be and invites us to imagine and work toward a more loving, just, and God-infused existence. And we do so, not only in times of crisis, but also in the day-to-dayness of our lives.

Given my first concern for ensuring that we do not forfeit the opportunity to acknowledge Hope's assurance and call and respond in the here and now, my second consideration has to do with embodied Hope's relationship to Jesus's gospel proclamation. Reflection upon Jesus's proclamation of the good news of God's unfolding reign, the kin(g)dom of God or kin(g)dom of heaven, and its potential as a symbol or metaphor of Hope, reinforces the foundation upon which embodied Hope rests.[16] As a metaphor of Hope, the kin(g)dom of God signifies what we can expect of God, of ourselves, and of our world in light of Jesus's ministerial vision. In Matt 4:17 and Mark 1:15, Jesus urges his followers to repent, to turn *away from* self- and other-destructive attitudes and practices and *toward* a new ethic in which love of God and love of neighbor as ourselves are normative patterns for human relationships. Jesus describes this new ethical dimension as the *kin(g)dom of*

---

15. See Copeland, *Enfleshing Freedom*.

16. Williams, *Sisters in the Wilderness*, 165–66; Brueggemann, *The Prophetic Imagination*, 22.

God or *kin(g)dom of heaven*. These metaphors suggest an alternative image of possibility, beckoning each of us to demonstrate, through the quality of our relationship with God, self, and others that the just and life-affirming world for which we yearn is a realizable possibility. The ethical implications of the gospel evoke my third concern, which queries the praxiological significance of an embodied theology of Hope. Preaching, together with other ministries of the church, amplifies and invites responsiveness to Hope's assurance and call. Through preaching, we remind congregations with whom we preach as ourselves of humanity's inherent identity as *imago Dei* and call to live as a nondistorting, nondestructive reflection of God's presence in the earth. Preaching also nurtures imaginative abundance and purposeful, Hope-filled action as articulations of Faith and expressions of Hope. Proclamation of the gospel through preaching, therefore, is an expression of Hope that bears witness to the possibility and efficacy of the new reality made evident in Jesus's gospel proclamation of God's emerging kin(g)dom.

Therefore, my approach to this dialogue is twofold. First, I approach this conversation convinced that preaching can serve as a conduit for eliminating distortion, revealing possibilities, and emboldening individuals and communities to live with Hope. Second, I posit that such is possible when undergirded by an embodied theology of Hope and grounded in Jesus's proclamation of the good news of God's unfolding reign, which biblical writes describe as the kin(g)dom of God or kin(g)dom of heaven.[17]

God Is Waiting for Us!

On Sunday, July 10, 2016, as we clergy processed down the aisle of the United Metropolitan Missionary Baptist Church, we were keenly aware of the grief, bewilderment, and longing that filled the space. People wanted to know if there was indeed reason to live with Hope, and if the answer is yes, where we might find Hope in times such as these. Is God still active in our world today? Does God still care about our individual and communal well-being, or has God given up on us? What role might the church play in preventing and alleviating the pain and grief of violence, suffering, and oppression? Can we mend our fractured world, heal the hurt that suffering engenders, and live true to our identity as *imago Dei*?

---

17. I use "kin(g)dom of God" and "kin(g)dom of heaven" interchangeably throughout the conversation. I also employ the parenthetical *g* as a way of acknowledging my own leanings toward kinship imagery while honoring traditional understandings of Jesus's gospel proclamation.

These questions resound throughout the Christian landscape, as pastoral leaders and congregations gather for worship in the wake of tragedies such as the events that shrouded the nation between July 5 and July 10, 2016. Discerning a faithful response is always complex. And naturally, given the vast diversity of Christian communities throughout the US and beyond, responses will vary depending upon one's context, commitments, and understandings of the church's mission and ministry. Some preachers and congregational leaders find it theologically prudent to steer clear of such complex questions, focusing instead on eternal salvation from sin and death and the gospel's significance for the lives of individual people of faith. The central task of the church, they reason, is soul salvation. Therefore, they caution against delving too deeply into sociopolitical and communal concerns lest it prove more disruptive than curative.

Another group of congregational leaders and preachers senses the need to do or say something but are hesitant about speaking. Agreeing with H. Richard Niebuhr that the church does not stand in opposition to society (Christ against culture), such leaders still struggle to find the proper balance of churchly and societal concern in Niebuhr's well-known taxonomy.[18] This level of discernment is especially needful given the polarized nature of US society and its demand that we choose sides in much of our public discourse. The danger of engaging in such discernment, of course, is that it may result in paralyzing indecision and so lead to failure—that is, to no response at all.

A third group of congregational leaders and preachers, seeking to grapple with the difficult questions the tragedies of July 5–10 and other societal concerns pose to the church's identity and ministry, chooses to respond more directly. With pastoral sensitivity to the needs of their congregations (often impacted directly), these pastoral leaders sense an imperative to address and redress the anguish and bewilderment their congregations feel. Degrees of homiletical discourse, lament, intercession, and direct action vary significantly between such congregations, as there is no one response appropriate to all situations. Yet, with prayerful discernment and a healthy dose of humility, such pastoral leaders seek to proclaim the Hope of the gospel as an alternative to the devastating sense of violation that suffering and oppression create.

On July 10, 2016, my church, United Metropolitan, was in the last category. We reflected as best we could upon the Hope of the gospel and its implications in light of the questions the week's events evoked. I was the worship leader that Sunday, and, as I recall, I welcomed the congregation

---

18. See Niebuhr, *Christ and Culture*.

by drawing attention to the events of the week and stumbling through a few words about how love is stronger than hate, and how we could not permit violence and death to have the final word. Our pastor, the Reverend Prince Raney Rivers, spoke much more eloquently.

As the preaching moment approached, the choir sang "The Potter's House," by V. Michael McKay, the sermonic selection for the day.[19] Pastor Rivers chose words from the prophet Hosea (Hos 11:1–10) as the sermon text, reiterating verses that the congregation had read earlier in the worship service. As he prepared the congregation to receive the message, he acknowledged the suffering, loss, and grief that surrounded us in that moment. Drawing inspiration from the sermonic selection, he spoke these words:

> I don't know about you, but I need some healing, need some peace; I just about ran out of joy last week, so I'm glad to be in the Lord's house. We talked about an earthquake in Haiti earlier, and last week felt like an earthquake. So, we are here today, celebrating and thanking God, and . . . listening for what the Spirit has to say.[20]

In response, the congregation offered a collective "amen," affirming the sentiment his words conveyed. Pastor Rivers's prayer sounded a similar note:

> Oh Merciful and Gracious God, we pause to give thanks to you once again, because we do know that you will have the last word. And we pray, Lord, that the word that you have for us today will stand us back up on our feet and get us ready to do what you would have for us to do. All these things we ask in the blessed name of Jesus, who is the Christ and who is your son and our savior. And the people of God said amen, amen.[21]

The sermon was the first in a five-sermon series, Prophetic Words in Modern Times. The sermon title was, "The God Who Will Not Give Up." Linking the events of the week to the words of Hosea and other biblical prophets, Pastor Rivers asserted,

> These are times when we need to hear what the prophets have to say. The prophets told us about justice; the prophets proclaimed to us the wisdom of God in time of national crisis. The prophets proclaimed Hope and a future, and we need to hear what they have to say.[22]

19. McKay, *The Potter's House*.
20. Rivers, "The God Who Will Not Give Up."
21. Rivers, "The God Who Will Not Give Up."
22. Rivers, "The God Who Will Not Give Up."

Reminding the congregation of the heartbreaking state of the nation, he highlighted the resounding question in Hosea. The state of affairs that breaks God's heart, Pastor Rivers proclaimed, is, "why do the people who God seems to love so much seem to love God so little?"[23]

As the sermon progressed, Pastor Rivers rehearsed ancient Israel's struggle to live faithful to the God who loved and called them, the same God whose heart breaks over the condition of our world today. Prompting the gathered community to remember, "God's steadfast love is our best and greatest Hope," he invited us, individually and communally, to discern the role that we might play in changing our world for the better: "While we may be waiting on God to change things in the world, the Scripture implies that there are times when God is waiting on people to make the change that we need to see!"[24]

I agree. God is waiting for us, urging us to prove God's presence in our world today. Embodied Hope reminds us that God, with wisdom and loving-kindness, created us *imago Dei*, a reflection of the divine. God also calls us to partnership, founded upon God's desire for *shalom* and made flesh in Jesus's ministerial vision and lived praxis. Partnership implies shared responsibility—that we have a role to play in ridding our world of violence; suffering; oppression; and evil, systemic injustice. We also have a role to play in the assurance of communal well-being whenever and wherever wholeness is lacking. Hope, therefore, calls us to a life of vocation, invites us to say yes to God's yes for creation and for our lives.

With this understanding, we discover that living with Hope is more extensive than responsive action or a right attitude in moments of distress. We aspire to live with Hope as a daily practice, to make God's presence known through our right relationship and high regard for the many others with whom we share our lives—through words of encouragement; through ministry of presence; through loving-kindness, celebration, creation care, lament; and, yes, the willingness to walk alongside others during the most devastating and tragic experiences of their lives.

This is a tall order, and it would be simpler if God did all the heavy lifting while humans reaped all the benefits. But that logic holds one fatal flaw. By virtue of our humanity and inherent identity as *imago Dei*, we bear an ethical responsibility to "bring to light" the God whose image we embody. God, the Creator and Impassioned Artist, views creation as good and very good, even in our flawed state. And Hope, the always-speaking voice of God's Spirit, stirs our imagination, daily reminding us that God's

---

23. Rivers, "The God Who Will Not Give Up."
24. Rivers, "The God Who Will Not Give Up."

dream for creation is becoming and can become an actuality despite all evidence to the contrary.

In the chapters that follow, I invite you into a sustained discussion of Hope as embodied presence of God's Spirit, of its significance for our lives, and of the role of preaching in emboldening individuals and communities to live with Hope. This Introduction lays the foundation for our conversation. Here I thought it important to contextualize our discussion so that we could remember that Hope is an ontological necessity, not simply at the conceptual level, but as lived experience and praxis. The Introduction also creates the scaffolding for our discussion of Hope as embodied theology, of Hope's efficacy in the lives of human persons, and of Hope's implications for the quality of our relationship with God, self, others, and the creation God calls good.

Chapter 1, "Towards an Embodied Theology of Hope," explores the necessity of embodied Hope with specificity, giving attention to its efficacy in the lives of human persons and its implications for the quality of our relationship with God, self, others, and the creation God calls good. Chapter 1 also introduces culturally induced despair, an insidious mechanism and enemy of Hope. Culturally induced despair and the negating and dehumanizing attitudes and practices it produces distort and distract us from living responsively to Hope's assurance and call

In Chapters 2 through 4, I employ the metaphor *language*, a heuristic device for revealing the powerful communicative, epistemological, and symbolic significance of image, myth, ideology, and theology for our patterns of thought, feeling, and interaction. Therefore, in each chapter, I invite consideration of the language's etymology, content, mode of communication, and implications for our lives. In Chapter 2, "Culturally Induced Despair Revealed," I identify *culturally induced despair* as a persistent threat to our ability to sense Hope's presence and embrace God's vision of *shalom*. Against the backdrop of persistently threatening individual and cultural realities, I reveal the insidious and deceptive nature of culturally induced despair and identify the deceptive language of despair as the system of communication through which culturally induced despair is propagated.

Under the title "Disclosing the Dangers," Chapter 3 expands our dialogue about culturally induced despair and its nefarious system of communication. Attending to culturally induced despair's theological and sociological implications, I identify two dangers. The first danger lurks in despair's potential for creating and perpetuating a distorted and deceptive view of reality and of our identity and capacity as human beings. The second danger arises in culturally induced despair's potential for creating imaginative dearth, for propagating the belief that life is static and unchangeable, and that new possibilities are unattainable. Highlighting two of the primary means by which Christian people of faith encounter the deceptive language of despair, this chapter explores the potential of iconic misrepresentation and of theological and ecclesial misrepresentation to cultivate patterns of perceiving, thinking, and behaving that provoke and sustain culturally induced despair.

The threat of culturally induced despair feels all-encompassing. Accepted as truth, its deceptive assertions provoke us to believe there are no alternatives to the world of violence, suffering, and oppression that currently exists. But this distorted view of reality does not have the final word. In Chapter 4, "The Anticipatory Language of Hope," I explore Hope as the antidote to culturally induced despair, giving attention to embodied Hope's potential for engendering anticipatory imagination and purposeful, Hope-filled action (lived praxis). This chapter will also explore the kin(g)dom of God as a metaphor of Hope, focusing significantly upon the links between Jesus's proclamation of the kin(g)dom of God or kin(g)dom heaven and Hope as theological praxis in our lives today.

Chapter 5, "The Disruptive and Energizing Power of Proclamation," draws our attention to the practice of preaching by revealing preaching's significance as a conduit of Hope and transformation. Preaching, grounded in an embodied theology of Hope, makes Hope's voice perceptible by eliminating distortion, revealing possibilities, and emboldening individuals and communities to live with Hope. The final chapter, "The Courageously Audacious Practice of Hope," expands our dialogue by naming and celebrating individuals and communities who exemplify the courage and audacity to live with Hope in seemingly impossible situations. Drawing upon the African American journey toward justice and equality as a case study and Rev. Dr. Martin Luther King Jr.'s dream of the beloved community as a heuristic backdrop, those of us desiring to preach an embodied theology of Hope today take a trek through history so as to gain wisdom from the journey. This is the path we will travel together as we explore Hope as embodied theology and lived praxis and the role of preaching in emboldening individuals and communities to live with Hope.

— 1 —

Toward an Embodied Theology of Hope

> We seriously doubt the possibility of the very things that we most want... For all that we dream about, we find ourselves content to live out the weary drama of the nightmare—to accept the is-ness of our lives as the ought and to find ways to short-circuit the Hope found in possibilities and daring to reach beyond what we ever thought ourselves capable of.[1]
>
> —Emilie Townes

Focus upon an embodied theology of Hope responds to a problem that has plagued humanity for millennia: our reluctance and, at times, inability to acknowledge each other and ourselves as *imago Dei*. Convinced of our fallenness and sinful nature, we tolerate domination, division, and discord as inevitable aspects of human identity. "We are only human," we come to believe, perpetuating the self-consoling epitaph of humanity's fated existence. We *are* only human, which in Christian theological anthropology marks us as beings created in the image of God. We are also overwhelmed by the idea that a loving Creator would gift humanity with the capacity to love as God loves. In glimpses and glances we wonder if we might be capable of such love. But filled with doubt, "we find ourselves content to live out the weary drama of the nightmare—to accept the is-ness of our lives as the ought."[2] Thereby we defer our dreams of a world in which all are well, and none are relegated to the margins or to a life of dearth. Thereby we grow dull to Hope's assurance and call, and abdicate the privilege and responsibility of lending our hands to God's redemptive work in the world. Thereby we come to believe we are incapable of living *imago Dei*.

1. Townes, *Breaking the Fine Rain of Death*, 179.
2. Townes, *Breaking the Fine Rain of Death*, 179.

Embodied Hope as a theological idea foregrounds our inherent identity as *imago Dei*. It is a conceptual metaphor for that which creates within human persons yearning for wholeness and well-being, the always-speaking voice of God's Spirit assuring us of God's power, faithfulness, and redemptive presence and calling us as fitting participants in God's loving, just, and restorative action in our world today. Hope is that *something within* that God gives to each of us by virtue of our God-createdness. We are beings created in the image of a creating God and made alive by God's vivifying *ruach* (the Hebrew word for "breath" or "wind"). And though we often doubt our own capacity for living as God desires, though we lose our way or become distracted by distorting conceptions of reality, Hope's assurance and call continually reminds us of who we are and of what we are capable. We are *imago Dei*, created to live as a nondistorting, nondestructive expression of God's presence in the world.

This chapter explores embodied Hope as a theological conception that nurtures our ability to live responsive to Hope's assurance and call. We begin our exploration by answering two questions: Why an embodied theology of Hope? And, what is embodied Hope? We give specific attention to Hope's implications for the *shalom* of God, human identity, and the call to Christian vocation. The chapter concludes by exploring the complexity of living responsive to Hope's assurance and call when the despairing realities of life suggest our efforts are futile. It introduces culturally induced despair as Hope's nemesis. Culturally induced despair prevents us from acknowledging our shared identity as *imago Dei* and our call to partnership with God. This final section serves as an entrée to Chapter 2 and Chapter 3 where we will explore the mechanistic interworking of culturally induced despair, followed by Chapter 4 and its exploration of the anticipatory language of Hope.

Why an Embodied Theology of Hope?

To consider embodied Hope as an expression of God's presence within is familiar ground for the Christian church, as Christian theology is largely incarnational. We worship God incarnate in "the bodily, concrete, marked, historical being, Jesus of Nazareth," who walked among us, died a physical death, and was resurrected as a sign of God's continuous concern for the well-being of creation.[3] When God decides to make Godself known to humanity, theologian M. Shawn Copeland writes, "God does so in human

---

3. Copeland, *Enfleshing Freedom*, 55.

flesh."[4] Therefore, she continues, "the body can never be simply one element among others in theological reflection." To negate the body, in other words, is to negate the creative wisdom of the God who formed us, vivified us with divine *ruach*, and designated us *imago Dei*. Yet we struggle to acknowledge our shared identity as *imago Dei* and similarly to acknowledge our capacity as fitting partners with God.

Steeped in an interpretive tradition that repeatedly portrays humanity as *fallen*, we convince ourselves that humans are inherently damaged and that our image is irreparably marred. The interpretive challenge is that the biblical narrative from which we draw our ideas about humanity's inherent flaws does not characterize humans as *fallen*. In Gen 3, humans awaken to the knowledge of good and evil, marking an end to innocence and altering their existence forever. At no point in this primordial story does God characterize them as *fallen*. Nor does God threaten to abandon them or tell them that they are no longer created in the divine image. Instead, we hear these words: "*See, the 'adam* [human] *has become like one of us, knowing good and evil*" (Gen 3:22). With this newfound knowledge, humans are required by God to leave the garden of innocence, never to return again. They have become *like* the Divine and must now take on the generative responsibility of choosing and producing good over evil as their daily praxis. Yet, despite the Scripture's emphasis upon humanity's newfound knowledge, the knowledge of good and evil, and the responsibilities thereof, many of us remain attached to interpretive traditions that foster stories of human fallenness and failure. As a result, we too often underestimate our potential for good and abdicate our ethical responsibility to echo God's presence in the day-to-dayness of our lives.

Why is interpretation or the interpretive lens through which we retell or propagate the biblical story important? Patricia J. Williams, reflecting upon the formative potential of story and myth, writes, "I do think that to a very great extent we dream our worlds into being. For better or worse, our customs and our laws, our culture and society are sustained by the myths we embrace, the stories we recirculate."[5] I am concerned that we have dreamed and are dreaming the present world of suffering and oppression into existence. Our stories, myths, and metaphors about who we are and about what we are capable of shape our shared existence (our *habitat*) and the attitudes and perceptions (our *habitus*) that sustain our shared existence.

Michael Warren, engaging the writings of the French social thinker Pierre Bourdieu, describes the interrelationship of *habitat* and *habitus* in

---

4. Copeland, *Enfleshing Freedom*, 56.
5. Williams, *Seeing a Color-Blind Future*, 16.

his insightful book, *At This Time, In This Place: The Spirit Embodied in the Local Assembly*:

> For Bourdieu, two histories intersect in each person. One is the *habitat*, or objectified history, accumulated over time in objects like machines, buildings, monuments, books, theories, customs, law, and so forth. The second is the *habitus*, the embodied history or matrix of perceptions, appreciations, and actions functioning as a kind of law written into each person's life from early upbringing. A habitus steeps a person in durable patterns of perceiving, thinking, and acting that are generally outside awareness but fixed in place by objective conditions of living, and perduring even after these conditions change.[6]

Our *habitus*—our perceiving, thinking and acting—when rife with images of domination, destruction, treachery, self- and other-contempt, and other forms of malice, obscures our ability to see one another and ourselves as *imago Dei*. It contributes to a distorted view of reality, persuading us that our shortcomings and failures, the flaws and brokenness of our world, are the definitive predictors of the future. We learn to anticipate and live into a perception of reality as fallen without recognizing that we possess the power to create new stories and new possibilities.

Patricia J. Williams similarly contends that suffering and oppression are perpetuated by "a habit of human imagination, deflective rhetoric, and hidden license."[7] Our directive images, the cultural images that order our lives together, create habits of human imagination of which we are often unaware. Over time, these habits become "constituted and established" as customs, laws, and social mores.[8] Paul Ricœur, in *History and Truth*, reminds us that cultural images and their resultant habits "have stability and internal history which transcend the chance happenings of the individual."[9] The images, stories, and myths that constitute our shared existence, in other words, gain sanction and potency as truth over time.

In US society, for example, negating cultural images have created and continue to create and perpetuate an insidious system of human valuation based upon race, gender, sexuality, class, materiality, education, age, body, physical ability, and other such indicators. These images give license to laws and social arrangements that disprivilege certain people groups while inordinately rewarding and privileging others. They also impact the well-being

---

6. Warren, *At This Time*, 107 (italics original).
7. Williams, *Seeing a Color-Blind Future*, 16.
8. Ricœur, *History and Truth*, 126.
9. Ricœur, *History and Truth*, 126.

of the earth and all who depend upon her resources, permitting overconsumption by those who possess greater privilege and material wealth, while denying basic life necessities, such as clean drinking water, food, and a safe place to live, to the poorest and most vulnerable in our world. When accepted as truth, negating cultural images shape a collective imagination. They constitute or establish patterns of thinking and behaving that reject the possibility of love, justice, and communal well-being as the normative shape of our lives together. When coupled with theological convictions that portray humans and the world in which we live as fallen, negating patterns of thinking and behaving become more potent.

Our problem, therefore, is not only our failure to acknowledge one another and ourselves as *imago Dei*. The problem with which we grapple includes the relational cost of habits of human imagination and practice that delimit our ability to see one another, the earth, and all living things as a reflection of the Creator's love. Relationally, negating habits of human imagination and practice perpetuate fatalistic thinking—the belief that our lives, our world, are governed by fate and that personal and social transformation is beyond our control. Fatalistic views of reality portray practices of love, justice, and peace (*shalom*) as *uncommon*, extraordinary exceptions to an otherwise infallible rule that represents humanity as flawed and fallen. Rather than emphasizing humanity's capacity to imagine and live toward a new reality, fatalistic thinking gives rise to "spiritual torpor"—apathy, indifference, lethargy, mercilessness, and presumed powerlessness regarding our ability to dream a new world into existence.[10]

What if we dreamt a new world into existence? What if we told stories of human potentiality and possibility? What if we remembered our identity as *imago Dei*—we Christians and all peoples of the earth? What if we created the foundation for a new *habitus* undergirding new patterns of perceiving, thinking, and acting? What if we dared to imagine and live in anticipation of God's reign fully realized? Ricœur writes, "It is in this sense that culture is established at the level of the tradition of the imaginary. Accordingly, it is at this level that we must search out the signs of the Kingdom to come."[11] What if we lived in anticipation of the kin(g)dom to come, of God's reign fully realized?

Embodied Hope anticipates the reign of God and invites us to participate in its continuous unfolding. It disrupts fatalistic thinking, nourishing our imaginative potential and emboldening us to view the world in which we live and ourselves as open to redemptive possibilities. Embodied Hope

---

10. Hess, *Caretakers*, 44–45.
11. Ricœur, *History and Truth*, 126.

also reminds us that we are human. We are beings created in the image of a creating God, and it is our vocation as human beings to live as an articulation of divine presence in our daily lives. With Hope, we dream a world in which love, justice, and *shalom* are normative expressions of human existence. With Hope, we join Jesus in announcing the end of captivity, oppression, perceptual distortion, and anything else that seeks to foreclose the future. And with Hope, we lend our hands in partnership with the Divine to make Jesus's ministerial vision an actuality.

What Is Embodied Hope?

Embodied Hope is a conceptual metaphor for Hope's presence in our lives. It is a language for describing *that which creates in each human being yearning for wholeness and well-being, the always-speaking voice of God's Spirit assuring us of God's presence, power, and fidelity and calling us toward loving, just, and restorative action*. It is a word spoken and an invitation given by way of God's presence within us. Gospel songwriter Lucie Eddie Campbell's hymn "Something Within" captures well Hope's presence: "*Something within that holdeth the reins, / Something within me that banishes pain; / Something within me I cannot explain, / All that I know is there's something within.*"[12] We know Hope as a sensate experience and disposition of heart and mind to which we endeavor to give expression, a *something-within* that theologians, philosophers, religious practitioners, and everyday people try to make intelligible through our language, practice, and artistic expressions. Hope is the spiritual tug that we sense, the holy indignation and righteous anger that we feel, the dream of justice that confronts us as truth. It is God's presence within us, beckoning and emboldening us to live as though the just and life-affirming existence for which we yearn is within our view. When we answer yes to God's call, when we lend our hands to God's restorative work, we make God's presence known in the earth. We also disclose something about who we are as *imago Dei*. In attitude and practice, proclamation and deed, we reveal our vocation as partners with God, permitting the presence of God's Spirit to fashion in us the courage to live with Hope.

Living with Hope is complicated. On the one hand, we possess the capacity to live with Hope by virtue of God's presence within us. However, the despairing realities of life often thwart our ability to sense Hope's presence and live in anticipation of God's new community. We will discuss the challenge of sensing Hope's voice in greater detail in Chapter 2. Here, I focus on

---

12. Campbell, "Something Within."

the ethical responsibility that ensues when we say yes to Hope's summons to imagine our world and lives together anew.

Embodied Hope is the impetus for new imagination and has implication for the quality of human relationship we create. It is a gift of divine favor of which humans are both recipients and stewards. Because it is an aspect of God's self-expression in our lives, Hope inspires and empowers us to live in just and life-affirming relationship with self, others, and the earth, our shared home. Accordingly, Hope opposes attitudes, practices, and social arrangements that perpetuate suffering, oppression, and other forms of malice and discord, calling us continually toward an ethic of love and care. The sisterly and brotherly love to which Hope beckons us recalls God's self-giving love extended to us through Jesus as well as Jesus's ministerial vision of a world in which all are welcome, and none are relegated to the margins. It also reminds us that our responsive love toward God—through worship, prayer, praise, thanksgiving, service, and the like—is indelibly connected to the love we hold for our sisters and brothers, known and unknown; for we are all one family. Embodied Hope is the voice of God's Spirit assuring of us God's presence, power, and faithfulness. It beckons us to live in just and life-affirming relationship with one another and thereby to prove ourselves good stewards of the gift we have received.

Three theological ideas give shape to my discussion of embodied Hope. The first is the assumption that God desires the well-being of creation, expressed most completely in the Hebrew conception of *shalom* and the ministerial vision of Jesus. The second is that Hope is an inherent aspect of humanity's identity as *imago Dei*. Consequently, humans possess the capacity to live as an expression of God's presence. And the third central theological idea, which builds upon the first two, is that humans have an ethical and moral responsibility, by virtue of our identity as imago Dei, to live in loving, just, and life-affirming relationship with one another, the earth, and all with whom we share the planet, as a sign of our love for God, others, and ourselves. Our vocation as human beings, in other words, is to live as a reflection of divine presence in the earth, made evident in the life and ministry of Jesus and in the many others who embrace his ministerial vision.

Embodied Hope and the *Shalom* of God

As a theological idea, embodied Hope assumes God's desire for the well-being of creation, the *shalom* of God. Reflecting upon *shalom* as an ideal for human relationship, Majorie Yudkin writes, "The Ideal of *shalom,* which should be understood as wholeness, is based on a model of God who is one, who unifies all polarities and apparently incompatible dualism into one."[13] Human embrace of this ideal tears down barriers and eliminates division, enhancing our ability to work toward the good of all without privileging one human community or geographic region over another.[14] *Shalom* implies the wholeness of creation, of life of every form, and of the earth our shared home. Yudkin also reminds us that wholeness as *shalom* requires a balance of justice (judgment) and love, not as opposing forces but as compatible and complementary models of relationship. "Integrity or wholeness requires not that we fulfill one model of relationship to the exclusion of the other," she writes, "but that we seek to create ourselves in God's image, by tempering justice with love, and moderating our love with concern for justice."[15] In other words, the *shalom* ideal cautions us to ensure that our quest for justice is laced with a desire for communal well-being, and that our offer of compassionate care does not become an end in itself but rather the attitude that fuels the work of justice. Embodied Hope awakens our desire for justice and love and thereby summons each of us to partnership with the Divine so that our world and we might experience *shalom* as a tangible reality in our lives.

Jesus's *ministerial* vision and life practices quintessentially exemplify a life fueled by the ideal of *shalom*. Theologian Delores Williams describes Jesus's ministerial vision as an invitation to his ancient and present-day followers to participate in the transformative ministry of creating social relations and material conditions that promote flourishing and well-being. Jesus announces this new relational paradigm by urging his followers to repent and to turn away from self- and other-destructive attitudes and practices—all while assuring us that the kin(g)dom of God is already taking shape in our midst.

Delores Williams's description of the kin(g)dom of God as a metaphor of Hope is apropos for this discussion:

> The kingdom of God is a metaphor of hope God gives those attempting to right the relations between self and self, between self and others, between self and God as prescribed in the sermon on the mount, in the golden rule and in the commandment to show love above all else.[16]

---

13. Yudkin, "The Shalom Ideal," 87.

14. Paradigms related to *the common good* often serve the privileged and do not address the power dynamics that dictate the Market. For an alternative view of the common good that begins with *care* for the most vulnerable rather than *production*, see Goudzwaard and de Lange, *Beyond Poverty and Affluence*.

15. Yudkin, "The Shalom Ideal," 87.

16. Williams, *Sisters in the Wilderness*, 165.

ence in our lives implies right relationship. As a metaphor of
 ...in(g)dom of God reveals the possibility of a world in which all
 ...urished in every domain of life, and none are relegated to places
 ... marginality. This is a relational existence that honors God, others, and self, and in which we experience *shalom* as a tangible reality.

Shalom does not emerge by happenstance. Reflecting upon Matthew, Mark, and Luke's descriptions of Jesus's ministerial vision, Williams writes, "The texts suggest that the spirit of God in Jesus came to show humans *life*—to show redemption through a perfect *ministerial* vision of righting relations between body (individual and community), mind (of humans and tradition), and spirit."[17] Jesus makes his ministerial vision known through acts of healing, delivering, restoring, and confronting. He eliminates strictures, dismantles structures, and transcends social and religious barriers so that those who had been deemed unworthy can experience the fullness of their humanity and identity as *imago Dei*. And to the dismay of those who sought to silence him, the social and religious naysayers of his time, Jesus devoted himself to disrupting old relational paradigms for the sake of a new community in which "water is thicker than blood, family is redefined, lepers are touched, and outcasts sit at the table," writes homiletician Barbara Lundblad.[18]

Despite efforts to obscure his vision (accusations, threats, testing, the inevitability of death), Jesus refused to deny relationship to those deemed unacceptable by social and religious elites or by everyday folk whose patterns of perceiving, thinking and acting (*habitus*) had become distorted. Instead, he persisted in "proclaiming the word of life that demanded the transformation of tradition so that life could be lived more abundantly."[19] Jesus lived and proclaimed God's *shalom*. Such proclamation is also possible today when people of faith and good conscience participate in Jesus's *ministerial* vision by engaging in the ethical thought and practice necessary to transform our *habitus* as well as the material conditions of our lives (*habitat*).

Embodied Hope and Human Identity

Hope as embodied theology also implies a theological anthropology that acknowledges the inherent connection of each human being with the Divine, our identity as *imago Dei*. It recognizes with theologian M. Shawn Copeland "that the body is a site and mediation of divine revelation; that the body

---

17. Williams, *Sisters in the Wilderness*, 164–65 (italics original).
18. Lundblad, *Transforming the Stone*, 53.
19. Williams, *Sisters in the Wilderness*, 165.

shapes human existence as relational and social, [and] that the creativity of the Triune God is manifested in differences of gender, race, and sexuality."[20] No human *body* is devoid of *imago Dei*. Therefore, our differences reveal something of the depth and breadth of God's creativity and of our potential as human beings. This remains true despite the "demonization in history, religion, culture, and society" of bodies deemed by various people and systems, in innumerable ways, unworthy of the image of God.[21] It also remains true despite miscarriages in acknowledging our own inherent being as *imago Dei*. We are all *imago Dei*, called to reflect God's presence in the earth. We reveal ourselves as fully human, in other words, when we acknowledge other people's inherent identity as *imago Dei* alongside our own. To dwell with another person is to dwell in the midst of *imago Dei*.

The apostle Paul makes a similar claim regarding humanity's identity during his speech before the Areopagus in Acts 17:16–28. Paul had been arguing in the synagogues with the Jewish teachers and in the marketplace with the Stoics, Epicureans, and other philosophers in defense of "the good news about Jesus and the resurrection." Exasperated by his argument, the other philosophers accuse him of proclaiming a foreign divinity and bring Paul before the Areopagite Council, the Greek high court, and demand he defend his religious views. Paul draws their attention to an altar with the inscription "To an unknown god" and declares the inscription is to "the God who made the world and everything in it, he who is Lord of heaven and earth" (v. 24a). Contrasting this God with the multiple gods of Athens and particularly with Zeus, Paul describes the *unknown God* as the One who requires neither shrine nor material representation, the self-existent One and Creator of the universe, who *"gives to all mortals life and breath and all things"* (vv. 24b–25).[22]

The Christian community reading this account would sense resonances of Gen 1:26–27 in Paul's words. But Paul's Athenian audience would hear in them a challenge to the idea that all of creation is indebted to Zeus, believed to be the god of the natural world.[23] Paul proclaims further that in this *unknown god* "'we live and move and have our being'; as even some of your own poets have said, 'For we too are his offspring.'" Again, Paul strikes a note of familiarity with his Athenian and Christian audiences. Christian

---

20. Copeland, *Enfleshing Freedom*, 2. Copeland includes two additional convictions in her theological anthropology, as she gives shape to her central argument: "that solidarity is a set of body practices; and that the Eucharist orders and transforms our bodies as the Body of Christ."

21. Copeland, *Enfleshing Freedom*, 2

22. Faber, "The Apostle and the Poet."

23. Faber, "The Apostle and the Poet."

readers will know that Paul is exalting the God of the Christian faith, the *I Am* or self-existent God of being revealed in Exod 3:13–15. But these words sound a different note for Paul's Athenian listeners. Paul borrows the latter portion of this verse from the well-known Greek poet of the time, Aratus, a text familiar to his Athenian listeners. But there is also a tension in his words. Rather than proclaiming that humanity is Zeus's offspring, as many of his listeners believed, Paul identifies the God of Jesus as the One in whom *"we live and move and have our being."*

Paul characterizes humans as God's *offspring* and by implication as siblings in God's family. God created us, formed us in God's own likeness, and breathed into us the capacity to live as an expression of divine presence on the earth. This includes living in loving, just, and life-affirming relationship with one another, living as one family. We bear God's image and are made alive by the breath of God, and our being and very existence is bound to the one who continually calls us toward *shalom*. We are *imago Dei*.

Hope, as an aspect and expression of divine presence, reminds us of God's desire for *shalom* and beckons us to embrace ways of being and relating that are laced with love and justice for all people. When we are able to sense Hope's presence, Hope awakens our imagination to possibilities that appear futile or nonsensical to us given the evidence around us, but not to God. Hope reminds us of God's power, faithfulness, and redemptive presence in our world today and of the manifold possibilities that exist when we heed Hope's assurance and call.

Embodied Hope and Human Vocation

Hope as embodied theology calls us to a life of vocation. It is an invitation to dream our world anew and lend our hands to making that dream a reality. Embodied Hope reminds us that God created within each human being the capacity to live toward a more loving, more just, more God-infused existence for all creation.

The biblical writers understood this capacity as humanity's vocation, the response that one "makes with his or her total self to the address of God and to the calling to partnership."[24] In the first of two Genesis creation stories (Gen 1), the Creator who speaks the celestial and terrestrial worlds into existence creates humanity for the purpose of living as an expression of divine presence in the earth:

---

24. Fowler, *Becoming Adult*, 74.

> Then God said, "Let us make humankind in our image, according to our likeness; and let them have dominion over the fish of the sea, and over the birds of the air, and over the cattle, and over all the wild animals of the earth, and over every creeping thing that creeps upon the earth." So God created humankind in his image, in the image of God he created them; male and female he created them (Gen 1:26–27).

With intentionality, the relational and communal God of creation makes humankind, male and female, in the divine image (*imago Dei*) and entrusts the worlds to humanity's care. As *imago Dei*, humans are given dominion over the earth and all her inhabitants, not to exploit and destroy them but to live as a manifestation of Godself.

The English word "manifest" has its origins in the Latin *manifestus*. The Latin rendering includes "bring to light" and "proved by evidence" along with more common meanings such as "palpable," "clear," "plain," "apparent," "evident," and "manifest." Drawing from these descriptions, to be human is to *bring to light* or *prove by evidence* the One in whose image we are created. Our identity as *imago Dei*, the image or likeness of God, speaks to our capacity to manifest our embodiment of God's loving and creative presence in the earth. Our lives, when we are faithful, reveal the God who gives us life, making God's presence among us perceptible through the quality of our relationship with each other, with other beings, and with the earth.

The biblical writers reveal God's desire that humans live in communion with all creation:

> God said, "See, I have given you every plant yielding seed that is upon the face of all the earth, and every tree with seed in its fruit; you shall have them for food. And to every beast of the earth, and to every bird of the air, and to everything that creeps on the earth, everything that has breath of life, I have given every green plant for food." And it was so. (Gen 1:29–30)

Through an inclusive image of communal flourishing, we discover that humans are to flourish alongside other living beings, including by consuming our share of the earth's abundant food supply and, by implication, other natural resources.[25] The narrative also assumes sufficient supply for all the earth's creatures. This image of abundance is appallingly distorted today, however, because of the overconsumption by some humans and the resultant deprivation of other humans, the earth, and nonhuman creatures.

25. See Johnson, *Ask the Beasts*, for an insightful and thorough discussion of humanity's place in the larger creation story.

Despite this distortion, God's desire for the well-being of creation calls us to partnership with the Divine as vigorously today as in the first days of human existence.

Our vocation, our role as partners, is to care for and promote flourishing in all that God has created. Even more, our vocation is to do this work as with the heart and mind of God. This includes caring for human community, other living beings, and the earth and her natural resources. We are *imago Dei*, called to manifest in thought and action God's presence in the earth.

The biblical writers intensify their assertion that humans are a reflection or manifestation of the Divine in the second creation story of Genesis (Gen 2). God as *divine sculptor* transforms dirt into a fleshly form, in Gen 2:7, until it is just as God intends. With hands still soiled from the dirt, the Sculptor kneels, bending and drawing close to the form, and with vivifying *ruach*, animates the first human (Hebrew: 'adam [Gen 2:7]), and by implication, 'adam's companion, the woman (Hebrew: 'ishshah [Gen 2:22]). They become living *souls* (Hebrew: *nephesh*), the very reflection of the Divine. The Creator's breath gives life, makes the human form *imago Dei* from the inside out, makes it a living soul, makes us 'adam.

James S. Bruckner notes that our common translation of the expression *nephesh* as "soul" falls short of its Hebrew connotation.[26] He writes, "A more accurate translation of the word-concept would be 'person in relation to' or 'bodily life in relationship with.'"[27] Therefore, humanity's soulish nature implies relationship with God and others. To be human is to be a fleshly reflection of the Divine (*imago Dei*), "a living physical being in relation to others."[28]

M. Shawn Copeland also reflects upon Gen 1–3 and similarly highlights humanity's identity as *imago Dei* and our capacity to live in relation with God and others:

> Three convictions central to theological anthropology derive from Christian interpretation of this narrative: (1) that human being, created in the image and likeness of God (*imago Dei*), have a distinct capacity for communion with God; (2) that human beings have a unique place in the cosmos God created; and (3) that human beings are made for communion with other living beings.[29]

26. Bruckner, "A Theological Description," 1–19.
27. Bruckner, "A Theological Description," 10.
28. Bruckner, "A Theological Description," 11.
29. Copeland, *Enfleshing Freedom*, 23–24.

We are created in the image of God (*imago Dei*) and, by virtue of our identity, possess the capacity to live in communion with God and with all that God has created.

To live in communion is to live in unity and intimacy with and with empathy for the cosmos God created. Communion is also reflective of the Greek κοινωνία (= *koinōnia*) to live in close and intimate relationship with another. Empathy, as an aspect of *koinōnia*, implies our ability to viscerally sense the thoughts, feelings, and experiences of another as though they are our own. God gives humans the capacity for empathy and fellowship—the ability to identify places of suffering and brokenness in human community and among other living beings so that we can discern the role that we might play in nurturing well-being and promoting flourishing. We are living souls, relational beings whose most ardent desire is the well-being of creation—self, others, earth, and other living being—and to live in relationship with God.

Preaching Hope as embodied theology acknowledges the *soulish*, relational nature of human identity and the vocation to which God invites us. It also acknowledges that our world is not as it should be, due in large part to humanity's failure to heed the always-speaking voice of God's Spirit and our call to vocation. Our vision of what might be possible is often distorted, and we struggle to sense the possibility of new life in the midst of the systemic chaos that gives rise to suffering and oppression in our world today. Yet, Christian communities of faith and people of good conscience throughout the world continue to gather, naming the reality of suffering and oppression but refusing to concede that such inadequacies are the inevitability of our existence. Instead, we gather together, reminding each other and ourselves that the Creator, with intentionality and care, gifted human beings with the capacity to live as an expression of divine presence on earth. Because we are *imago Dei*, our vocation is to seek the well-being of creation; to coexist with all that God calls good, envisioning our world anew and permitting our lives to arc toward the loving, just, and life-affirming existence for which our souls so deeply yearn.

Culturally Induced Despair: An Adversary of Hope

We embody Hope. No matter our adeptness at sensing or living responsive to Hope's assurance and call, Hope continually reminds us of God's enduring concern for the well-being of creation and call to partnership. No longer must we remain bound to habits of human imagination and practices that perpetuate violence, suffering, and oppression. No longer must we tolerate attitudes, practices, laws, mores, or systems that distort our ability to see each other as *imago Dei*. God's abiding presence within frees us to live with Hope, a response made tangible when we lend our hands to God's redemptive and restorative work in the world.

Living with Hope is no simple matter. Not only does it necessitate a new angle of vision regarding our capacity for loving, just, and life-affirming relationship. Living with Hope entails identifying, disrupting, and ultimately dismantling negating and dehumanizing systems and constructs that distort and distract us from living responsive to Hope's assurance and call. This includes negating and dehumanizing patterns of perceiving, thinking, imagining, and behaving embedded in our social and political institutions as well as our religious fellowships. Living with Hope also necessitates remediation of the relational cost negation and dehumanization exact. That is, when people of faith and good conscience underestimate our ability to live with Hope, when we undervalue our capacity to live in loving, just, and life-affirming relationship with others, we contribute to and perpetuate relational fractures that negate *shalom* as a realizable possibility. Underestimating our capacity to live with Hope, therefore, functions as another form of distortion and distraction.

The distractions we encounter distort reality. Such distractions negate the possibility of a qualitatively better state of existence and so place us at risk for culturally induced despair. Over time, distortion dampens our sensitivity to Hope's assurance and call. As we will discuss, culturally induced despair is an insidious mechanism: Given that it both produces and is sustained by distortion and negation, culturally induced despair works through and is resonant in negating and dehumanizing sociopolitical, attitudinal, ideological, theological, and ecclesiastical constructs and practices. It both cultivates and thrives upon a distorted perception of reality and of the possibilities that exist when we lend our hands to God's restorative work in the world.

Despair, as a theological concept, is not new to the Christian church. Thomas Aquinas (and a number of other moral theologians following his lead) conceived of despair as a sin that undermines the theological virtue *Hope*.[30] Regarding Hope, Aquinas writes, "The principal object of hope, precisely as it is a virtue, *is God*. And since this is the very definition of a theological virtue . . . it clearly follows that hope is a theological virtue."[31] Despair, on the other hand, constitutes "a voluntary refusal to trust that God

---

30. Thomas Aquinas, *Summa Theologiæ*.
31. Thomas Aquinas, *Summa Theologiæ*, 17 (italics added).

makes salvation genuinely possible" to repentant sinners.[32] And, since God is the object of our hoping or anticipating, "we should hope for nothing less from God than [God's] very self."[33] Therefore, the good for which we *properly hope* is "indeed eternal blessedness" or "beatitude," God's matchless and limitless presence in our lives.[34]

Hope, in Aquinas's conception, is more than desire or expectation. Hope is a theological virtue that comes from God and *is God*. It is a "disposition of spirit" that prompts us to attain to God as the source and end of our hoping.[35] And, while it is permissible to anticipate other good things, Aquinas teaches that these things are secondary and in "subordination to eternal happiness" (blessedness, beatitude, beatification).[36] Our dreams and desires are "subordinated to God as the ultimate end sought and as the primary source of getting it."[37] Therefore, the believer's task, and I take some liberty with this interpretation of Aquinas, is to synchronize our heart with the heart of God, to make God's commitments our commitments so that the end to which we live is indelibly connected to God's desire for creation and for our lives.

Aquinas does not explicitly speak of Hope as an aspect of humanity's inherent identity as *imago Dei*, as I do. But, his assertion that Hope, as a disposition of the human spirit, comes from God and *is God* is compelling. Therein we sense Aquinas's tacit acknowledgment of God's communion and enduring presence with human beings or (as I suggest) of the Spirit's presence within. We also sense resonances of a divine summons to human beings to lean into God as the One who gives meaning to life and to the

---

32. Thomas Aquinas, *Summa Theologiæ*, 81. Thomas Aquinas continues with this reflection on despair: "Now, the mind's true appraisal about God acknowledges that he grants pardon to sinners and brings men to salvation, in accord with the words of Ezekiel, I do not desire the death of the sinner, but that he be converted and live (Ezekiel 18, 23). Contrariwise, false opinion envisions God as denying pardon to the repentant sinner, or as not converting sinners to himself through justifying grace. And so, the act of hope, squaring with true judgment, is praiseworthy and virtuous; while the opposite attitude, which is despair, reflecting as it does a false view of God, is vicious and sinful" (89).

33. Thomas Aquinas, *Summa Theologiæ*, 9.

34. Thomas Aquinas, *Summa Theologiæ*, 9. See footnote (c) by volume editor and translator William J. Hill: "A perfect knowledge of beatitude would be nothing less than the very experience of its in beatific vision; man's awareness of it in this life is only in the obscurity of faith and in dependence upon images and analogies. Cf. *I Corinthians* 13, 12; 2, 9. The response is suggesting that there is a positive content and value in the concept of the good to express some true meaning about blessedness to the human mind."

35. Thomas Aquinas, *Summa Theologiæ*, 7.

36. Thomas Aquinas, *Summa Theologiæ*, 11.

37. Thomas Aquinas, *Summa Theologiæ*, 11.

practice of living with Hope, which has implications for humanity's vocational call to exemplify God's presence in the earth.

Also compelling is Aquinas's characterization of despair as a disposition that opposes Hope, though our points of departure differ. Aquinas is concerned with ensuring we acknowledge God as the source and ground of Hope. For Aquinas, that for which we hope, or the object of our hoping, is eternal beatification, which only comes from God. Despair opposes Hope because despair represents "a turning away from God," a denial of God in search of some fleeting, transient good.[38] More specifically, despair signifies a denial of God's salvific intent toward humanity, promoting a false appraisal of God and God's activity in the world.[39] "The mind's true appraisal about God," Aquinas writes, "acknowledges that [God] grants pardon to sinners and brings [people] to salvation."[40] Therefore, Aquinas characterizes despair as a "mortal sin," that which misrepresents and negates God's intent toward salvation for all who repent.[41] A secondary concern for Aquinas is despair's propagative nature, as is evident in his characterization of despair as "not only sinful itself, but a source for further sin."[42] Despair opposes Hope, Aquinas asserts, both because it promotes a negative appraisal of God's salvific intent and because it is a source of further sin.[43]

How is my point of departure different? Aquinas is concerned with despair as a rejection of God's intent to save repentant sinners. I am primarily concerned with the sociocultural and theological roots of despair and their impact upon our ability to live with Hope and acknowledge our shared identity as *imago Dei*. While eternal beautification may be ultimate, both communally and individually, my desire is to amplify Hope's assurance of God's power, faithfulness, and redemptive presence as well as Hope's invitation that we lend our hands to God's loving, just, and restorative work in the world today. I introduce the concept *culturally induced despair* as a means of naming and unpacking these concerns.

---

38. Thomas Aquinas, *Summa Theologiæ*, 11.

39. Thomas Aquinas, *Summa Theologiæ*, 89. "Contrariwise, false opinion envisions God as denying pardon to the repentant sinner, or as not converting sinners to himself through justifying grace. And so, the act of hope, squaring with true judgment, is praiseworthy and virtuous; while the opposite attitude, which is despair, reflecting as it does a false view of God, is vicious and sinful."

40. Thomas Aquinas, *Summa Theologiæ*, 89.

41. Thomas Aquinas, *Summa Theologiæ*, 187. Glossary definition of a mortal sin: a sin "in which a creaturely thing is preferred to God, one deserving of eternal punishment."

42. Thomas Aquinas, *Summa Theologiæ*, 187.

43. Thomas Aquinas, *Summa Theologiæ*, 7.

Culturally induced despair is an insidious mechanism. It is an embodiment of hopelessness that draws energy from the multiple manifestations and intersecting nature of violence, suffering, oppression, and other dehumanizing conditions evident in our shared existence. Its impact is far-reaching and dangerous. This is so because culturally induced despair both produces and is sustained by negating and dehumanizing sociopolitical, attitudinal, ideological, theological, and ecclesiastical constructions and the de-creating (negating and dehumanizing) patterns of perceiving, thinking, and behaving they promote. When de-creating thoughts and practices constitute our *habitus*, they prevent us from acknowledging our shared identity as *imago Dei* and call to partnership with God. De-creation also obscures our interconnectedness as human community as well as our bond with all other aspects of creation. Eventually, especially when left uncontested, de-creating thoughts and practices plunge us into the depths of despair exacerbated by meaninglessness, anxiety, distress, exhaustion, and imaginative dearth. These conditions prevent us from imagining life anew, thereby negating the possibility of an alternative reality. In magnitude, scope, and complexity, culturally induced despair's de-creating effect distorts our shared identity as *imago Dei* and delimits our ability to sense Hope's assurance and call.

Feelings of despair resulting from inadequate sociopolitical, attitudinal, ideological, theological, and ecclesiastical constructions is not sinful despair. It is neither a rejection of God in search of some other transient good nor a denial of God's salvific intent. Our experience of culturally induced despair is more reflective of another of Aquinas's conceptions. Aquinas argues that "it would not be a sin" if someone were to despair over circumstances we perceive ourselves as having no capacity to change, "as for example, if a doctor were to despair over the cure of someone fatally ill, or if someone were to despair of ever acquiring wealth."[44] The doctor, in other words, perceives herself as powerless to change the circumstances of her patient's life. Similarly, culturally induced despair takes root when we feel powerless to change the disparaging circumstances of our lives. When we experience a sense of powerlessness about our capacity to remediate violence, suffering, oppression, and other dehumanizing realities that inundate our shared existence. The danger that culturally induced despair poses for our shared existence, therefore, is not that it leads to a negation of God's salvific intent. Culturally induced despair is dangerous because it diminishes our facility in sensing the voice of Hope and thus our capacity for living as a reflection of God's love and care for humanity, the earth, and other living beings. Sin, if sin must be named, is rooted in the de-creating or dehumanizing and oppressive

---

44. Thomas Aquinas, *Summa Theologiæ*, 91.

structures, ideologies, and theologies in church and society that prevent us from sensing Hope's presence and correspondingly from living responsive to Hope's assurance and call. The violence, suffering, oppression, and other forms of dehumanization that culturally induced despair produces are indeed sinful. More precisely, writes James Cone, "when suffering is inflicted upon the oppressed, it is evil and we must struggle against it."[45] Culturally induced despair, though not sinful despair, creates the conditions necessary for sin to take root by dulling our sensitivity to Hope's voices.

Culturally induced despair and the sinful practices it produces do not have the final word. Hope, the always-speaking voice of God's Spirit continuously calls us toward loving, just, and life-affirming relationship with self, others, and the earth our shared home. Therefore, our task as gospel proclaimers and purveyors of Hope is twofold. First and foremost, our challenge is to live responsive to Hope's assurance and call as we invite others to do the same. Living with Hope entails engaging in concrete practices of Hope indicative of God's desire for universal *shalom*. It also entails acknowledging others' and our own identity as *imago Dei*, as beings created in God's image and animated by God's breath. Second, our task involves identifying, disrupting, and ultimately dismantling negating and dehumanizing systems and constructs that distort and distract us from living responsive to Hope's assurance and call, including those embedded in our social, political, and religious institutions. We embark upon a conversation about the second task in the next two chapters. In Chapters 4 and 5 we will talk more specifically about Hope's anticipatory language and amplifying the voice of Hope through preaching and other Christian practices.

---

45. Cone, *God of the Oppressed*, 177. Cone also makes a distinction between suffering inflicted upon the oppressed and the call upon Christians to suffer with Christ when he writes, "but when suffering arises out of the struggle against suffering, as in the fight against injustice, we accept it as a constituent of our calling and thus voluntarily suffer, because there is no freedom independent of the fight for justice."

— 2 —

Culturally Induced Despair Revealed

> The world is not as it should be, and ... the brokenness we experience cuts deep into our social fabric and has done so for a long time. This recognition of the pervasive, insidious, and historically persistent forces of destruction at work in the world sits at the heart of the feminist movement.[1]
>
> —Serene Jones

AT THE CONCLUSION OF Chapter 1 we situated culturally induced despair within a larger theological conversation about Hope and despair. Highlighting its distinctiveness from Aquinas's conception of sinful despair, we signaled culturally induced despair's mechanistic threat to our ability to sense and respond to Hope's assurance and call. Unlike the "mortal sin" of despair that Aquinas identifies, culturally induced despair, a deceptive mechanism, is not concerned with negating God's salvific intent toward humanity. Culturally induced despair produces futility, the feeling that our efforts toward remediating sociocultural and religious inadequacies in the present and toward the future are pointless. This is not sinful despair. However, the negating and dehumanizing conditions that sustain culturally induced despair, toward which it also contributes, are indeed sinful, as they diminish our ability to acknowledge our own and one another's identity as *imago Dei* as well as our capacity to sense and respond to Hope's assurance and call.

In this chapter, we explore culturally induced despair's insidious and mechanistic nature and the threat it poses to our identity as *imago Dei* and to our ability to live with Hope. As a primary focus, we will identify and deconstruct the socially fabricated shared system of communication

---

1. Jones, *Feminist Theory*, 96.

through which culturally induced despair transmits and reproduces its distorting messages, and the ways this system diminishes our capacity to live responsive to Hope's assurance and call. The deceptive language of despair is the medium through which we receive culturally induced despair's negating and dehumanizing messages. Through various channels, the deceptive language of despair propagates the notion that violence, suffering, oppression and other forms of dehumanization are not only natural, normal, and acceptable; they are humanity's inevitable fate. The channels through which such notions flow also perpetuate the belief that our humanness makes us incapable of living in loving, just, and life-affirming relationship with God, self, and others, which also negates our shared identity as *imago Dei*. We explore the first four of those channels in the current chapter: (1) seemingly innocuous colloquial expressions, (2) idioms of exasperation, (3) social conventions, and (4) constituent elements of our known world. In Chapter 3, we extend the conversation to include culturally induced despair's resonance within five additional channels, namely, negating images, myths, ideologies, theologies, and ecclesial commitments, and the threat they pose to our ability to live with Hope and to acknowledge our shared identity as *imago Dei*.

An Insidious Mechanism of Despair

I have described culturally induced despair as an insidious mechanism. It is an embodiment of hopelessness that draws energy from the multiple manifestations and intersecting nature of violence, suffering, oppression, and other forms of dehumanization evident in our shared existence. Culturally induced despair takes root when we come to believe that violence, suffering, oppression, and other dehumanizing conditions are "natural, normal, and inevitable parts of everyday life," to borrow again from Patricia Hill Collins.[2] Though our hearts long for wholeness and well-being, the chaotic state of our existence fuels the notion that we and our world are irreparably flawed and fallen and that there is little we can do about it. Such claims, when permitted to fester, distort our perception of reality and diminish our capacity to sense Hope's assurance and call. They give rise to culturally induced

---

2. Collins, *Black Feminist Thought*, 69. Referencing the impact of controlling images, Collins argues that "controlling images [of Black womanhood] are designed to make racism, sexism, poverty, and other forms of social injustice appear to be natural, normal, and inevitable parts of everyday life." I appropriate her understanding of the negating impact of such images throughout this writing and expand it to include the ways "controlling images" of many sorts are resonant in the channels through which culturally induced despair seeks to distort our vision of reality.

despair, an insidious mechanism that co-opts our imaginative potential as well as our attitudes, practices, and deeply held beliefs. And it does so oftentimes without our conscious consent.

We are overwhelmed by the state of our world, and questions abound regarding the efficacy of our efforts toward actualizing the loving, just, and life-affirming existence for which we so deeply yearn. Why continue to fight what appears to be a losing battle? Why imagine our lives anew when change seems implausible? Are seeking the well-being of all people or toppling systems of oppression and dehumanization reasonable endeavors? Is it reasonable to imagine a world in which everyone receives food, clothing, and shelter enough for a healthy and comfortable life? Is procuring clean water, medicines, and other lifesaving and life-sustaining balms for the masses of people around the globe a worthwhile expenditure of our resources? Is it really *our* responsibility to save the earth and other living beings from annihilation? As we consider the relevancy of our theological commitments and religious assumptions, further questions arise. What significance does God's vision of *shalom* and Jesus's proclamation of the kin(g)dom of God hold for our world today? What are we to make of Isaiah and Micah's prophetic vision of a time when we "shall not lift up [the] sword against" one another (Isa 2:4; Mic 4:3), or of Amos's call for justice to "roll down like waters, and righteousness like an ever-flowing stream" (Amos 5:24)? Are their prophetic utterances mere echoes from an ancient past that hold no relevance for our lives today? Must we continue to live in anticipation of God's kin(g)dom fully realized, or shall we simply resign ourselves to the givenness of life?

Culturally induced despair's fatalistic construal of life pressures us to respond to such questions by wringing our hands in anguish. To ignore Hope's assurance and call is to adopt the fatalistic notion that what exists in the present is determinative of the future; it is to simply "live out the weary drama of the nightmare" as a more plausible direction for our lives.[3] To concede that the tiered systems of power that bequeath privilege to some and inflict suffering upon others are impervious to transformation, and that such systems are both normal and morally just and right. Fatalistic impulses constrain and deceive us, pressing us to give up and declare our "innocence with an accent of despair."[4] For though our actions (or lack thereof) may serve

---

3. Townes, *Breaking the Fine Rain of Death*, 179.

4. Weil, "The Love of God," 35. Reflecting upon the biblical character Job's response to his physical, psychic, and material affliction, Weil describes Job's impulse to believe his friends' accusation that his affliction is due to some sin that he has committed. Job, of course, is innocent, though tempted to believe otherwise. Therefore, Weil writes, "If Job cries out his innocence with an accent of despair, it is because he himself can

to perpetuate the same violence, suffering, oppression, and dehumanization we wish to eliminate, culturally induced despair prompts us to declare with innocence, "This was never my intent."

In this sense, culturally induced despair affords solace of a sort. It permits us to abdicate the social responsibility to which Jesus called us when he proclaimed love of God and neighbor as the foundation upon which the Law and Prophets rest. Culturally induced despair also veils the social responsibility Jesus himself demonstrated when he stood with and among the most vulnerable of his time, healing, delivering, restoring, and providing while advocating on their behalf to religious elites, zealots, and everyday people of faith. Further, culturally induced despair makes the chaotic state of our world appear tolerable by assuring us we are already doing the best we can to resolve the cultural ills of our time. Assuaged of our fears that we have not done enough, in the sway of culturally induced despair we succumb to the belief that our problems are too difficult and numerous to remediate; that ensuring the well-being of the many is too much to ask of us; that what really matters is the well-being of *my* family, community, or nation. Overtaken by culturally induced despair, we come to believe that other people must fend for themselves, that preserving the planet and other living things is beyond the scope of human responsibility, that God and God alone can solve our problems. Culturally induced despair's insidious consolation exempts us from moral accountability and invites tacit denial of our identity as *imago Dei* and our role as participants in God's redemptive work.

Adopting such a despondent disposition toward life rarely results from a conscious decision to embrace culturally induced despair. Becoming despondent is more often a matter of pragmatism, exhaustion, or both. For some, choosing a pragmatic response to seemingly intractable sociocultural or religious ills seems the best they can do. A student's response to my repeated emphasis upon living toward a loving, just, and life-affirming world for all people during lectures for my Introduction to Preaching class reveals such exhaustion. "You keep talking about the world," he exclaimed, "but I am just trying to deal with my small congregation in rural North Carolina. Thinking about the world is too much." His point is well-taken. The "world" is immense, and no one person or community can respond to all the world's problems. Yet thinking about the world or a more universal

---

no longer believe it; within himself, his own soul takes the side of his friends. Job implores the testimony of God himself, because he can no longer hear the testimony of his own conscience; it is no longer anything more than an abstract and dead souvenir (memory)." The converse may also be true: that we declare ourselves innocent though on some level aware that we have participated in the oppressive structures we wish to topple. I borrow Weil's quote to highlight this latter response.

understanding of *shalom* is also important. It reminds us that our efforts toward alleviating distress in one community must not intensify the distress of other vulnerable communities. It also helpfully reminds us that eliminating a distressful or oppressive situation in our own community is not an end in itself—meaning that our work is not done when our community is well. Hope invites our participation and contributions to the broader work of alleviating violence, suffering, oppression, and other dehumanizing conditions throughout the world, no matter where our point of entry might be. For this is the work to which the gospel invites us, and the work culturally induced despair seeks to confound.

As an insidious mechanism, culturally induced despair surreptitiously gains a foothold when we lose sight of the larger ministry to which our efforts contribute. It persistently and repetitively solicits our allegiance to the distorted notion that we cannot care for ourselves and others at the same time. Culturally induced despair also evokes practices indicative of hopelessness, such as silence about and resignation to the way things are. Silence, resignation, and other despairing practices make violence, suffering, oppression, and numerous forms of dehumanization permissible and tolerable formulations, allowing them to fester and spread their malignancy throughout our known world.[5] In this respect, though not a mortal sin of the sort Aquinas describes, culturally induced despair is both destructive and propagative (a source of further negation and dehumanization). Its ultimate goal is to divert our attention away from God's vision of *shalom* so as to replace our dreams of a world where wholeness and well-being are the normative expression of human relationship with tacit resignation to the disorder and insufficiency that currently exists.

America's response to the 9/11 attacks on the World Trade Center and two other locations in the US provides a fitting example of the power of culturally induced despair to distract us from God's vision of *shalom*. Overwhelmed with grief and disheartened regarding the possibility of *shalom*, we found ourselves standing on the precipice of culturally induced despair, not just on September 11, 2001, but in the weeks, months, and years following these horrific attacks. These events disrupted our sense of well-being and reminded us of our volatility and vulnerability as a nation and as individual people. War was imminent, and "fear that the world we know will be taken away from us by people that we don't know if we don't take it away from them first" drove many of us to concur that war was our only alternative.[6] Even as

---

5. See Young, "Five Faces of Oppression."

6. Taylor, Baccalaureate address at Wake Forest University on May 14, 2006 (based on my contemporaneous notes).

we prayed, "*Thy kingdom come, thy will be done, on earth as it is in heaven*," we questioned the feasibility and advisability of a world in which love of God, neighbor, and self are guiding principles for our lives. "How are we to love people who do not appear to love us?" we asked, questioning the efficacy of peace when retaliation appeared the better alternative.

In a 2016 article for *Missio Alliance*, Derek Vreeland, Discipleship Pastor at Word of Life Church in St Joseph, Missouri, reflects upon his experience of 9/11.[7] He, like many Christians, initially supported the so-called war on terror as a viable response to the 9/11 attacks. But fifteen years later, Vreeland reevaluates his decision, challenging Christians to reflect upon how we will remember this difficult moment in history. I quote him at length:

> How Will We Remember? "Never forget" became a national motto after 9/11. Certainly, none of us will. The images of collapsing buildings, smoke, fire, and dust-covered faces will remain branded in our collective memories forever. No doubt we will remember, but how will we remember? This question is not for the American "we," but the Christian "we." How will we—who have been taught to forgive others their trespasses and love those who position themselves as an enemy—remember 9/11? We could choose to settle our thoughts on the wrongdoing, a path that leads to retaliation, or at least the desire for retaliation in some form. Some followers of Christ have gone this way. I did so in the months that followed 9/11. I applauded the so-called "war on terror," as a reasonable response to 9/11, not understanding at that time that a war on terrorism is essentially a never-ending war, a giving in to the continuous cycle of retaliation.
>
> Our desire for retaliation results in part from transmitting our pain instead of transforming it as Richard Rohr advises. He writes: "If we do not transform our pain, we will most assuredly transmit it. If we cannot find a way to make our wounds into sacred wounds, we invariably give up on life and humanity." War is a way of giving up on humanity, at least a giving up on the life of our perceived enemy. This kind of remembering, a kind of remembering that fuels a desire for retaliation, is not compatible with the way of Jesus. We need a better way to remember. We need to remember rightly.[8]

---

7. Vreeland, "A Christian Memory of 9/11."
8. Vreeland, "A Christian Memory of 9/11."

Culturally induced despair keeps us in the loop of painful remembering, clouding our desire to transform our pain. When we persist in this way of thinking, perceiving, and behaving, when we emphasize retaliation over peace, and when our efforts to protect ourselves are not tempered with love, compassion, and grace, we weaken our capacity for imagining and working toward alternative possibilities. As our imaginative potential weakens, culturally induced despair again finds a foothold.

We experience culturally induced despair, in other words, not because we do not believe in God as the source of salvation, as salvation is not our subject of discontent. We experience culturally induced despair when we lose sight of God's desire for *shalom* and of Hope's assurance and call. Culturally induced despair in full sway leads us to assent, either willingly or inadvertently, to the distorting assertion that violence, suffering, and oppression are natural, normal, acceptable, and inevitably woven into the fabric of our existence. Though opportunities for transformation exist, culturally induced despair promotes the notion that we are trapped in a closed world of oppression and disillusionment from which there is no escape.[9] And, absent a physical or psychic route of escape, we indeed feel trapped and hopeless. Over time, we come to believe that transforming our pain, our fears, or the places of insufficiency in our world is an impossible task for which we have no facility. Or worse, we hold that transformation and restoration are no longer a necessity. Gradually, such feelings and dispositions dampen our sensitivity to the voice of Hope, our ability to image alternatives, and our desire to live in partnership with the faithful God of Creation who is, even now, making all things new.

The Communicative Potency of Culturally Induced Despair

The feelings, dispositions, and practices that attend culturally induced despair do not arise ex nihilo. They develop over time. They also develop in response to a socially constructed shared system of communication that breeds doubt regarding our identity as *imago Dei* and our capacity to live in life-affirming relationship with God, others, and self. I refer to this nefarious communication system as *the deceptive language of despair,* a metaphor for the multiple means by which we encounter culturally induced despair's assertion that we and our world are irredeemably flawed and fallen. Sinful, dehumanizing cultural realities (secular and religious) feed and legitimize this system, coalescing to create a language, a system for communicating and

---

9. Freire, *Pedagogy of the Oppressed*, 31.

convincing us that violence, suffering, oppression, and other forms of dehumanization are indelibly dyed into the fabric of our society.

As a sociological concept, *fabric of society* denotes a society's culture, the various strands by which we give shape to our known world or οἰκουμένη.[10] Our known world is the world we create and inhabit together, the world that becomes perceptible as a society's cultural threads come together to create a fabric. Raymond Williams defines *culture* as "the *signifying system* through which . . . a social order is communicated, reproduced, experienced and explored."[11] Culture represents the multiple and complex ways of being, thinking, relating, and behaving a society deems acceptable: its "whole way of life."[12] These attitudes and practices may include but are not limited to various ethnic customs, foodways, artistic expressions, and intellectual contributions. Such attitudes and practices may also evince a society's rejection of customs, ways, expressions, and contributions it deems unacceptable, such as US society's rejection of Black people of African descent's cultural contributions for much of its history prior to the mid twentieth century.[13] Culture, in this way of thinking, is a comprehensive concept that includes a particular society's values, mores, practices, social conventions, and norms; its images, myths, spoken and written words, ideologies and theologies; its artistic and creative expressions; its domestic and international laws, rules, policies, and regulations; as well as the structures, systems, and institutions it establishes to administer and sustain the world we create together.

There is a reciprocal relationship between a society's culture and the various attitudes and practices that give shape to that culture. Michael Warren, drawing insight from Raymond Williams, notes, "though culture communicates a particular social order, that order itself is, in turn, shaped by its system of signifying."[14] Not only does culture communicate and exert a formative impact upon our individual and communal lives. Our attitudes, practices, thoughts, and other forms of expression communicate and reproduce culture. Culture, in this respect, is neither naturally occurring nor neutral in its formative potential. It is a human construction determined by all the dynamics of power and privilege evident in human relationship, "a signifying system keeping a social order in place."[15]

---

10. Gr. οἰκουμένη (*oikoumenē*) signifies the inhabited earth or the world we inhabit, our "known world."

11. Williams, *The Sociology of Culture*, 13.

12. Williams, *The Sociology of Culture*, 13.

13. See Du Bois's reflection on Black American's desire to live as "co-workers in the kingdom of culture," in *The Souls of Black Folk*.

14. Warren, *Seeing through the Media*, 46–47.

15. Warren, *Seeing through the Media*, 46.

Each person's experience of culture, and thus of our known world, is highly contextualized. We come to know this world and its culture by way of kinship and friendship connections, formal and informal educational experiences, social relationships, political discourse, formal and informal structures, corporate gatherings (religious and nonreligious), and other means by which we encounter one another and the systems that govern our society. Consequently, the quality of our interaction with and within the various entities, structures, and relational paradigms that constitute our society's culture significantly influences the manner by which each of us perceives and experiences our known world. These interactions impact what we know, and oftentimes what we are able to know or imagine. This is important because a society's culture is not simply a compilation of its formal assertions. The manner by which a society embraces or discounts, in word and practice, the values and ideals it espouses also contribute to a society's culture. The US Declaration of Independence's ideal that all people are created equal, for example, makes a formal assertion about US culture. However, persistent and repetitive inequality throughout the nation's history, frequently sanctioned by law, calls into question the veracity of this formal assertion. Equality as a realizable cultural ideal requires intentional and tenacious effort toward eliminating the structures that perpetuate inequality. It also requires building the infrastructure necessary to secure an equal and just society for all. Realizing the ideal of equality, in other words, does not occur by happenstance or as a result of formal assertions. It requires cultural and systemic embodiment. When a society and its members fail to live into or stop striving toward its most honorable and life-giving ideals, that society becomes a channel for propagating the deceptive language of despair.

A society that propagates the deceptive language of despair also exposes its members to the threat of culturally induced despair. This type of society fosters its own vulnerability, including disharmony among its members. The longer we live in such vulnerable and disharmonious society, the more susceptible we become to the deceptive language of despair's portrayal of our known world and of one another as irreparably flawed and disfigured. The deceptive language of despair nefariously and repetitively transmits the distorting assertion that oppressive and dehumanizing attitudes and practices are acceptable if not normal ways of being and relating in our known world. When such attitudes and practices (read: racist, sexist, xenophobic, classist, homophobic, ageist, extremist, or self-hating attitudes and practices) tinge the constituent elements of our culture, and when we respond with tolerance rather than contestation, we give license to the deceptive language of despair. Over time, tinges become recalcitrant dispositions of heart and mind. They appear to us to be permanent stains upon the fabric of our society, sociocultural conditions that will last forever.[16] The façade of permanence, the idea that current conditions will never end, thwarts our ability to dream beyond the boundaries of what currently exists. Our inertia when met with the façade of permanence tempers our collective desire to respond to God's appeal that we expunge the stain of dehumanization from the fabric of our society.

Transmitting and Reproducing the Deceptive Language of Despair

The deceptive language of despair's transmission and reproduction are dependent upon dysfunctional dynamics within and across the various cultural elements that give shape to our known world. And where such dysfunction exists, the deceptive language of despair insidiously pervades our common practices and consequently, our perception of what might be possible for our lives together. More specifically, the deceptive language of despair contributes to a bifurcated system of valuation that deems some groups worthy and deserving of greater social privilege and freedom of expression than others. Such systems also, with a comparable level of intensity, relegate particular groups to the margins of society, to spaces where social privilege is a scarce commodity and freedom is tenuous at best. The deceptive language of despair, in other words, surreptitiously infiltrates our deeply held assumption about each other as well as our determinations about what we deem normative for our known world. It catches us unaware, making us unwitting participants in transmitting and reproducing its fatalistic view of reality.

Four communication channels for the deceptive language of despair are worth exploring, both because the channels have potential for perpetuating bifurcated valuation systems, and because of the channels' likelihood for cultivating ways of perceiving, thinking and behaving that diminish our capacity to sense Hope's assurance and call. Among these communication channels are common colloquial expressions, idiomatic expressions, and cultural assumptions—especially those that are deeply entrenched enough as to be considered innocuous or at most only minimally offensive. Also included are conduits of despair concealed within constituent cultural elements, within the systems, structures, and institutions we create to provide

---

16. See Brueggemann's discussion of the "royal consciousness" in Brueggemann, *The Prophetic Imagination*.

order to our shared existence. By these and other channels, the deceptive language of despair makes its distorting message known.

Negating and Dehumanizing Colloquial and Idiomatic Expressions

Failing to examine even mundane assumptions about proper attire, hairstyles, foodways, and worship practices can increase our exposure to the deceptive language of despair's distorting messages. Minimizing exposure includes attentiveness to valuative resonances emanating from explicitly negating as well as seemingly innocuous colloquial expressions and figures of speech. Consider, for example, Christian religious language delineating the distinction between "high-church" and "low-church" worship traditions. The designation "high churchmen" was originally used in Elizabethan England (between 1558 and 1603) to refer to "the group in the Church of England which [stressed] her historical continuity with Catholic Christianity, and hence [upheld] a 'high' conception of the episcopate and of the nature of the Sacraments."[17] Despite the historical roots of the term "high church," in US society today the term has become associated with what is often thought of as better church. The valuative tone assigned to "high church" situates it within the deceptive language of despair's bifurcated system—a system that deems, in this instance, some worship practices far better than others and more deserving of social and religious sanction.

Other colloquial expressions embody and transmit a much more nefarious history. Colloquial descriptors such as "dumb jock," "dumb blonde," "nagging woman," "holy roller," "dumb Southerner," "welfare queen," "Black brute," "baby mamma," "stud," and "bitch"—not to mention numerous other racialized and sexualized terms that perpetuate stereotypes—negate and objectify. Objectification characterizes people as things rather than as subjects worthy of dignity and respect; thus, these terms also negate and obscure our shared identity as *imago Dei*. Objectifying colloquial expressions, seeing that they objectify, are by no means innocuous. Inasmuch as they negate and characterize particular people and groups as less deserving of power, privilege, freedom, and dignity (subjectivity) than others, those colloquialisms noted above, and other objectifying expressions perpetuate the deceptive language of despair's negating and dehumanizing system of valuation. Theologian Patricia Hill Collins refers to such expressions as "controlling images," characterizations that sanction oppression and marginalization,

---

17. Addleshaw, *The High Church Tradition*; Cross ed., *The Oxford Dictionary*; Hein, "The High Church."

often made concrete in our laws and regulations.[18] By recirculating objectifying colloquial expressions or holding them as ideological certainties, we become complicit in transmitting and reproducing the deceptive language of despair's dehumanizing messages.

In addition to colloquial expression, we might also consider the role common idioms and social conventions play in transmitting and reproducing the deceptive language of despair. Consider, for example, common idioms of distress or exasperation, such as "I am starving!" or "This is about to kill me!" Surely, the great majority of us do not actually mean we are starving or that we are close to death, but we employ such idioms in order to express our level of discomfort in the moment, albeit with exaggerated expressions. Other idioms such as "This is just the way that things are," "We are only human," "There's only so much we can do," "Who knows what would happen if . . . ," "What difference does it make?," "It doesn't really matter what we do," and the like pose a greater risk for transmitting and reproducing the deceptive language of despair. We make these pronouncements as expressions of exasperation or distress, as a means of assuaging our fears or tempering our concerns regarding the pervasiveness of violence, suffering, oppression, or other forms of dehumanization. With such words, accompanied by a shoulder shrug, lowered eyes, deep sighs, head-shaking, or other such gestures, we give voice to our discontent and lament the material conditions of our existence. We also express wariness through these idioms, both about the possibility of transformation, and about our own or others' facility or *will* to create the change for which we long. Though spoken without despairing intent, these and other idiomatic expressions, through their regularity and presumed harmlessness, give occasion to the deceptive language of despair.

How is this possible? Repeatedly weaving seemingly harmless idioms into our common vernacular enhances our attachment to them as potential truths about our world and about our capacity for transformation. Over time, these *idioms-become-truths* exert a formative impact upon our lives, producing and reproducing long-lasting patterns of perceiving, thinking, and behaving drenched in despair. Such expressions also contribute to the despairing attitudes and practices to which such idioms give rise, such as avoiding, ignoring, dismissing, tolerating, detaching, qualifying, hiding, and the like. Subtly and seductively, seemingly innocuous idiomatic expressions take on an ideological quality, increasing our susceptibility to becoming conduits for the deceptive language of despair's destructive messages.

Cognitively, despairing assertions and actions make the world as it exists in the present appear coherent (intelligible, cognitively acceptable)

---

18. Collins, *Black Feminist Thought*, 69–96.

and less threatening. They decrease the dissonance between the world as it exists and the world we wish to see. They also assuage our fear that we have not done enough to usher the world we imagine into existence. Expressions such as "We are already doing the most we can" (meaning, the most we will) to tackle and eliminate deplorable attitudes and practices in our nation afford us comfort. Such assertions function as benign benedictions, as benevolent pats on the back, even as deplorable conditions persist—crippling poverty among the most vulnerable in the nation; maltreatment of women, men, and children seeking refuge from violence and political persecution; disparate, class-based access to educational opportunities; disparate and class-based access to healthcare; the persistence of fresh-food deserts in poor communities; race-based mass incarceration; numerous embodiments and expressions of sexism, racism, and heteronormativity; and inadequate intervention to redress drug addiction, including the methamphetamine and crack epidemics ravaging far too many communities throughout the US. Coherence makes such conditions tolerable, which cultivates assent to the idea that violence, suffering, oppression, and other forms of dehumanization are natural, normal, acceptable, and inevitable ways of being and relating.

Emotively, despairing assertions and actions amplify the futility of dreaming or imagining life anew. They diminish our sense of connectedness with God, our mutuality with each other, and our shared responsibility for creation. In *Celebration and Experience in Preaching*, homiletician Henry Mitchell reveals the importance of the emotions and of preaching with the emotive consciousness in mind.[19] Noting the apostle Paul's emphasis upon faith, hope and love as "three of the greatest goals in life" (1 Cor 13:13), Mitchell emphasizes the formative potential of higher emotions as well as the deformative potential of lower, negative emotions.[20] Higher emotions cultivate and reinforce practices indicative of the gospel's emphasis upon wholeness and well-being. Despairing words and actions power "low emotions" such as hatred, fear, shame, guilt, apathy, hopelessness, and heartlessness while also diminishing "high emotions" such as love, empathy, compassion, holy indignation, joyful and sorrowful weeping, and mutuality.[21]

In her insightful publication titled *Suffering*, Dorothee Soelle further elucidates the powerful impact of the emotions upon our ways of being and relating, with attention to apathy.[22] Soelle describes apathy as a "social condi-

---

19. Mitchell, *Celebration and Experience*.
20. Mitchell, *Celebration and Experience*, 26.
21. Mitchell, *Celebration and Experience*, 32.
22. Soelle, *Suffering*, 36.

tion in which people are so dominated by the goal of avoiding suffering that it becomes a goal to avoid human relationships and contacts altogether."[23] Instead of fostering compassion for those who suffer, apathy turns us inward, permitting us to ignore the suffering of others. Apathy becomes more deeply entrenched when we possess the material resources and, I might add, geographic distance to shield ourselves from the suffering that pervades our existence. In other words, writes Soelle, "private prosperity obscures public poverty."[24] Such obliviousness to the state of our world deprives us of the privilege of living in loving, just, and restorative relationship with others and thus of the opportunity to live with Hope. Our challenge, therefore, as gospel proclaimers and people of good conscience, is to keep raising these subtle, despairing words and actions to consciousness; to keep naming them even as we speak and practice them, so that we remind ourselves to keep saying yes to God's yes for our lives and for creation as an important means by which we resist the deceptive language of despair's seductive lure.

Students in my Community Engagement Fellows Seminar at Wesley Theological Seminary encountered this challenge as they sought to remain steadfast and discern meaning in the Hope-filled practices they had already embraced. The Fellows Program invites students who are discerning a vocational call to community engagement through public theology, urban ministry, and missional church ministry to participate in a three-year cohort experience.[25] During these three years, they explore their area of specialization as well as develop and implement a project that responds to a need or concern about which they are passionate. The projects are indicative of each student's sense of vocational identity and commitment to the practice of *shalom*. Yet, members of this passionate and action-oriented group of community-engaged individuals found themselves questioning the efficacy of their efforts to lend their hands to God's redemptive and restorative work in the world.

"Is our work in vain? Are we making a difference? Or are we just spinning our wheels and doing something that makes us feels good with no lasting result?" During my first year with the program, and in the year following, students raised these and similar questions on several occasions. In light of the persistent ferocity of dehumanizing cultural realities they daily encountered, they wondered if their work and the work of their predecessors had brought or would yield any lasting result. Though they

23. Soelle, *Suffering*, 36.
24. Soelle, *Suffering*, 40.
25. See Wesley Theological Seminary, *The Community Engagement Institute* (web page).

remained passionate about their work, they also expressed consternation that they were confronting and responding to many of the same problems their forebears in the fight for justice had addressed, issues they thought would certainly have become passé by the twenty-first century. These and other questions captured our imagination: What lasting change resulted from the women's suffrage, civil rights, and anti-apartheid movements of the past or from the first steps toward the Poor People's Campaign in the 1960s? What does it mean that we are still addressing many of the same problems today? And what, if anything, should we expect of our current efforts toward transformation? From their vantage point, the evidence—persistent poverty; abuse of women and children; violence against Black- and Brown-bodied people; anti-Muslim, antigay, anti-immigrant, and racist rhetoric; to name a few intractable issues—seemed to reinforce the notion that nothing has or will change.

Such questions are necessary. They reveal that even as we engage in practices of Hope—as we persist in loving, restoring, resisting, emboldening, welcoming—the ferocity and seeming changeless nature of negating and dehumanizing cultural realities can cause us to doubt the veracity of our efforts toward *shalom*. But questioning is only one element of the conversation. As we strain to remember that *shalom* is a realizable possibility, Hope assures us that "the arc of the moral universe is long, but it bends toward justice," though ever so slowly and arduously.[26] In every uncertain moment, Hope is present, calling to remembrance our identity as *imago Dei* and our capacity to live as an expression of God's presence in the earth. Echoing the words of the apostle Paul to the Church at Corinth, Hope encourages, "We are afflicted in every way but not crushed; perplexed, but not driven to despair; persecuted, but not forsaken; struck down but not destroyed" (see 2 Cor 4:8-12). Our task, Paul continues, is to make the life of Jesus visible through our words and actions, not as a form of politically correct speech or behavior but as an expression of our identity as *imago Dei* and of our determination to live with Hope. We might consider, therefore, moderating our use of idioms of exasperation and distress, especially idiomatic expressions that characterize negating and dehumanizing cultural realities as changeless, as a means of resisting the deceptive language of despair's impact upon our patterns of imagining, perceiving, thinking, and behaving.

---

26. Parker, popularized by King, "Remaining Awake."

Negating and Dehumanizing Social Conventions

In addition to its resonance in colloquial expressions and idioms of exasperation and distress, the deceptive language of despair also finds opportunity in social conventions thought to be shared by all members of society. Because many of us believe such conventions to be normative and fair, their devaluating resonances are difficult to detect, as they appear innocuous. Among these seemingly innocuous conventions are regulations, evident in some professional and business settings in the US, that prescribe, among other aspects of self-presentation, *proper* hairstyles for the workplace. Rules that regulate hairstyles have been particularly troublesome for Black and other ethnic-minority women, especially regulations prohibiting hairstyles that fit with the tight curl of many ethnic women's natural hair.

On December 5, 2017, the Eleventh-Circuit Court of Appeals declined the Equal Employment Opportunity Commission's (EEOC's) petition to rehear a case in which Catastrophe Management Solutions refused to honor their job offer to Chastity Jones, an African American woman.[27] The company initially hired Ms. Jones but subsequently rescinded the offer when she refused to alter her hairstyle. Per policy, the company characterized Ms. Jones's hairstyle, natural locks (or dreadlocks), as "excessive" and against company policy, and the courts agreed.[28] Specifically, the appeals court ruled that "banning dreadlocks in the workplace under a race-neutral grooming policy—without more—does not constitute intentional race-based discrimination."[29] The ruling continued, indicating that "dreadlocks are not, according to the EEOC's proposed amended complaint, an immutable characteristic of black individuals."[30] In other words, the Eleventh-Circuit Court of Appeals determined that Ms. Jones possessed the ability to change her hairstyle, as a hairstyle is not an unalterable aspect of identity.

As a Black woman with natural hair locks, I am keenly aware of the difficulty Black women face in navigating the contours of US culture, especially in light of social conventions related to forms of self-presentation and personal grooming in professional spaces.[31] The de facto assumption among

---

27. Little, "It's Still Legal."

28. Little, "It's Still Legal."

29. *Equal Employment Opportunity Commission vs. Catastrophe Management Solutions.*

30. *Equal Employment Opportunity Commission vs. Catastrophe Management Solutions.*

31. I currently serve as a faculty member in an academic community in which little emphasis is given to how one chooses to wear their hair or their attire; therefore, people enjoy a great deal of freedom in these areas. I am not aware of a situation in which I

many in US society is that appropriately coiffed and beautiful hair is represented either by long and straight hair devoid of texture or, as popularized in media portrayals of Black women and other women with melanin-kissed skin, by thick and long curly hair with just a slight hint of texture. For many Black women, achieving such hairstyles demands a great deal of processing to their natural hair or significant expenditures on hair augmentations, such as weaves, extensions, or other such products.[32] Though many Black women opt for natural hairstyles, "these styles are not universally embraced by the larger society and are typically seen as less attractive or flattering than straight hair," creating a dilemma for Black women.[33] Should not Black women, with women of all ethnic and racial groups in the US, possess the freedom to choose the hairstyle they desire, including styles that are more consonant with the tight curl of their natural hair?

The 2017 case is not the first time the courts have been tasked with issuing a ruling regarding a woman's hair and the workplace. (These cases are most often filed by Black or other ethnic-minority women.[34]) In their insightful article, "The Hair Dilemma: Conform to Mainstream Expectations or Emphasize Racial Identity," Duke University professors Ashleigh Shelby Rosette and Tracy L. Dumas write, "Women and minorities suffer a disadvantage in crafting this professional image due to negative stereotypes, lower expectations, and workplace norms that run counter to their cultural values and that reward white male standards of behavior and appearance."[35] While all women are required to negotiate their professional identity in the workplace within the "paradox of femininity and attractiveness, . . . minority women often feel they must compensate for both their gender and race in attempting to present a professional image that will render them *credible* to their co-workers."[36]

The courts' decisions in these cases, though legally allowable, intentionally or unwittingly perpetuate racial bias regarding the unruliness and

---

have been denied a job opportunity because of my hair. But I have been on the receiving end of numerous microaggressions about my hair (about what it evokes for others) and have listened to others express oftentimes ridiculous misconceptions and curiosities about Black people's hair. Prior to my time in academia, I served in a number of professional positions in which rules regarding *proper* attire and grooming were significantly more pronounced.

32. Rosette and Dumas, "The Hair Dilemma," 410.

33. Rosette and Dumas, "The Hair Dilemma," 411.

34. Griffin "How Natural Black Hair." See also Randle "I Am Not My Hair"; Patton, "Hey Girl"; Davis, "Afro Images"; Carr, "The Paraphernalia of Suffering."

35. Rosette and Dumas, "The Hair Dilemma," 407. See also, Collins, *Black Feminist Thought*, 69–96.

36. Rosette and Dumas, "The Hair Dilemma," 408 (italics added).

unacceptability of Black and other ethnic-minority women's hair. Biases such as these arise from and contribute to the deceptive language of despair's bifurcated systems of valuation. Biased ideas about Black women's hair call Black women's credibility in the workplace and in other sectors of society into question, not because Black women have somehow demonstrated a lack of credibility, but because standards of beauty and self-presentation are assumed to communicate a person's value to society. Linking beauty standards and self-presentation norms with an assumption of one's value to society creates a peculiar correlation at best, which stifles our ability to live with Hope. The bifurcated systems of valuation to which racial and other cultural biases contribute not only threaten Black and other ethnic women's ability to navigate the contours of US culture. Bifurcated systems of valuation also rob all who perpetuate them of the capacity to truly live in just and life-affirming relationship with Black women and with the numerous others whom US culture far too often relegates to the margins.

Social conventions thought to be proper for all members of society are not limited to hair. They include the presumed rightness or properness of particular foodways, artistic expressions, manners of dress, language conventions, learning styles, teaching paradigms, institutional affiliations, and other such indicators to which society assigns value. The dominant paradigm for teaching and learning in the US, for example, remains didactic, which privileges students who demonstrate strengths in verbal or logical learning, or both, despite the vast number of students who possess significant strengths in other styles of learning. Students who do not fit the traditional paradigm are marked *exceptional* (a word often negatively construed), suggesting they are an exception to the rule or to the normal way of learning. How much more might we advance the work of *shalom* and nurture wholeness and well-being if we were to embrace educational paradigms that acknowledge and value the diverse learners who populate our educational institutions? Again, bifurcated systems of valuation deprive us of the ability to honor one another as *imago Dei* and as deserving recipients of God's *shalom*.

Negating and Dehumanizing Constituent Cultural Elements

Among the most disruptive channels through which the deceptive language of despair transmits and reproduces its negating and dehumanizing messages are those concealed within constituent cultural elements of our known world. Constituent cultural elements include the structures, systems, and institutions we create to provide order and to communicate the norms, values, and mores we deem appropriate to our shared existence. They also include the attitudes and practices that produce and sustain this order as well as the ways of perceiving, thinking and behaving shaped by our participation in it. At their best, constituent elements, such as educational institutions, religious communities, families, governing bodies, businesses, and industries embody, transmit, and reproduce our highest ideals and most noble aspirations. They acknowledge and amplify our interconnectedness with one another and all creation as well as our great potential as agents of restoration and compassionate care. And at their most destructive, they promote acquiescence to the negating and dehumanizing notion that violence, suffering, oppression, and other dehumanizing conditions are natural, normal, acceptable, and inevitable expressions of our shared existence.

In *Seeing a Color-Blind Future*, Patricia J. Williams laments racism's deep entrenchment in US culture. In response, she issues a moral imperative encouraging us to acknowledge our "common, ordinary humanity" with all other human beings.

> I am certain that the solution to racism lies in our ability to see its ubiquity but not to concede its inevitability. It lies in the collective and institutional power to make change, at least as much as with the individual will to change. *It also lies in the absolute moral imperative to break the childish, deadly circularity of centuries of blindness to the shimmering brilliance of our common, ordinary humanity.* I do believe wholeheartedly that there are lessons to be gleaned from the practiced commitment to the community of all people.[37]

The nation's practice of obscuring or denying racism's deep stain upon its cultural fabric makes US citizens particularly vulnerable to the deceptive language of despair's negating and dehumanizing assertions.

Systemically, obscuring or denying legitimizes discriminatory practices and inequitable institutional constructions that relegate some to the margins of society while centering and inordinately rewarding others. Obscuring and denying racism and other forms of dehumanization also permits the nation, its citizens, and the church to abdicate moral accountability for the bifurcated system of valuation that both produces and is sustained by racism's hardy persistence in US culture. As a result, obscuring and denying permit racism and other dehumanizing constructs to clothe themselves in the accouterments of each new era and maintain their net effect. Therefore, American citizens are vulnerable to despair's deceptive language not because the majority of U.S. citizens overtly champion racism

---

37. Williams, *Seeing a Color-Blind Future*, 68 (italics added).

and other forms of dehumanization. Indeed our vulnerability consists in the systemic silence about and negation of such a legacy's existence despite its deep stain upon the fabric our society.

When the guiding principles and organizational configurations of our social and religious institutions promote discriminatory practices that bequeath privilege to some (generally White men) while simultaneously disprivileging others (generally racial and ethnic minorities and women), they give license to the deceptive language of despair. When we prioritize the accumulation of wealth over the well-being of our neighbors, we give license to the deceptive language of despair. When we consume and recirculate negating rhetoric about immigrants and other marginalized communities, we give license to the deceptive language of despair. When we remain silent in the face of injustices or evince reticence about lending our hands to God's restorative work, we give license to the deceptive language of despair.

Afforded such license and opportunity, the deceptive language of despair distracts us from God's vision of *shalom* and diminishes our capacity to sense and respond to Hope's assurance and call. The trajectory of our world appears fixed and its course unchangeable. Having convinced us of this idea, the deceptive language of despair next lulls us into believing that the pursuit and accumulation of wealth, power, and pleasure without regard for the impact of such pursuit upon the environment or on the lives of others, especially the poorest and most vulnerable in our world, is a necessary and acceptable pattern for life. Over time and absent contestation, this pessimistic view of reality becomes rooted in our durable patterns of perceiving, thinking, and behaving. Pessimism produces acquiescence to the way things are, and acquiescence undermines our ability to live responsive to Hope assurance and call.

Acquiescence co-opts our imaginative potential. Over and against images of flourishing grounded in mutuality and communal well-being, the deceptive language of despair's invitation to acquiesce functions to convince us that current distributions of power, privilege, material possessions, and access to basic human rights are as they should be, and that existing social arrangements, such as those promoted by the US and our allies, are morally right and just. Through the deceptive language of despair, we are urged to accept social arrangements rife with violence, suffering, oppression, and other forms of dehumanization as the best we can do with the resources available to us (read: human rights, political power, material wealth, natural resources). The invitation to acquiesce also encourages us to cosign policies and practices that bifurcate access to those resources along lines of race, ethnicity, class, gender, sexual orientation, age, physical and cognitive ability, religion, national identity, and other dividing constructs. Similar to the unjust biblical prophets excoriated in Mic 3:5, "who cry 'Peace' / when they have something to eat, / but declare war against those / who put nothing into their mouths," those who acquiesce to despair deceptively declare "Peace" even as violence, suffering, and oppression ravage our sisters and brothers. In this respect, the deceptive language of despair's invitation to acquiesce risks making us prophets of our own undoing.

The invitation to acquiesce is difficult to decline—a difficulty we sense most viscerally with reference to policies, practices, or preferences from which we gain personal benefit or privilege. I discovered this several years ago after accepting a new faculty position. I called my insurance provider's helpline to seek assistance identifying a physician in my area. I provided the necessary insurance information and described my needs. To my surprise, and despite my request for names of private physicians, the helpline representative repeatedly directed me to family-practice facilities and clinics in the area. In the course of the conversation, I mentioned that I was new to the faculty at my institution and expressed my surprise that the plan did not include private physicians. And then it happened: The helpline representative made an about-face, chiding me for not noting earlier in the conversation my position on the faculty. She then proceeded to provide a list of excellent physicians in the area, from which I was able to choose a suitable doctor. After a bit of investigation, I discovered that my insurance plan was no different from plans available to the numerous staff and service employees at my institution. Yet my privileged position as faculty afforded me access to options that were presumably withheld from other employees. I make this assumption because the representative I had called initially assumed that I was one of those "other employees." And while I recounted the story to administrators and wrote an email of complaint to the insurance provider, I also benefited from the preferential status that my position as faculty afforded me.

My experience is but one example of how invitations to acquiesce to inequitable social arrangements present themselves. Cynthia Hudley's investigation of policies and practices that guide funding for K–12 public education in the US adds to our understanding of this deceptive lure.[38] Hudley, now retired professor of education at UC Santa Barbara, notes that we have done little to close the rather significant gap in the availability of resources between "urban schools" and schools in "high-poverty" neighborhoods and schools in middle-class and affluent neighborhoods. In addition to pointing out deteriorating physical plants, Hudley notes in her 2013 investigation that teachers at all levels in urban and high-poverty schools

---

38. Hudley, "Education and Urban Schools."

"report having to work with outdated textbooks in short supply; outdated computers and other kinds of technology; and inadequate or nonexistent science equipment, materials and labs."[39] Such conditions "diminish student engagement and achievement" and render inaccessible the opportunity to learn and excel at the same level as students at well-resourced schools.[40] Families who possess the material resources necessary to ensure their children attend well-resourced schools fare significantly better than those who rely upon underresourced public schools in neighborhoods that are similarly underresourced. Accepting these conditions as the best we can do, or ignoring them and assuming that the plight of urban and high-poverty schools is not *our* problem evince acquiescence, a practice that perpetuates the disparate distribution of resources among public schools.

The persistence of toxic environmental conditions that disproportionately target poor communities and communities of color provides another example of the invitation to acquiesce. Not only do these conditions evince inequity, they also evoke important questions about our willingness to consent to policies and practices that deny or diminish racially and economically marginalized people's access to safe living environments and other life-sustaining resources. Theologian Dwight N. Hopkins's insightful article, "Holistic Health and Healing: Environmental Racism and Ecological Justice," details the problem.[41] In an in-depth analysis of the environmental movement in the US, Hopkins reveals the impact of unsafe environmental conditions upon working-class and poor communities of color. Highlighting their risk of exposure to toxic environmental conditions, he writes, "millions of African Americans, Latinos, Pacific Islanders, and Native Americans are trapped in polluted environments because of their race and color."[42] As a consequence, "inhabitants of these communities are exposed to greater health and environmental risks than is the general population."[43] These communities, alongside other poor communities, such as coal-mining communities in Appalachia and other regions of the US, do not have the same opportunities as other Americans "to breathe clean air, drink clean water, enjoy clean parks and playgrounds, or work in a clean, safe environment."[44]

39. Hudley, "Education and Urban Schools."

40. Hudley, "Education and Urban Schools."

41. Hopkins, "Holistic Health and Healing." See also, Lee, "Beyond Toxic Wastes and Race"; Bullard, "Introduction"; and Bullard, "Anatomy of Environmental Racism"; Schade, *Creation-Crisis Preaching*; Pinn, "Of God, Money, and Earth"; Rasmussen "Environmental Racism."

42. Hopkins, "Holistic Health and Healing," 16.

43. Hopkins, "Holistic Health and Healing," 16.

44. Hopkins, "Holistic Health and Healing," 10.

This is due in part to their lack of sufficient economic resources to move out of contaminated areas. But it also reflects the continual failure of will on the part of local and federal political leaders to effect policy changes that would eliminate toxic environmental conditions in poor communities.

Hopkins makes this point more poignantly in his comments regarding racism and environmental policy decisions.

> Devastation is an understatement when applied to people of color's holistic health; that is to say, environmental and social wellness. Environmental racism undergirds decisions about contaminated fish consumption, air pollution, hazardous toxic sites, urban incinerators and landfills, lead poisoning in children, Native American land rights, the use of technologies in sustainable development, and farm workers' proximity to pesticides.[45]

Environmental racism, and environmental classism, sanctions and sustains unsafe and unhealthy living conditions for poor communities, a disproportionate number of which are communities of color.

Hopkins's insights about environmental racism and my added emphasis upon environmental classism are difficult to hear because they remind us that we cannot remain oblivious to the problems that persist in racially and economically marginalized communities throughout our nation. For example, the problem of lead-contaminated drinking water in Flint, Michigan, which was identified in 2014, has persisted for more than five years. This issue dominated the headlines and national news coverage throughout 2016 accompanied by an immense public outcry for solutions. But eventually, the story dropped from the headlines and in some cases from public consciousness as the crisis continued well into 2019, more than five years after the problem was originally made public.

Another example, less prominent in the headlines, are the continual increases in black lung disease among coal miners in central Appalachian coal-mining states. A May 2018 NPR report revealed a steady increase of black lung disease since its 2012 and 2016 investigations, including an increase of "30 percent in West Virginia and 16 percent each in Kentucky and Virginia" since 2016.[46] Robert Cohen, an occupational health researcher at the University of Illinois Chicago, who was interviewed for the report says, "You know, it's something we should not be seeing . . . at all and we're seeing thousands of cases still in the 21st century."[47] Environmental racism and

---

45. Hopkins, "Holistic Health and Healing," 16.
46. Berkes, "New Studies Confirm a Surge."
47. Berkes, "New Studies Confirm a Surge."

classism are not acceptable expressions of our lives together; they are not the best that we can do given the resources available to us.

These problems beckon our collective concern as a nation and as people of faith. They also highlight the deceptive language of despair's potential for misrepresenting negating social realities as normal, acceptable, and indelibly woven into the fabric of our society. When we ignore these problems or accept the despairing assertion that we are already doing the best we can do, we risk consenting to the deceptive language of despair's distorting message that we have already exhausted restorative possibilities for our known world.

How is this possible? Responses are numerous. In some instances, the deceptive language of despair functions to convince us that we are incapable of simultaneously caring for others and ourselves. As a mechanism that promotes acquiescence to what is given, the deceptive language of despair stokes the flames of self-centeredness, so as to convince us that prioritizing our own material well-being, and oftentimes our material excesses, is preferable to considering the well-being of others. The deceptive language of despair similarly stokes self-centeredness among those of us experiencing dearth in our individual and collective lives. Even as we sense the sting of oppression, the deceptive language of despair invites us to fix our eyes upon our own needs and our needs alone, concealing the possibility of collective action, such as pooling our material, intellectual, spiritual, or corporal resources to meet the needs of the many. Snared in its deceptive web, we become consumed with mere survival and lose sight of our potential for imagining alternative possibilities.

Nancy Lynn Westfield, religious educator and practical theologian, describes *mere survival* as "hunkering down, rudimentary maintenance, the struggle to meet necessity."[48] Survival of this sort evinces estrangement, isolation, insecurity, doubt, fear, reticence, and resignation to endure suffering without anticipation of change. Opposing theologian Delores Williams's assertion that "God, through Jesus, [gives] humankind new vision to see the resources for positive, abundant relational life," mere survival evinces adaptation to the way that things are.[49] Williams describes survival as engaging in the "ethical thought and practice upon which to build positive, productive quality of life."[50] It is creative and productive, not rudimentary and stagnant. Westfield's emphasis upon resilience similarly orients us toward creating and producing, as resilience "speaks of elements of Hope and the ability to

---

48. Westfield, *Dear Sisters*, 7.
49. Williams, *Sisters in the Wilderness*, 165.
50. Williams, *Sisters in the Wilderness*, 165.

dream past moments, days, years of desperation."[51] The practice of resilience (Westfield) and *new vision to see resources for positive abundant relational life* (Williams) evinces a refusal to accept the deceptive language of despair's assertion that reality is fixed and impervious to transformation.

By every means the deceptive language of despair seeks to dampen our desire to live with Hope. It repeatedly promotes the notion that we and our world are irredeemable flawed and fallen and that efforts toward transformation are futile at best. It also contributes to and keeps alive a bifurcated system of valuation designed to convince us that inequitable distributions of power, privilege, material resources and rights are paradigmatically acceptable, if not normal. Escaping the deceptive language of despair's distorted construal of reality is tough. We encounter its negating and dehumanizing assertions in such unexpected cultural forms as colloquial and idiomatic expressions, social conventions, and constituent cultural elements—including in the assumptions, mores, attitudes, practices, systems, structures, and institutions that give form to our known world. Over time, the deceptive language of despair functions to assuage our fears that we have not done enough. It creates moral and social allowances that permit people of faith and good conscience to abdicate our responsibility to love our neighbor as ourselves. For if the deceptive language of despair's dehumanizing assertions are true; if negating social realities are permanent and there are no more transformative possibilities left to explore, what need is there to live with Hope or lend our hands to God's restorative work in the world? Of what necessity is living into our identity as *imago Dei* in such a world?

Questions such as these invite acquiescence to the deceptive language of despair's negating and dehumanizing assertions, and acquiescence gives rise to culturally induced despair. Culturally induced despair makes itself known systemically and attitudinally. Systemically, the persistence of dysfunctional and inequitable social arrangements evinces social embrace of culturally induced despair's construal of reality. Attitudinally, culturally induced despair gives rise to an immense sense of hopelessness regarding the state of our world and humanity's ability to live true to our identity as *imago Dei*. Hopelessness ensues when we resign ourselves to the notion that the violence, suffering oppression, and dehumanization of the present are determinative of the future, views often held most resolutely by those who benefit from current social arrangements. Hopelessness, that is, is not principally a possession of the poor and dispossessed. Walter Brueggemann's reflection on hopelessness is apropos. He writes:

---

51. Westfield, "Toward a Womanist Approach," 524.

> Because hope has such a revolutionary function, *it is more likely that failure to hope—hopelessness—happens among the affluent, the prosperous, the successful, the employable, the competent, for whom the present system works well.* We are the ones who are likely to be seduced into taking the present political, economic, intellectual systems too seriously and to equating it with reality. Indeed, it is prudent to take it that way, because that is where the jobs and benefits are. The more one benefits from the rewards of the system, the more one is enraptured with the system, until it feels like the only game in town and the whole game.[52]

As an insidious cultural mechanism, culturally induced despair legitimizes exclusionary practices that deprive others of the rights and privileges we desire for our own affinity and identity group or groups. And it presents such constructions as *the only game in town and the whole game*. In this static view of reality, dehumanization and oppression become acceptable expressions of human relationship, rendering those who are most adversely impacted "permissible victims," per Frances Wood, and those whom the system rewards admissible beneficiaries.[53]

The vast reality of violence, suffering, oppression, and other dehumanizing conditions is horrific and painful, of this there is no doubt. As Serene Jones has said, "The world is not as it should be, and the brokenness we experience cuts deep into our social fabric and has done so for a long time."[54] Such conditions exert a claim upon our lives, affording each of us an opportunity to discover the place, as Frederick Buechner writes, where our "deep gladness and the world's deep hunger meet."[55] Culturally induced despair seeks to silence this call to vocation and with it the voice of Hope. But hopelessness and despair do not have the final word. Hope's assurance and call resonates within, assuring us of God's redemptive presence and reminding us of our call to vocation. We are *imago Dei*, created to live as a reflection of divine presence in the earth, especially at such a time as this. And, like "Rachel weeping for her children," we will not be consoled (Jer 31:15; Matt 2:18).[56]

---

52. Brueggemann, *Hope Within History*, 81 (italics added).
53. Wood, "'Take My Yoke,'" 46.
54. Jones, *Feminist Theory*, 96.
55. Buechner, *Wishful Thinking*, 95.
56. In Jeremiah, the prophet anticipates the return of the Hebrew people from Babylonian exile, asserting that God hears their cry and will respond: "Thus says the Lord: / A voice is heard in Ramah, / lamentations and bitter weeping. / Rachel is weeping for her children; she refuses to be comforted for her children, / because they are no more" (31:15). In response to her cry, the prophet continues, "Thus says the Lord:

To be clear, I am not advocating a life of perpetual anxiety or psychic restlessness about negating social realities, though moments of restlessness, discontent, and anxious anticipation may very well become necessary. Restlessness reminds us that we do not carry the weight of the world upon our shoulders alone, as humans are but one partner in this restorative work. We are coworkers with God, participants in the restorative and redemptive work of the Divine. As coworkers, we embrace the difficult yet necessary task of identifying and naming (deconstructing) the channels by which culturally induced despair communicates its destructive messages—an important step toward eliminating distortion and cultivating attitudes and practices of Hope. It is imperative, therefore, that we remain ever cognizant of our inherent identity as *imago Dei* and of our vocational call to live as a reflection of God's presence in the earth.

/ Keep your voice from weeping, / and your eyes from tears; / for there is a reward for your work, says the Lord: / they shall come back from the land of the enemy; / there is hope for your future, says the Lord: / your children shall come back to their own country" (31:16–17). In the New Testament, the Gospel of Matthew (2:18) quotes Jer 3:15 as a response to the events that necessitate Joseph and Mary's escape to Egypt with their young son, Jesus. King Herod, who has heard of Jesus's birth, issues an edict to kill all the children in and around Bethlehem who were two years old or under (Matt 2:16). Jer 31:15 fittingly expresses the grief mothers throughout Bethlehem must have experienced over the death of their children.

3

Disclosing the Dangers of Culturally Induced Despair

Common rituals and mythologies are agencies of symbolic socialization and control. They demonstrate how society works by dramatizing its norms and values. They are essential parts of the general system of messages that cultivates prevailing outlooks (which is why we call it culture) and regulates social relationships. This system of messages, with its story-telling function, make people perceive as real and normal and right that which fits the established social order.[1]

—George Gerbner and Larry Gross

Living with Hope, we are discovering, is a complex matter. It is far more than wishful thinking, blind faith, or indolently awaiting the day when God will make all things new. Living with Hope is a practice, our considered and active response to Hope's assurance and call. Responding to Hope's call evinces our acknowledgment of God's redemptive presence in the world and acceptance of our vocational call to become coworkers with the Divine. As coworkers, we also acknowledge our identity as *imago Dei* and the vast potential we hold for living as a reflection of God's presence in the earth. And we bear an ethical responsibility to do so in a nondistorting, nondestructive manner. For though we may acknowledge our identity as *imago Dei*, if we adopt distorted ways of perceiving, thinking, and behaving; if we acquiesce to the notion that violence, suffering, oppression, and other forms of dehumanization are acceptable and inevitable; if we misconstrue god-likeness as the power to dominate and subjugate; then

1. Gerbner and Gross, "Living with Television," 363–64.

we present to one another and to ourselves a distorted image of God. Why is this important? Because acquiescence to dysfunctional and inequitable social arrangements or to the view that things must always remain the same, especially when we or our identity group or groups inordinately benefit from such arrangements, gives culturally induced despair opportunity to propagate its distorted construal of reality.

In Chapter 2, we explored culturally induced despair's sociopolitical and attitudinal impact upon our ability to sense Hope's presence and to acknowledge our shared identity as *imago Dei*. Culturally induced despair, we revealed, is an insidious mechanism that co-opts our imaginative potential and subsequently our attitudes and practices, oftentimes without our conscious consent. We also identified four channels through which culturally induced despair transmits and reproduces its deceptive messages, including seemingly innocuous colloquial expressions, idioms of exasperation, commonly held cultural assumptions, and constituent elements of our known world. These channels coalesce to create a communication system, the deceptive language of despair, which functions to distort our view of reality and distract us from Hope's assurance and call. In this chapter, we extend the conversation to include five additional channels, namely, negating images, myths, ideologies, theologies, and ecclesial commitments and the threat they pose to our ability to live with Hope and acknowledge our shared identity as *imago Dei*. Alongside those identified in chapter 2, these channels and their underlying constructs transmit and reproduce the deceptive language of despair. Accepted as truth, despairing assertions degrade our imaginative potential, robbing us of the capacity to envisage beyond the boundaries of our present reality.

We begin our discussion by exploring the power and potential of human imagination. Paul Ricœur, Maxine Green, Maria Harris, Paulo Freire, and Henry Giroux's reflection on the imagination will aid us in identifying both its possibilities as well as the danger of imaginative dearth. Their wisdom and insights also undergird our consideration of the roles negating and dehumanizing images, myths, ideologies, theologies, and ecclesiological commitments play in constituting habits of human imagination that diminish our capacity to sense Hope's assurance and call, to acknowledge our shared identity as *imago Dei*, and to dream our world anew. Several additional dialogue partners will enrich our conversation: Michael Warren's *Seeing through the Media: A Religious View of Communication and Cultural Analysis* and bell hook's *Black Looks: Race and Representation* will guide our discussion about the iconic nature and formative potential of media images.[2]

2. Warren, *Seeing through the Media*.

These works, alongside Marlon T. Riggs's documentary film *Ethnic Notions*, will ground our exploration of iconic images as a reservoir from which culturally induced despair's distorting messages flow.[3] The deceptive language of despair also propagates its messages via negating and dehumanizing ideologies and myths, and through the binary constructions that support and perpetuate them. Patricia Hill Collins's discussion of binary thinking in *Black Feminist Thought: Knowledge, Consciousness and the Politics of Empowerment* and Sander Gilman's exploration of nineteenth-century iconography in "Black Bodies, White Bodies: Toward an Iconography of Female Sexuality in Late Nineteenth-Century Art, Medicine, and Literature" will guide our exploration in this area.[4] Justo L. González's *The Story of Christianity*, volume 1 and Obery M. Hendricks's *The Politics of Jesus: Rediscovering the True Revolutionary Nature of Jesus's Teachings and How They Have Been Corrupted* will aid our exploration of theology's and ecclesiology's potential as conduits of despair.[5] My own interpretive reading of Jesus's and the early church's foundational theological commitment to loving God and neighbor will further this dialogue and analysis of culturally induced despair's theological and ecclesial resonance. My desire is that investigating the channels through which culturally induced despair communicates its deceptive messages will embolden us to interrupt its transmission and reproduction and to seek pathways for cultivating ways of perceiving, thinking, and behaving that are indicative of living with Hope.

Disclosing the Dangers of Imaginative Dearth

The imagination is one of our most significant capacities as human beings. It makes possible our ability to dream our world into existence and has been the impetus for transformative and emancipatory thought and action for millennia. As we will discuss later, the imagination has also been the source evil doings—hence the necessity for an ethical foundation upon which to ground our imaginings. By way of Hope-infused imagination, we envisage our world as in the process of transformation, as successively moving toward the end of violence, suffering, oppression, and dehumanization in every form, and progressively becoming a reality in which war as a course of study will come to an end and all creation shall bask in the glory of God's *shalom*. But something stands in our way. Our challenge, and precisely the reason imagination is important, is that the deceptive language of despair's

3. Riggs, prod. and dir., *Ethnic Notions*.
4. Collins, *Black Feminist Thought*; Gilman, "Black Bodies, White Bodies."
5. González, *The Story of Christianity*; Hendricks, *The Politics of Jesus*.

resonance in the various twists and turns of life can thwart our imaginative potential and fill us with despair. Our imagination can be left wanting when we give sustained assent to the notion that alternatives are impossible or worse, that change is unnecessary. This applies whether we are disaffected and overwhelmed by the chaos and insufficiency of the present or whether (as Walter Brueggemann suggests) we are satiated by static religion, comfort, privilege, and power.[6] Therefore, I identify imaginative dearth fueled by the deceptive language of despair as the primary threat to our ability to live with Hope and imagine our world anew.

Gripped by imaginative dearth, we experience a pronounced dissipation of the imagination's radiance, radius, and creativeness, as we lean ever so closely toward culturally induced despair. In such a state of seizure, alternative arrangements appear to us as nonsense, as fanciful ideations devoid of grounding in reality. Maria Harris notes this danger when she writes, "A tendency exists in some to limit the meaning of imagination to fantasy or make-believe, even to assume it refers to a kind of nonserious dabbling or dilettantism of the mind."[7] Labeled as products of just such narrow, fantasy-producing imagination and so viewed as having no apparent or acknowledged grounding in reality, proposals that promote more loving, just, and life-affirming existence for all are often dismissed as implausible or viewed with suspicion. Dismissals of this sort limit our ability to imagine our world anew and live responsively to Hope's assurance and call. We become adept at bemoaning social, political, and religious ills and, lacking fruitful imagination, we come to believe our critique is itself the change we seek. More dangerously, imaginative dearth can lead us to reject life-affirming alternatives to our current situation, especially those with which we are unfamiliar.

Culturally induced despair's mechanistic proficiency to seize our imaginative potential and thwart our ability to dream our world anew made itself known as I taught with a group of pastoral leaders during the summer of 2019. We had been engaged in a very generative conversation about embodied Hope and the importance of the imagination for our ability to live with Hope and wanted to think more deeply about the implications of these ideas for our ministry settings. As a culminating exercise, I asked participants to gather in small groups and together imagine how we and our world would be different if we took Jesus's ministerial vision seriously and committed ourselves to creating a loving, just, and life-affirming existence for all creation. I prefaced the exercise by clarifying, "This exercise is an invitation for us to activate our imagination. It is not a fanciful exercise, but rather

6. Brueggemann, *The Prophetic Imagination*, 28–37.
7. Harris, *Teaching and Religious Imagination*, 30.

a purposeful practice, as imagining is the initial step toward realization." Drawing wisdom from Brueggemann's cultural critique that "our culture is competent to implement almost anything and to imagine almost nothing,"[8] I offered an additional note: "This is an invitation to imagine, not manage or worry about a plan of implementation. There is a place for plans and implementation, for concretely living in anticipation or *living with Hope*, but here we focus on imagining."

The groups, with laptop, pen, and pad in hand, gathered to begin their work. At the conclusion of the exercise, I asked each group to share their vision of possibility. Some imagined the possibility of food, clothing, and shelter for everyone; environments free of carbon emissions and other polluting agents; international peace among nations; the dismantling of the multiple isms that divide us; an end to interreligious discord; global reconciliation; and the like. But others found imagining a new reality a more difficult task. Fixed upon the chaotic state of our present reality, some leaders became preoccupied with identifying social, political, and religious ills and naming the physical and psychic pain they create. They also spoke words of lament and discontent, an important step toward acknowledging that our world is not as it should be. But they could not imagine a day when such ills would no longer exist:

"Will the day ever come when people will view my son with autism as a whole person?"

"Will the church ever fully accept and affirm me for who I am?"

"Is it reasonable to think that racism, sexism, and homophobia will end in my lifetime?"

"When will we stop looking askance at people with mental and emotional illnesses?"

As these leaders voiced their discontent, they also echoed the sentiment that such ills will never end—a sentiment too deeply entrenched to abandon, despite the pain it evokes. Imaginative dearth anchors us to places of pain and discontent with no apparent route of escape.

There is a more sinister side to imaginative dearth, as I intimate above. When experiencing imaginative dearth, we may dismiss or belittle efforts toward transformation, or we may misconstrue such efforts as malevolent, reacting with disdain or very often with unfounded fear. The reasons for such cynicism and fearfulness are various. In some instances, disdain and cynicism arise because of the untested quality of new ideas and latent fears about the fragility of systems and structures upon which we rely. In other instances, there is a more elemental reason; we are simply wedded to the

---

8. Brueggemann, *The Prophetic Imagination*, 40.

way things are, as this is the world we know and feel competent to navigate, and we are unwilling to see it change. Very often, however, those who summarily reject new ideas view them as malevolent. In their novelty, new ideas and proposals press the social, political, and religious boundaries of current systems and structures, at times threatening to dismantle them or require of them significant change.

Christian debates about proposals to affirm women's ordination and pastoral leadership or the ordination and pastoral appointments of LGBTQAI individuals reveal well this sinister side of imaginative dearth. Those who vociferously and adamantly reject such proposals likely view them as a threat to the well-being of the church, and perhaps as a threat made by people with malevolent intentions for the gathered community. In their way of thinking, proponents of LGBTQAI and women's ordination are intent upon destroying the Christian faith and must be stopped. Successfully advocating for change in these and other difficult areas begins, I am convinced, at the level of the imaginary. It will require our openness to imagining the possibility of change, which might include giving voice to both the nightmarish images that flood our consciousness and the images of loving, just, and reconciling Christian communities in which all are welcomed as sisters and brothers. What would it mean, for example, if we acknowledge our shared commitment to the gospel? What if we afforded to women and LGBTQAI individuals the dignity and respect necessary to freely and with grace exercise their gifts (including their gifts for congregational leadership) alongside all others in the Christian church? How might our attitudes, policies, and practices change if we engaged in such acts of hospitality, love, and justice? And how might God work more expansively in our midst if we truly believed the Creator whose Spirit animates each of us for the work of the ministry is no respecter of persons and shows no partiality (see Acts 10:34)? Questions like these and the honest reflection they invite open us to the theological conviction that God's *shalom* is still a realizable possibility. They also move us another step closer to resisting culturally induced despair's drain upon our imaginative potential.

I name imaginative dearth as a problem because whatever the underlying causes, and there may be many, our attachment to unjust and life-denying structures and systems in church and society can so degrade our imaginative potential that we become complicit in negating God's just intent and desire for *shalom*. Imaginative dearth also traps us in a state of hopeless and discontent, or it makes us oblivious to the suffering of others, unaware in either case that we possess the capacity to imagine life otherwise. Thus, fertile and life-giving imagination is needed to power our sense of identity as *imago Dei* and our capacity to live with Hope.

Cultivating Fertile and Life-Giving Imagination

In *History and Truth*, philosopher Paul Ricœur stresses the imagination's significance for our inherent potential as human beings. Against notions of the imagination as constituted by fanciful or childish ideations, Ricœur describes the imagination as the seat of human possibility. The imagination, he advises, has three functions: metaphysical, explorative and prospective, and mytho-poetic, all of which enhance our ability to live with Hope.[9] The imagination's metaphysical function, Ricœur writes, "cannot be reduced to a simple projection of vital, unconscious or repressed desire."[10] Humanity's inherent capacity to imagine, to envisage and conceive of possibilities that do not exist in the present, powers our ability to propose futures and live toward their actualization. In this sense the imagination is also visionary and generative, as imagining our lives anew reveals vistas of possibility yet unexplored. Ricœur describes this quality of the imagination as its "prospective and explorative function"—imagination's ability to live in anticipation of the futures we envisage, even when evidence suggests our efforts to build such futures are likely futile.[11] Many Christians, for example, echo Jesus's assertion that God's kin(g)dom is drawing near, even as the signs of the time suggest its remoteness. Yet Christians continually pray, "thy kingdom come, they will be done, on earth as it is in heaven," daily exploring possibilities and living in anticipation of God's kin(g)dom fully realized. The imagination's prospective and explorative function, in other words, is not constrained by what exists, or limited by what seems probable. Despite evidence that humans lack the capacity to imagine and live toward new realities, humans do posses this capacity.

Given the imagination's metaphysical and explorative and prospective functions, Ricœur surmises, the imagination "is, *par excellence*, the instituting and constituting of what is humanly possible. In imagining possibilities, [humans] act as prophet[s] of [their] own existence."[12] At our fullest *capacity* as human being, when we are living most intently as *imago Dei*, we act as *"prophets of [our] own existence."*[13] Biblical prophets were visionaries who, under God's influence, critiqued the oppressive systems of their times and proposed new realities. Their prophecies were far from fanciful ideations; they were contextually significant, concrete proposals of an

---

9. Ricœur, *History and Truth*, 126.
10. Ricœur, *History and Truth*, 126.
11. Ricœur, *History and Truth*, 127.
12. Ricœur, *History and Truth*, 127 (italics original).
13. Ricœur, *History and Truth*, 127 (italics added).

"alternative community" indicative of God's fidelity and desire for *shalom*.[14] To that end, Jeremiah, Isaiah, Micah, Amos, and other biblical prophets sought to energize everyday people "to engage the promise of newness that is at work in our history with God."[15] And when people failed to respond, biblical prophets called them to repent, to turn away from that which fosters oppression and toward the life-giving and liberating light of God. As prophets of our own existence, humans possess the potential to envisage and live toward restorative possibilities in our world today. Imagining and restoring includes holding each other and ourselves accountable as we make decisions and expend the energy and resources necessary to create and establish new relational paradigms that prioritize the wellbeing of the many and relegate none to the margins or to a life of dearth.

So, why is the imagination important to our conversation about embodied Hope? Ricœur writes, "We can then begin to understand in what sense we may speak of a redemption through imagination: by means of dreams of innocence and reconciliation, hope works to the fullest human capacity."[16] Hope is at work in the imagination, enlivening us to dream a world in which reconciliation is the normative expression of our shared existence. The imagination, in this sense, affords redemptive or restorative possibilities. Redemption through imagination, however, does not occur by chance or as the result of a thought exercise. Redemption requires us to embrace new *myths* about who we are and of what we consist, "not in the positivistic sense of legend or fable," Ricœur explains, "but in the phenomenological sense of religion, in the sense of a meaningful story of the destiny of the whole human race."[17] He refers to this as the imagination's "mytho-poetic function," our ability to re-story our lives and open our world to redemptive possibilities. How might our lives be different, for example, if our stories amplified humanity's inherent identity as *imago Dei* and our potential for living as a nondistorting expression of divine presence in the earth rather than humanity's perpetual flawedness, fallenness, guilt, and shame? What if we re-storied our lives? I invite our consideration of these questions because according to Ricœur, "every *real* conversion, is first a revolution at the level of our directive images."[18] By telling new stories and envisioning our world anew, we enhance our ability to live with Hope and strengthen our resistance to imaginative dearth.

14. Brueggemann, *The Prophetic Imagination*, 59.
15. Brueggemann, *The Prophetic Imagination*, 60.
16. Ricœur, *History and Truth*, 127.
17. Ricœur, *History and Truth*, 127.
18. Ricœur, *History and Truth*, 127 (italics original).

In *Teaching and Religious Imagination*, educational theorist Maria Harris adds to our discussion of the imagination by proposing a religious conception of the imagination. "A religious perspective," Harris writes, "is a way to value, to approach a human activity from a particular angle of vision, where the particularity leads to certain choices."[19] Harris's emphasis upon religious imagination is an invitation to approach the act of imagining from a decidedly religious point of view. To that end, Harris elucidates four aspects of religious imagination. The first is the *contemplative imagination*, which includes our ability to approach "the other as a Thou."[20] It is an invitation to set aside our preconceptions, preoccupations, and unsubstantiated interpretations and approach each person, situation, practice, and matter as a "Thou" worthy of reflective consideration. To contemplate is to acknowledge the subjectivity of the many others with whom we share our lives. It "calls for a totally engaged bodily presence: attending, listening, being-with, and existing fully in the presence of Being."[21] In preaching, contemplation might include attentive and appreciative reflection upon the task of preaching, the people with whom we preach, the spaces in which we gather, and the Scripture from which we draw wisdom and theological insight. Contemplative imagination intentionally and unapologetically amplifies radical subjectivity, which includes acknowledging our own inherent value and right to dignity and respect as *imago Dei*.

The *ascetic imagination*, a second element of religious imagination, emphasizes detachment, "the letting be of being, the standing back in order not to violate."[22] Ascetic imagination invites empathy and, where necessary, sympathy. It draws our attention to existing power dynamics and the need to rectifying questionable motives and biases, lest we reinscribe the inequities we desire to eliminate. A third form of imagination, the *creative imagination*, invites individuals and communities of faith to view our formal and informal ministerial endeavors as creating new possibilities.[23] This form of imagining counsels us to ask, on each occasion, if our preaching, teaching, fellowship, stewardship, and the like are reflective of the gospel's emphasis upon wholeness and well-being for all creation. Harris's final element, the *sacramental imagination*, invites us to view our engagements and ministerial endeavors as "a sacrament, a symbolic, ritual

---

19. Harris, *Teaching and Religious Imagination*, 11.
20. Harris, *Teaching and Religious Imagination*, 21.
21. Harris, *Teaching and Religious Imagination*, 21.
22. Harris, *Teaching and Religious Imagination*, 21.
23. Harris, *Teaching and Religious Imagination*, 21.

form through which the holy is mediated."[24] We endeavor to live each day, in word and deed, as a reflection of the One whose image we bear and whose breath enlivens our souls.

Both Ricœur's philosophical conception and Harris's religious perspective reveal our potential for imagining and living toward a just and life-affirming future, even as the *how* of its actualization remains obscure. Thus, Ricœur's reminder: "Every *real* conversion, is first a revolution at the level of our directive images."[25] Imagination empowers us to envisage our world anew and commit ourselves to seeing that vision become a reality; to re-story our lives—to create new myths or meaningful stories and recover older, neglected ones that urge us more intently toward reconciliation as a normative expression of human relationship. A religious point of view adds value to the act of imagining and re-storying. It invites us to view each encounter as dialogue with a Thou and cautions us against manipulation and abuse as we engage in the sacramental work of creating new realities. Concurrence with these and other life-affirming conceptions of the imagination inevitably arc us toward God's vision of *shalom* for all creation. A religious conception of imagination orients our imaginative potential toward wholeness and wellbeing while shielding us against imaginative dearth.

Resisting Imaginative Dearth

Our conversation thus far has focused on the imagination's life-affirming qualities and their potential for shielding us against imaginative dearth. But what must be said of reifying and life-denying imaginings? As surely as we possess the capacity for imagining a qualitatively better state of life, we are similarly capable of imagining and perpetuating realities rife with violence, suffering, oppression, and other forms of dehumanization. Mindful of this double-edged quality of the imagination, educational theorist Maxine Greene, in *The Dialectic of Freedom,* explores the danger imaginative dearth poses for our ability to imagine and establish humane and humanizing communities.[26] Drawing attention to the multiple systemic and structural obstacles that contribute to imaginative dearth, she reminds us that obstacles, though impediments, are not insurmountable. They are "artifacts, human creations" that diminish our imaginative potential and ability to live with Hope.[27]

---

24. Harris, *Teaching and Religious Imagination,* 22.
25. Ricœur, *History and Truth,* 127 (italics original).
26. Greene, *The Dialectic,* 4.
27. Greene, *The Dialectic,* 9.

In his groundbreaking work *Pedagogy of the Oppressed*, educational theorist Paulo Freire refers to such obstacles or artifacts as "limiting situations."[28] Limiting situations obscure our ability to "perceive social, political, and economic contradiction, and to take action against the oppressive elements of reality."[29] Hopelessness and imaginative dearth ensues when we perceive obstacles as immovable or impervious to transformation. We feel hopeless and experience culturally induced despair, not because limiting situations are in fact insurmountable, but because we perceive them as such. Our perception of reality is important because "when people cannot name alternatives, imagine a better state of things, share with others a project of change, they are likely to remain anchored or submerged, even as they proudly assert their autonomy."[30] Without redress, limiting situations produce imaginative dearth and limit our ability to actualize the loving, just, and life-affirming world we desire.

The process of resisting imaginative dearth involves critical thought, imaginative abundance, and concrete action. Critical thought is the process by which we delineate the limit-situation's or obstacle's cause—what creates and sustains it and how. In this way we reveal the obstacle's operating system as well as its limiting impact upon our lives. In addition to exposing obstacles, resisting imaginative dearth requires imagining an alternative reality, including its contours and life-affirming possibilities. Assuming we dismantle and eliminate negating obstacles, what alternative world might we desire to establish? This task can be daunting, as the pastoral leaders I mentioned previously illustrate, because it requires us to do more than critique the inadequacies of our world. We must also imagine and consider alternatives. Resisting imaginative dearth, therefore, requires us to maintain a necessary tension between critical thought and imaginative abundance by permitting critical thought to inform imaginative abundance and vice versa. Exposing despair is not an end in itself; nor is imagining new possibilities. We must acknowledge and bring despairing realities to light while refusing to consent to their claim to permanence. And we must dream and establish new paradigms without neglecting the difficult task of precisely exposing and dismantling existing structures and systems of oppression and dehumanization. Only then can we "through transforming action . . . create a

---

28. Freire, *Pedagogy of the Oppressed*, 31. Freire uses "limiting situations" and "limit situations" interchangeably.

29. Freire, *Pedagogy of the Oppressed*, 17. The ultimate goal of Freire's problem-posing education is conscientization (*conscientização*), which he describes as "learning to perceive social, political, and economic contradictions, and to take action against the oppressive elements of reality."

30. Greene, *The Dialectic*, 9.

new situation, one which makes possible the pursuit of a fuller humanity."[31] Through critical thought and imaginative abundance, we can "perceive the reality of oppression not as a closed world from which there is no exit, but as a limiting situation which [we] can transform."[32] When critical thought, imaginative abundance, and concrete action coalesce in service to God's *shalom*, we can indeed resist imaginative dearth.

Jesus's life and ministry evinces a bold effort toward resisting imaginative dearth and envisioning life anew. Jesus was born into and began his ministry in an extremely bifurcated society, especially with regard to class, ethnicity, gender, and religious orientation. As a practicing Jew, he understood well the religious lines of demarcation between Jews and other ethnic and religious groups, as well as the religious importance of observing the purity laws that delineated clean from unclean. As a resident in the Roman Empire, he also understood well the social divisions of his time. In Jesus's world, people deemed unclean or otherwise socially or religiously unacceptable, including those living with sustained illnesses and disabilities, were literally relegated to the margins of society. Therefore, Jesus begins his ministry by inviting people to turn away from the bifurcated systems that ordered their existence and toward a new reality, God's kin(g)dom on earth.

As an expression of that reality, Jesus urges his followers, then and now, to ground our ethical thought and practice in the commands to love God with our total being (Deut 6:45) and love our neighbor as ourselves (Lev. 19:18). He also repeatedly demonstrates such love by transgressing the social and religious boundaries of his time, a practice met with disdain by first-century religious and social elites. Among his many transgressions is that Jesus heals without bias, including those believed to be living with infectious diseases. He expels demons of multiple kinds, touches and calls the dead to life, eats with tax collectors and sinners, meets with the Pharisee Nicodemus by night (paying no deference to our modern-day criticism of Nicodemus) and welcomes those relegated to the social and religious margins to sit at table with him. His most grievous social transgressions, however, involve his willingness to love across the metaphorical aisles of his time. In addition to Jesus's multiple encounters with people of his own racial and ethnic group, he also engages and affirmed people of maligned ethnicities, such as the Samaritan woman who meets Jesus at a well in her region and the Canaanite woman whom Jesus reluctantly but ultimately assists. He even casts a Samaritan passerby who aids an injured man on the roadside as the definitive exemplar of *agape* in his parable about neighbor

---

31. Freire, *Pedagogy of the Oppressed*, 29.
32. Freire, *Pedagogy of the Oppressed*, 31.

love; we refer to this man today as the good Samaritan, often unaware of how offensive this story might have been to the religious and social elites of Jesus's day. Those who stood in opposition to this new vision of possibility decry Jesus's efforts as blasphemous, treasonous, and godless. Yet Jesus persisted in advancing his ministerial vision, proclaiming the kin(g)dom of God and teaching the radical possibility of dwelling together as kin in this new community. Despite opposition, betrayal, and the looming possibility of death, Jesus resisted imaginative dearth.

Imaginative dearth remains a threat to our ability to embrace and live toward Jesus's vision of a new reality. When the imagination degrades, our capacity to live with Hope similarly degrades. This is so because over and against Hope's invitation to lend our hands to God's redemptive and restorative work in the world, imaginative dearth thwarts our ability to conceive of a qualitatively better state of existence. Reifying and life-denying imagining give rise to imaginative dearth. Permitted to fester, these dehumanizing imaginings co-opt our imaginative potential and diminish our capacity to embrace and sustain the attitudes and practices necessary to create a loving, just, and life-affirming existence for all creation. It seems important, therefore, that we explore in greater detail the means by which culturally induced despair propagates its negating and dehumanizing messages and their impact upon our ability to imagine our world anew.

Image as Communicative Channel

Media images are everywhere, presumptuously telling us who we are, what and whom we should value, and of what we are capable. They re-present the world to us with a full complement of proposition about the state of reality and what we can and cannot do to eradicate the multiple ills that plague our known world and beyond. In *Seeing through the Media,* Michael Warren cautions against uncritically viewing media images, noting that most people "have little idea of how images function in shaping their consciousness."[33] Most of the media images we encounter are iconic and representational in nature, meaning they have implications for our lived experiences.[34] Iconic images re-present "some person, place, object, event, or narrative," and by way of this re-presentation, make claims and value judgements often accepted as truth. Iconic images are also "pictures we see with our eyes rather than with our 'mind's eye,' the imagination," depictions many believe are

---

33. Warren, *Seeing through the Media,* 122.

34. Warren, *Seeing through the Media,* 123. See also, Miles, *Image as Insight*; Miles, "Vision"; Rossi and Soukup, eds., *Mass Media*; Dowler, "Media Consumption."

innocuous.[35] We internalize these images and the truths they propose at a level distinguishable from cognition, without pausing to "think about them, understand how they work, make judgments about their value," or consider whose interest they serve.[36] Consequently, we rarely raise to consciousness their potential for shaping our perception of reality as well as our ways of being and relating. This is not to suggest all iconic representations function negatively; they do not. Still, uncritical acceptance of iconic images as truth, whether negatively or positively understood, has implications for our durable patterns of perceiving, thinking, and behaving.

Iconic representations, in other words, possess formative potential. Because they are viewed but not critically considered, iconic representations can and often do shape patterns of perceiving, thinking, and behaving without the viewers' awareness or consent.[37] As an example, uncritically affirming the validity of iconic images that repetitively and consistently represent particular individuals and communities as harmless, trustworthy, and desirable predisposes us and our institutions to over-valuate the targeted group's contributions to society and overly presume their innocence. Accordingly, society generally responds to these "desirable groups" in a non-threatening and non-defensive manner, which allows group members greater freedom of movement, access to power and privilege, and greater latitude regarding their actions. Inappropriate or bad behaviors among members of such groups are often excused as anomalous and out of character, as the behaviors of "bad actors," and are not deemed representative of the entire identity group. Likewise, when we uncritically accept as truth iconic images that persistently represent particular individuals and communities as dangerous and undesirable, we develop predispositions that lean us toward undervaluation or devaluation of those individuals and communities. Rather than acknowledging their shared humanity with all people, society (we and our institutions) assumes their malevolence or potential for such and withhold from them privileges freely given to more desirable individuals and communities. Inappropriate or bad behaviors among members of such groups are often viewed as more egregious than inappropriate or bad behaviors from members of other groups. And bad actors are viewed as representative of the entire identity group, reinforcing and deepening negative preconceptions regarding all members of the group. The same might be applied to places and things characteristically portrayed as either good or bad, valuable or worthless, such as the binary of dark and light, in which darkness is

---

35. Warren, *Seeing through the Media*, 123.
36. Warren, *Seeing through the Media*, 135, 140.
37. Warren, *Seeing through the Media*, 135.

almost exclusively characterized as death-dealing and nonproductive and light as life-giving and generative.

These and other patterns of perceiving, thinking, and behaving are indicative of the formative potential of iconic representations. An aspect of that formation is iconic images' potential to elicit mimetic behavior—behavior that mimics or responds in accordance with the representations we encounter. Michael Warren observes, drawing from René Girard's philosophical exploration of mimesis—that humans are mimetic by nature.[38] Our tendency is to imitate behaviors, attitudes, and characteristics we see in others, including those represented by iconic images. Religious groups, for example, utilize iconic imagery (paintings, symbols, sculptures, and other such representations) as means of reminding adherents that they are connected to a particular tradition and as means of "inviting [them] to imitate the qualities of the person or reality represented by the icon."[39] In response, adherents are expected to internalize the values, character traits, and relational practices indicative of the icon. For example, the iconic symbol of a cross is representative of Christian ideals and practices. More complex images, such as moving pictures with sound, and images more similar to our lived experiences, possess greater mimetic potential.[40] The stronger the perceived similarity of an iconic image to ourselves or our experience (such as an image of people belonging to our same sex, race, age, or social group), the more likely it becomes that we will "make a connection between ourselves and the person" depicted in the image.[41] The iconic image of Michelle Obama as first lady of the United States, for example, serves to enhance many Black women's perception of themselves as members of US society whose contributions matter. This is so because the similarities people perceive between the iconic image and themselves contribute to their self-understanding. We reimagine who we are in the world in light of this new experience or connection with an iconic image.

Adding to Warren's emphasis upon familiarity (similarity) and complexity, one's frequency and constancy of exposure to iconic images also enhance the formative power of such images. Frequency and constancy of exposure to an iconic images imply its legitimacy and increase the probability that viewers will accept the representation as an accurate reflection of the

---

38. Warren, *Seeing through the Media*, 135. See also, Girard, *The Girard Reader*.

39. Warren, *Seeing through the Media*, 129.

40. Warren, *Seeing through the Media*, See Chapter 5 for a detailed discussion of three types of iconic images—single-frame representations; graphic representations in sequential, internally coherent frames; and graphic representations in sequential, internally incoherent, but externally coherent frames—and their mimetic potential.

41. Warren, *Seeing through the Media*, 129.

real world. Representations become self-validating, not because we have assessed, quantified, or critically reflected upon them, but simply because they are so pervasive as to appear to us as truth. This is especially the case when the social and religious valuation attributed to people, things, and places remains consistent across multiple representational contexts (e.g., on television; in movies, newspapers, or magazines; on billboards and websites; or in live settings). Repetitive representations of women as emotionally volatile and thus less powerful and intellectually capable than men across multiple platforms, for example, assign to women a lesser value than men in a society where power and intelligence are associated with emotional stoicism. Similarly, repetitive representations in Christian circles of poor people as in need of "soul salvation" assign to poor individuals and communities a lesser value than affluent communities have, in a society where godliness is too often associated with material wealth and power. Coding poverty as sin permits Christian communities to ignore systemic injustices inherent in sinful, oppressive, and discriminatory structures that deny poor people access to the monetary and material resources, educational opportunities, and other forms of social currency necessary to live whole, healthy, and fulfilled lives. Even more, such coding allows Christians, if we so desire, to focus exclusively upon soul salvation while abdicating our ethical responsibility to stand alongside those whom Jesus calls blessed in Matt 5:1–12.

Why is attention to repetition and constancy of exposure important? Four dangers to our ability to live with Hope and acknowledge our shared identity as *imago Dei* arise from repetitive and constant exposure to negating representations. The first is their potential for eliciting and fueling biases of which we are often unaware. If we are surrounded by negating images, such biases appear to us as truth (as in the example above about people living in poverty). If we take biases as truth, we miss their malevolent quality. Biased attitudes and their resultant practices can lead us to believe that efforts to eliminate racist, sexist, classist, homophobic, heterosexist, and xenophobic rhetoric, attitudes, and practices are nothing more than so-called political correctness—right speaking with no lasting significance for the quality of our lives together. Awash in such beliefs, we risk abdicating our ethical responsibility to regard each other as *imago Dei*. We also risk legitimizing actions that violate others or that deprive others of their freedom to safely move about the world, to access resources, and to experience fruitful and happy lives. Similarly, biases in favor of exnominated groups—groups whose race, gender, sexual identity, ethnicity, and the like are considered normative and thus remain unnamed—can lead us to overvalue the worth of these groups and their contributions to society, a societal overvaluing that also serves to justify bestowing on these groups inordinate privilege and freedom.

A related danger from repetition of and constancy of exposure to negating iconic images is their potential for clouding our ability to notice and affirm actions or other characteristics that conflict with our perception of or what we believe we already know about the represented group. Our attachment to negating representations—the presumption that such representations are reliable and accurate—suppresses our ability to incorporate affirming images into our imaginative horizon. Positive representations become less believable than the dominant portrayal, reaffirming our biases as truth. Confident in this knowledge, we dismiss or reject affirming images as unreliable or anomalous, as these positive representations defy assumed facts. What we perceive as reliable and accurate, in effect, distorts our ability to perceive otherwise.

Power dynamics operational in the media industry and in US society reveal a third danger from repetitive and constant exposure to negating, iconic images. By and large, those without power have little to no control over how they are represented in the media, and thus over how they are perceived through the media. bell hooks, in her important work *Black Looks: Race and Representation,* contends that those who control the production and dissemination of images in US society also possess the power to construct and sustain systems of domination.[42] With specific attention to the power dynamic involved in constructing and perpetuating White supremacist patriarchy, hooks writes,

> Long before white supremacists ever reached the shores of what we now call the United States, they constructed images of Blackness and Black people to uphold and affirm their notions of racial superiority, their political imperialism, their will to dominate and enslave. From slavery on, white supremacists have recognized that control over images is central to the maintenance of any system of racial domination.[43]

Racist constructions of reality seem credible and normative, not simply because prejudiced or biased attitudes persist. They appear credible because media moguls responsible for disseminating images possess the institutional, political, structural, and economic power necessary to circulate racialized images to the masses of people as reliable representations of Blackness. Power creates sustainability and implies credibility.

42. hooks, *Teaching to Transgress.*
43. hooks, *Teaching to Transgress,* 2.

In *Feminism Unmodified,* Catherine MacKinnon, associate professor of law at the University of Minnesota Law School, makes a similar case.[44] She argues that to "have power" means that the constructions of reality that one proposes is accepted as credible while those "without power" are stripped of credibility despite their perspective on reality. The world as defined by the powerful becomes "proof," in other words, despite objective evidence to the contrary. Elucidating this point, MacKinnon writes, "The world is not entirely the way the powerful say it is or want to believe it is. If it appears to be, it is because power constructs the appearance of reality by silencing the voices of the powerless, by excluding them from access to authoritative discourse."[45] The dynamic relationship between power and the construction of reality creates a dilemma for all of us. Iconic images, when repetitively presented and re-presented by those who control the media, constrict the content and limits of our imagination. They not only limit what we know, but also what we are able to know. Given such limitations, we too risk silencing and rejecting voices of opposition in favor of the "appearance of reality" the powerful want to promote. We essentially reify dominant and commonly accepted representations of reality.

A fourth danger of repetition and constancy of exposure to negating iconic images is their potential as tools of socialization. Supplementing hooks's and MacKinnon's concerns about the media's role in creating images, George Gerbner and Larry Gross grapple with the media's potential for constructing and representing the symbolic world of their choosing and then socializing us to it. Gerbner and Gross's instructive article, "Living with Television: The Violence Profile," reveals the power of rituals and myths, when interwoven into social platforms such as television, to enculturate viewers to values and norms that "fit the established social order."[46] Far from radical representations designed to challenge existing norms and practices, Gerbner and Gross contend that media images "are part of the general system of messages that cultivate prevailing outlooks (which is why we call it culture) and regulates social relationships."[47] With regard to television, one of the most prevalent media platforms, and its role in the larger enculturation process, Gerbner and Gross continue: "Its chief cultural function is to spread and stabilize social patterns,

44. MacKinnon, *Feminism Unmodified.*
45. MacKinnon, *Feminism Unmodified,* 164
46. Gerbner and Gross, "Living with Television."
47. Gerbner and Gross, "Living with Television," 363–64. See also, Downing and Husband, *Representing 'Race'*; Dines and Humez, eds., *Gender, Race and Class in Media*; Garcia, ed., *Contested Images*; Spears, *Race and Ideology*; Nilsen and Turner, eds., *The Colorblind Screen*; Hall and Jhally, *Representation & the Media*; Warren, *Seeing through the Media*; Wykes and Gunter, *The Media and Body Image*; hooks, *Black Looks.*

to cultivate not change but resistance to change. Television is a medium of the socialization of most people into standardized roles and behaviors. Its function is, in a word, enculturation."[48]

Media images and other iconic representations socialize us to ways of being and relating that are consonant with dominant ideas, values, and relational paradigms. They also dismiss or present for comic relief ideas, values, and relational paradigms that depart from standardized and presumed-acceptable roles and behavior. Noting this tension, Gerbner and Gross contend that the media's symbolic world is one "in which violence prevails and power is largely in the hands of middle-aged white males while other groups are symbolically erased or grossly under-represented and stereotyped."[49] The world, they propose, is rightly ruled by "middle-aged white males," posing a significant challenge for individuals and communities viewed as auxiliary or *other*.[50] The media re-presents the world to us in a manner that perpetuates social arrangements, power structures and valuation systems that those who control the media deem normative. And because of the repetitive and constant nature of media representations, such images function to legitimize disparate social and religious arrangements as normative, acceptable, and inevitable for our lives.

The dangerous potential of negating representations to cloud our ability to perceive our world from a new angle of vision has historical precedence. In his documentary film *Ethnic Notions*, Marlon Riggs explores the historical construction of racialized and sexualized representations of people of African descent.[51] Through a process of careful excavation and analysis of historical documents—movies and films, advertisements, photos (private and personal), televised performances, newspaper clippings, and personal journals—Riggs unearths a stunning and shocking array of negating racialized and sexualized representations of African Americans from the antebellum period into the mid-twentieth century. These images not only supported the ideology of Black inferiority that undergirded policies denying Black people freedom and enfranchisement in America. They also reinforced an ideology of White superiority, which shaped White people's sense of identity, social imagination, and behavior toward people of African descent and all non-Europeans.

Lawrence Levine, esteemed historian at the University of California Berkeley, describes the formative power of these images. Commenting, in

---

48. Gerbner and Gross, "Living with Television," 366.
49. Gerbner and Gross, "Living with Television," 366.
50. Gerbner and Gross, "Living with Television," 366.
51. Riggs, prod. and dir., *Ethnic Notions*.

one segment of *Ethnic Notions* on the grossly disfigured and dehumanizing images of Black people commonly circulated during the Jim Crow era, Levine grapples with their appeal to the masses of White people.

> Blacks don't really look like that, so why is it so appealing to people to think they look like that, to pretend they look like that, to look at icons that look like that? *You look at them often enough Blacks begin to look like that even if they don't* . . . They've had great impact on our society. They actually tell us both about the inner desires of the people who create and consume them and also, they tell us about some of the forces that shape reality for a large portion of our population.[52]

Despite White people's knowledge that Black people "don't really look like that," the images depicted in Riggs's documentary shaped the social imagination and consciousness of many White Americans well into the mid-to-late twentieth century.

We encounter iconic images through multiple mediums. We have also discussed several means by which the mimetic potential of iconic images can increase. Connections between people and images can increase because of the particular platform through which they are disseminated, because of their similarity with our real lives and so their familiarity to us, and because of their constancy and repetitiveness. We also noted four dangers that arise from repetitive and constant exposure to negating representations across multiple platforms: these dangers include the potential of images for promoting unconscious bias and so limiting our ability to challenge biases, and the potential of images to be used as tools to reify power and enculturate a worldview in accordance with existing structure of power and domination.

A final concern is worth noting. Those of us who proclaim the gospel also function in the minds of many as iconic representations of the Christian faith. While all Christians are encouraged to live as ambassadors of Christ, as in 2 Cor 5:11–21, people of faith accord to pastors and other ministers of the gospel greater esteem and a higher level of trust that we will adhere to the gospel's claims regarding love, faith, and hope. I name these expectations because it is our challenge to remember that when religious leaders publicly, from pulpits and in other arenas, propagate negating and dehumanizing rhetoric and representations about race, ethnicity, gender, sexual identity, legal status, religious orientation, denominational affiliation, and the like, we expose the congregations with whom we preach to the threat of culturally induced despair. This is so because people who uncritically align themselves with our attitudes and practices are as susceptible to imitating them as they

---

52. Riggs, prod. and dir., *Ethnic Notions* (italics added).

would be if such perspectives were televised, presented on their favorite website, or displayed on a billboard. Our delegated role as icon imbues us with the potential for either enlivening and emboldening the people with whom we preach to live with Hope or thrusting them more deeply into the depths of despair. The perspectives we propagate, the rhetorical word pictures we paint, and the tangible images we incorporate exert a formative impact upon those who trust us to speak God's salvific love into the present moment. Thus we must endeavor even more to live with Hope and, in word and deed, to honor our shared inherent identity as *imago Dei*.

Ideology and Myth as Communicative Channels

In addition to lurking in the destructive potential of negating and dehumanizing iconic representations, the deceptive language of despair finds opportunity in the ideologies and myths we embrace and hold as truth. Gustavo Gutiérrez describes ideology as a reading of reality that "tends to dogmatize all that has not succeeded in separating itself from it or has fallen under its influence."[53] Ideologies are more than beliefs or commonly held notions. They are presumed certainties about the way things are, even when irrational or devoid of reliable evidence. Ideologies function to explain or justify a particular viewpoint or reading of reality, often attributing them to mythological conceptions about a particular group's inherent superiority or inferiority or to assumptions regarding God's divine will. Ideologies that support unrestrained environmental consumption and manipulation, for example, appeal to biblical interpretive traditions that afford humans dominance over the natural world. Ideologies that support patriarchy—that assert male dominance and women's subordination to men in social, civic, familial and ecclesial contexts—also appeal to biblical writings, as do assumptions regarding White racial superiority, such as manifest destiny, White supremacy and the like. These and other ideologies are dogmatic in nature, negating and often demonizing all other systems of thought and practice.

Myths, in their simplest form, are the stories we create and recirculate to give meaning to our lives and to the world in which we live. In *Seeing a Color-Blind Future*, Patricia J. Williams reminds us that we produce and reproduce or world "by the myths we embrace, the stories we recirculate."[54] The myths we embrace have implications for our vision of reality. Wendy

---

53. Gutiérrez, *A Theology of Liberation*, 137.
54. Williams, *Seeing a Color-Blind Future*, 16.

Doniger, in *The Implied Spider: Politics and Theology in Myth*, is also concerned with the power of myth to shape our view of reality:

> A myth is not a lie or false statement to be contrasted with truth or reality or fact or history ... But in the history of religions, the term *myth* has far more often been used to mean "truth." What makes this ambiguity possible is that *a myth is above all a story that is believed, believed to be true, and that people continue to believe despite sometimes massive evidence that it is, in fact, a lie.*[55]

Myths are powerful precisely because individuals and communities believe them to be true. They function as valid representations of what *ought to be* and, conversely, of what *ought not be*. As we tell and retell the same stories or myths, they produce and reproduce conceptions about who we are and of what we consist as human beings and as members of particular identity or affinity groups. They also shape our understanding of the world in which we live and of the many others with whom we share our lives. But unlike ideologies, myths are not inherently static and dogmatic. Myths can be told from various perspectives, depending upon the storyteller, the identified main character, or the context in which the myth is told. This is so, writes Doniger, because myths possess the "ability to contain in latent form several different attitudes to the events that it depicts."[56] These various attitudes allow "each different telling to draw out, as it were, the attitude that it finds compatible."[57]

Elizabeth Johnson illustrates this well in *Ask the Beasts: Darwin and the God of Love*. Johnson describes Gen 1 and 2, as "poetic, mythic narratives teaching religious truth about the relation of human beings and the world to God."[58] In tracing the history of these stories, Johnson notes that despite the centrality of God as Creator of the whole universe in these stories, theology narrowed its focus over the centuries from the broad view of God's creative endeavor to an almost exclusively anthropocentric view of creation. "Our special identity, capacities, roles, sinfulness, and need for salvation became the all-consuming interest," writes Johnson.[59] Lost was theology's emphasis upon the natural world's intrinsic worth. Instead, interpreters came to believe "the natural world was simply there as something God created for human use."[60] The internal structure of the story remained the same, but the various

---

55. Doniger, *The Implied Spider*, 2 (italics added).
56. Doniger, *The Implied Spider*, 84.
57. Doniger, *The Implied Spider*, 84.
58. Johnson, *Ask the Beasts*, 184 (Kindle).
59. Johnson, *Ask the Beasts*, 3 (Kindle).
60. Johnson, *Ask the Beasts*, 3 (Kindle).

storytellers chose new points of emphasis. Consequently, "theology," Johnson asserts, "lost touch with the universe."[61] The perspective or attitude from which a community tells and passes on its mythic stories to future generations has implications for that community's sense of the world as well as for its relationship with other human beings and the natural world.

Ideology and myth, while not the same, share common threads. One of those threads is that both are tools by which we make meaning of our lives. Both make the world appear coherent and accessible. A second thread is that both ideology and myth can fall prey to promoting totalizing dogmatic readings of reality. That is, ideologies and myths, when viewed as the only possible conceptions of reality, become all-encompassing and exclusive of all other readings or perspectives. When an ideology, or a myth that fuels an ideology, becomes all-encompassing and exclusive, it becomes dangerous. Therein we discover the danger of negating and dehumanizing ideologies and the myths that keep them alive—racism, sexism, classism, heteronormativity, White supremacy, anti-Semitism, and the various political ideologies to which many (perhaps even we) pledge allegiance. Negating ideologies and myths rest upon a dualistic conception of reality—one that assigns value to people, systems of thought, mental processes, and things in oppositional terms. In this dualistic structure, one element's value lies in direct opposition to the contrasting element's value, giving birth to the many disparate paradigms evident in our world today—*us* and *them*, *me* and *other*, *secular* and *sacred*, *body* and *spirit*, *right* and *wrong*, *good* and *evil*, *light* and *dark*, *acceptable* and *unacceptable*, *intellect* and *emotion*, *normal* and *abnormal*.

Binary thinking fuels this dualistic view of reality. Dualism's binary construction perpetuates the assumption that we are hard-wired for living in polarized rather than complementary relationship. This way of understanding human relationship promotes divisions based upon phenotype, ethnicity, nationality, sex, gender, sexual orientation, emotionality, religion, material and monetary wealth, age, ability and other such differentiating markers. And while it is true that these and other differences exist among human beings, binary thinking does more than acknowledge that people are different. It creates and perpetuates culturally induced despair's bifurcated system of valuation, designating some identities or identity markers as preferable, normative, and of value while consigning their perceived opposites to the category *other*. In this way of thinking, writes Patricia Hill Collins, "one part is not simply different from its counterpart; it is inherently opposed to

---

61. Johnson, *Ask the Beasts*, 3 (Kindle).

its 'other.'"[62] Culturally induced despair would declare, "Whites and Blacks, males and females, thought and feeling are not complementary counterparts—they are fundamentally different entities related only through their definition as opposites."[63] Sexual dualism, for example, construes maleness (and gendered masculinity) as inherently superior and more valuable than its opposite or *other,* femaleness (and gendered femininity). This dualistic view and its binary system of valuation sanctions patriarchy as the natural order for human relationship and, as a consequence, the oppression and subordination of women and of the feminine. In like manner, White supremacist ideologies linked to the binary Black/White (or White/non-White) justify in the minds of their devotees White nationalist attitudes and actions. These include outward shows of animus and disregard toward all non-Whites through rallies and marches as well as acts of violence against their perceived *other(s)*. White nationalist ideologies were on display in the August 2017 "Unite the Right" rally in Charlottesville, Virginia. Representations of individuals and communities as *other*, especially when repetitive and consistent across contexts, fuels binary thinking and sanctions oppressive ideologies and actions.

In opposition to the theological conception and biblical characterization of humans as *imago Dei,* binary thinking also perpetuates a distorted view of human relationship. It categorizes people according to observable differences or by our association with or relationship to other individuals (nation, family, tribe) rather than acknowledging our shared identity as human, as *imago Dei*. Binary thinking encourages us to ignore the complexity of human identity and relationship, to disregard the web of human interconnectedness across various categories, and the vast continuum of human identities even within readily perceived identity groups. More dangerously, binary thinking possesses the potential for promoting and reifying bias, discrimination, hatred, and violence through its suggestion that some of us are more valuable and deserving of human dignity and respect than others of us.

Sander L. Gilman's insightful article, "Black Bodies, White Bodies," reveals the danger of binary thinking as well as the dangerous alliance between

---

62. Collins, *Black Feminist Thought,* 70. Collins as well as other theological thinkers employ the concept "other" to refer to the objectified and devalued "other" or opposite in a binary construction. This use is different from the theological use of "the Other" to refer to God as other than human beings. See also Collins, *A Different Heaven and Earth*; Grant, *White Women's Christ and Black Women's Jesus*; Doniger, *The Implied Spider*.

63. Collins, *Black Feminist Thought,* 70.

negating representations and oppressive ideologies.[64] Gilman explores "the function of visual conventions as the primary means by which we perceive and transmit our understanding of the world about us."[65] With attention to nineteenth-century iconography, Gilman provides an extensive analysis of how the icon of the Hottentot female, representing all Black women, and European prostitutes, representing the sexualized (White) woman, were conflated to create a class of women regarded as separate from and completely other than the nonsexualized, "pure" White woman.

Gilman indicates in agreement with Warren that visual images, especially those in paintings and portraits, consist almost exclusively of icons that re-present rather than present reality. His concern, however, is not with art's mimetic quality, though he acknowledges such qualities may exist. Gilman is more concerned with the ideological potential of iconography (iconic representation in art), especially artistic renderings of an individual or groups of individuals, to shape our perception of reality.

> Even with a modest nod to supposedly mimetic portrayals it is apparent that, when individuals are shown within a work of art (no matter how broadly defined), *the ideologically charged iconographic nature of the representation dominates.* And it dominates in a very specific manner, for the representation of individuals implies the creation of some greater class or classes to which the individual is seen to belong. The resulting stereotype may be overt, as in the case of caricatures, or covert, as in eighteenth-century portraitures. But they serve to focus the viewer's attention on the relationship between the portrayed individual and the general qualities ascribed to the class. Specific individual realities are thus given mythic extension through association with the qualities of a class.[66]

From the observer's perspective, all members of the class to which the model is seen to belong are the same, resulting in a homogeneous image—a prevailing stereotype of the group. Therefore, the conflation of the White sexualized woman and the Hottentot female created a class of women that were considered other than as well as inferior to the nonsexualized iconic representation of the presumed-respectable White woman.

The ideological and mythic potency of such artistic renderings is enhanced because they are "composed of fragments of the real world,

---

64. Gilman, "Black Bodies, White Bodies."
65. Gilman, "Black Bodies, White Bodies," 204.
66. Gilman, "Black Bodies, White Bodies," 204 (italics added).

perceived through the ideological bias of the observer," writes Gilman[67] Skin color and hair texture, for example, represented valid physical difference between many people of African descent and those of European descent. But in a binary understanding of reality in which the values of better or worse, superior or inferior, good or evil are applied, or when tales about the origin of differences are attached, observable differences diminish into stereotype and dehumanizing myth. Many in the European scientific community, for example, believed differences in physiognomy (observable characteristics) were indicative of Black women's inferiority to White women. They also promoted the notion that Black people or people of African descent "were a separate (and needless to say, lower) race, as different from the European as the proverbial orangutan."[68] Sadly, these distinctions were well accepted throughout Europe during the nineteenth century with little question or concern about their validity, which added to their potency as tools of dehumanization and negation.

Our ability to create stories (myths) and to pass those mythic stories on to future generations is an important aspect of our identity as human beings. Equally important is our ability to ask questions and make meaning of our lives, to form varying systems of belief, relationship, and governance. They are among the gifts we possess as sentient beings. Also significant is our capacity for living in loving and just relationship with each other and with the natural world. This includes our ability to imagine possibilities for our lives together that honor the inherent worth of all that God has created and that promote its well-being. Our challenge is to live within the tension these human capacities create: to both affirm and exercise our various abilities while also acknowledging the freedom of others to do the same without violation or exploitation. Meeting that challenge means remaining attentive to the stories that we tell and the ideological positions we take.

67. Gilman, "Black Bodies, White Bodies," 204.
68. Gilman, "Black Bodies, White Bodies," 216. Gilman specifically highlights an essay by J. J. Virey, a nineteenth-century European scientist, and Virey's reliance upon the work of his contemporary, George Cuvier. Gilman's insights are worth highlighting: "In this essay, Virey summarized his (and his contemporaries') views on the sexual nature of black females in terms of acceptable medical discourse. According to him, their 'voluptuousness's is 'developed to a degree of lascivity unknown in our climate, for their sexual organs are much more developed than those of whites.' Elsewhere, Virey cites the Hottentot woman as the epitome of this sexual lasciviousness and stresses the relationship between her physiology and her physiognomy (her 'hideous form' and her 'horrible flattened nose'). His central proof is a discussion of the unique structure of the Hottentot female's sexual parts, the description of which he takes from the anatomical studies published by . . . Georges Cuvier. According to Cuvier, the black female looks different. Her physiognomy, her skin color, the form of her genitalia label her as inherently different" (213).

It also includes resisting totalizing perspectives and their negating and dehumanizing impact upon the many others with whom we share our lives. Therefore, it is worth repeating that the danger of negating ideologies and myths is their dogmatic and totalizing potential. They become absolute, especially when supported by scientific research presumed to be objective. Negating ideologies and myths are also indicative of a dualistic understanding of reality, typified by binary thinking and by the system of valuation that accompanies such patterns of thought. This dualistic understanding of reality contributes to the deceptive language of despair's negating assertions regarding the state of our world, our identity as *imago Dei,* and our ability to live with Hope. Uncritical assent to such negating assertions places us at risk for imaginative dearth, diminishing our capacity to imagine our world anew and live toward its actualization.

Theology and Ecclesial Practice as Communicative Channels

Theological and ecclesial distortion represent a third medium by which the deceptive language of despair propagates its negating and dehumanizing message. Often characterized as necessary evils, negating and dehumanizing theologies and ecclesial commitments permit us to sidestep central tenets of the faith in order to advance oppressive ideologies, policies, and practices in church and society. They likewise enable us to abdicate moral responsibility for the harm such policies and practices inflict. The Virginia General Assembly's determination in 1642 that baptism has no bearing upon enslaved individuals' physical status as bond or free permitted Christian people of faith to enslave Christian brothers and sisters and support the institution of slavery with no sense of guilt or moral accountability.[69] Moral abdication was also evident in the noticeable silence from many churches when former US president Donald J. Trump's administration separated more than a thousand immigrant children from their families beginning in April 2018 with no plan for families' reunification.[70] Theological and ecclesial distortion, in other words, demonstrates the church's and its adherents' sometimes fickle relationship with basic tenets of the faith and the moral peril such fickleness produces.

Consider, for example, the extent to which we are willing to misappropriate Scripture in order to defend *our* social, political, or personal agendas. Which tenets of the faith are we willing to vacate or suspend in favor of

69. "An Act for Suppressing Outlying Slaves."
70. Cummings, "Child Separation."

disparate distributions of power and privilege in our ecclesial communities, families, or larger society? In what situations might we consider the command to love God with the entirety of our being and love our neighbor as ourselves an inconvenience or an antiquated law to which we are no longer obligated? Likewise, when does Jesus's emphasis upon living in anticipation of the kin(g)dom of God become a stumbling block to our personal ambitions and pursuits? What exploitative practices are we willing to ignore or *unknow* in order to secure our own well-being? In what situations might we misrepresent sinful oppressive structures as God's permissive or expressed will? These questions arrest and beckon us, not because we do not know the correct answer or how we should respond. They challenge us because we, like the early church and generations of Christian since, live within the tension of Jesus's gospel proclamation and the attitudes and practices we perceive as necessary to navigate life in the present age. We desire to live with Hope, to live responsive to Hope's assurance and call, to lend our hands to God's loving, just, and restorative work in the world. But not unlike our predecessors, we live within the tension of our desire to live and proclaim the gospel and competing interests that call into question the gospel's efficacy for our ability to survive and thrive in our world today.

The tension to which I refer is rooted in the challenge Jesus's most basic praxiological teaching presents. Specifically, his reiteration of the Mosaic law's creedal injunction to love God with our total being (Deut 6:4–5) and the Holiness Code's warning against vengeance and its command to love our neighbor as ourselves, an essential sign of holiness (Lev 19:18). These two commandments originally functioned as a system to order ancient Israelites' relationship with God, with others in their community, and the nations they encountered along the way. Jesus proposes a more expansive understanding, however, when he identifies love of God and neighbor as the foundation upon which the law and the prophets rests as well as the ethical code by which citizens of God's kin(g)dom should live.

But why these two commandments? In Deut 6:4–5, the location of the first commandment, the phrase *shema Yisrael* ("Hear, O Israel") alerts the community to the gravity of the command they are about to receive: "Hear, O Israel: The Lord is our God, the Lord alone. You shall love the LORD your God with all your heart, and with all your soul, and with all your might." So significant were these words for the life and practice of ancient Israel that they were told to keep the words of this commandment in their hearts, bind them on their hands, fix them as an emblem or frontlet on their foreheads, and write them on the doorposts and gates of their homes. Similarly, Jesus calls upon his followers to pledge their allegiance to God alone, to love God with every aspect of our being—with our affection, our intellect, our strength, our very existence (Matt 22:37-38; Mark 12:29-30; Luke 10:27). And while we receive no instruction to affix the commandment to our bodies or to the entrances of our homes, Jesus identifies the command to love God with our total being as the first of the great commandments on which *hangs all the law and the prophets.*

The second commandment, Lev 19:18, speaks more specifically to the quality of our relationship with the many others with whom we share our lives. Again, with attention to relationships within the ancient Israelite community, God commands, "You shall not take vengeance or bear a grudge against any of your people, but you shall love your neighbor as yourself: I am the LORD." And again, Jesus universalizes this commandment to include all who would follow him, as is evident in the Synoptic Gospel accounts of Jesus's teachings (Matt 22:39; Mark 12:31; Luke 10:27b). In Luke's Gospel (10:25-36), Jesus confirms the importance of the commands to love God and love neighbor in his response to a lawyer's question, "What must I do to inherit eternal life?" Jesus answers his question with a question: "What is written in the law?" to which the lawyer responds by quoting Deut 6:5 and Lev 19:18b. Jesus assures the man that he has given the correct answer, but the man, "wanting to justify himself," poses another question: "And who is my neighbor?" In response, Jesus tells a story or parable about a man who had been beaten nearly to death while traveling along the way, and of the three people who had opportunity to help him—a priest, a Levite, and a Samaritan. Jews and Samaritans had been at odds with one other for centuries and had no dealings with each other, making the Samaritan a most unlikely character for Jesus to include in this story about loving one's neighbor. More shocking is the fact that Jesus characterizes the Samaritan as the one who demonstrates neighbor love and as the one whose behavior his presumably Jewish audience should endeavor to emulate, instructing them, "Go and do likewise" (Luke 10:37). Neighbor love, Jesus's illustrates, extends well beyond the multiple boundaries and delineating systems that function to divide us from one another.

Mark's Gospel account also highlights the importance of neighbor love. In Mark 12 a scribe overhears a conversation (or rather a heated dispute) between Jesus and some Sadducees about the resurrection and marital relationships (vv. 18-27). Pleased with Jesus's response to the Sadducees, the scribe interrupts their conversation and asks Jesus, "Which commandment is the first of all?" Jesus cites Deut 6:4-5 and Lev 19:18b as one commandment (not two), noting, "there is no other commandment greater than these" (v. 31). The scribe, a reconciling presence in the conversation, affirms Jesus's response, adding that the love of God and neighbor is "more important than all burnt offerings and sacrifices" (v. 33). In response, and perhaps with a degree of surprise and relief, Jesus acknowledges his and the scribe's shared wisdom as well as the scribe's nearness to the kin(g)dom of God (v. 34). Again, in speaking with a scribe, Jesus chooses as exemplar of the *royal law* (see Jas 2:8) a character viewed as suspect by many who followed Jesus.

Matthew's Gospel, like the Gospel of Luke, portrays Jesus as responding to a lawyer's query regarding the greatest commandment in the law. In Matthew's account, Jesus responds by identifying the commandment to "love the Lord your God" with all your heart, soul, and mind as "the greatest and first commandment" (22:37–38). Then he reiterates a commandment he had previously highlighted during a conversation with a young man about eternal life. In Matt 19, Jesus had responded to a young man's query by drawing his attention to the commandments against committing murder, committing adultery, stealing, bearing false witness, and dishonoring one's parents. Jesus concluded his response by adding, "also, you shall love your neighbor as yourself" (v. 19). When the young man replied, "I have kept all these, what do I still lack?" (v. 20), Jesus told him to sell his possessions and give the money to the poor (v. 21)—another unexpected response. In Matt 22:39 Jesus reemphasizes the same commandment, calling to remembrance his earlier conversation with the young man. But this time he also reveals another truth; that loving our neighbor is of similar importance as or "like unto" loving God. Jesus's earlier conversation in Matt 19 is instructive for his conversation with the lawyer in Matt 22. That is, his encouragement to the young man to sell his possessions and give them to the poor demonstrates something of the expansive love to which Jesus invites his larger audience in Matt 22, and to which he invites us today. Loving our neighbor may require us to relinquish some of our own possessions for the well-being of others.

The commandments to love God and love neighbor as ourselves also became foundational for the early church and remain so for the church today. James, in his letter (or moral teaching) to "the twelve tribes in the Dispersion" (1:1), characterizes the command to "love your neighbor as yourself" as an essential element of the *royal law* (2:8). Thus, James devotes a significant portion of his correspondence to discussions about the quality of our relationship with each other, especially in light of our tendency toward class-based division and partiality in favor of people with greater material resources. Class-based division and partiality clouded the church's ability to see itself as a reconciling community for all people. James underscores this problem earlier in chapter 2, asking, "My brothers and sisters, do you with your acts of favoritism really believe in our glorious Lord Jesus Christ?" (2:1). Continuing this line of questioning, he writes, "For if a person with gold rings and in fine clothes comes into your assembly and if a poor person in dirty clothes also comes in, and if you take notice of the one wearing the fine clothes and say, 'Have a seat here, please,' while to the one who is poor you say, 'Stand there,' or 'Sit at my feet,' have you not made distinctions among yourselves and become judges with evil thoughts?" (2:1–2). Throughout his writing, James invites his community to consider the gravity of their actions, for by their preferential treatment of the rich they were in attitude and practice neglecting their neighbor and violating the *royal law*.

Ultimately, James reveals, Christian communities should be places where those who are weak, ill, and otherwise broken can call for the elders of the church for relief without fear of mistreatment or marginalization (see Jas 5:13–15). That is, at our best, Christian communities become Hope-filled bodies in which and with which we can confess our sins and find forgiveness. Infused by the love of Christ for all people, we also exemplify an eagerness to attend to the material needs of our sisters and brothers while lifting each other in prayer, fully assured that in our time of need someone will likewise pray for us and walk by our side.

In 1 John 4:11–21, the writer places even greater emphasis upon loving God and loving neighbor as ourselves by indicating that loving God is inseparable from loving our brothers and sisters:

> [11] Beloved, since God loved us so much, we also ought to love one another. [12] No one has ever seen God; if we love one another, God lives in us, and his love is perfected in us. [13] By this we know that we abide in him and he in us, because he has given us of his Spirit. [14] And we have seen and do testify that the Father has sent his Son as the Savior of the world. [15] God abides in those who confess that Jesus is the Son of God, and they abide in God. [16] So we have known and believe the love that God has for us. God is love, and those who abide in love abide in God, and God abides in them . . . [19] We love because God first loved us. [20] Those who say, "I love God," and hate their brothers or sisters, are liars; for those who do not love a brother or sister whom they have seen, cannot love God whom they have not seen. [21] *The commandment we have from him is this: those who love God must love their brothers and sisters also.*

Neighbor love is more than a good practice. The writer of 1 John is emphatic in his assertion that loving God and loving our brothers and sisters are inextricably connected. God abides in us, 1 John reveals, gifting us with the capacity to live as an expression of God's presence in the day-to-dayness of our lives, for as God is, "so are we in this world" (v. 17). Therefore, we cannot claim to love God and ignore the needs of our sisters and brothers.

Or, as James suggests, "faith without works is dead" (2:14–26). That is, faith absent tangible expression God's loving care for our sisters and brothers can hardly be considered faith at all.

The commandment to love God and neighbor, as universalized in Jesus's teachings and as expanded by the early church, opens wide the gates of God's community to those deemed outsiders by church and society. In the ancient church, these included Samaritans, Syrophoenicians, and other Gentiles. Also included were women, children, slaves, and those who because of their physical and psychological infirmities or because of the material conditions of their lives had been relegated to the margins of society. The commands to love God and neighbor remain the foundation for the church's ethical praxis. Together they animate the church and each of us individually to engage in acts of love and compassionate care for all people, and to do so as an expression of our identity as *imago Dei* and commitment to the way of Jesus the Christ.

Discerning what it means to live as followers of Jesus and, as per our primordial faith, as *imago Dei* was a persistent concern in the early church. Initially, the commands to love God and neighbor gave meaning to their lives and to their identity in and with Jesus as the Christ. Love of God and neighbor also sustained the church as they, in breathless anticipation, remained resolute in their belief that Jesus was God's chosen Messiah and would come again to receive those who had remained faithful in love and compassionate care. But Jesus did not return to receive the faithful, requiring the church and individual people of faith to reimagine their lives in light of the delay of the parousia, the Messiah's eschatological return.[71]

The Delay of the Parousia

The anticipatory fervor and commitment to love and compassionate care that defined the early church was grounded in their belief in the Messiah's soon return. They were convinced, writes Alexander E. Stewart, that "the long-awaited Messiah had come, had died, had risen from the dead, had ascended to heaven and had poured out the eschatological gift of the Holy Spirit."[72] They were also aware "that the final resurrection and judgment had not yet happened and they were waiting for Jesus the Messiah to return to bring the final consummation and the new heavens and earth."[73] Liv-

---

71. See Riggans, "The Parousia"; Ladd, "Pondering the Parousia"; Hiers, "The Problem of the Delay"; Stewart, "The Temporary Messianic Kingdom."

72. Stewart, "The Temporary Messianic Kingdom," 264.

73. Stewart, "The Temporary Messianic Kingdom," 264.

ing in anticipation of Jesus's messianic return was an act of faith for the early church. The parousia also represented an end to the persecution early Christians experienced at the hands of the Roman Empire and the Jewish religious leaders as well as an end to the material lack that so defined their existence. The Messiah's return would make all things new. But the newness they anticipated had not materialized. John's image of God's new Jerusalem coming down to earth from the heavens in the book of Revelation remained in the not-yet.[74] Even as people awaited his return and engaged in practices of love and compassionate care, Jesus's promised soon return did not materialize in their lifetimes (or in the lifetime of their children or grandchildren). Thus, New Testament writers, in addition to encouraging the church to remain faithful in its praxis of love and compassionate care, also endeavored to give meaning to the parousia's delay.[75]

Gospel writings, including the Gospel of Mark, sought to mediate the church's anxiety by assuring the faithful that some would not "taste death" until they would see God's kin(g)dom fully and powerfully realized (Mark 9:1). Other New Testament writings, such as the book of Hebrews, sought to enliven the church's anticipation of the Messiah's return by characterizing Jesus as a faithful and eternal high priest who would sustain them as they awaited the day of the Lord. In chapter 3 of the book of Hebrews, for example, the writer encourages the church to follow Jesus's example of faithfulness to "the one who appointed him" (vv. 1–2). The church, the writer asserts, is God's house to which Jesus remained faithful "as a son" (v. 6). Thus, the writer encourages the church to "hold firm the confidence and the pride that belongs to hope" (v. 6). Later, in chapter 5, the writer quotes the liturgist of Ps 110:4, identifying Jesus as "a priest forever after the order of Melchizedek" (v. 6). Melchizedek, priest and king of Salem in the Hebrew Scriptures (see Gen 14:17–18), preceded the Hebrew people's identity

---

74. See Hiers, "The Problem of the Delay," 145–55. According to Hiers, in an effort to account for the delay of the parousia, Luke omits elements of Mark's Gospel account and tailors his own account to explain the delay: "On the one hand, he [Luke] undertakes to show that Jesus had not mistakenly believed or proclaimed that the Parousia was near. On the other hand, Luke holds before his own contemporaries—who might still have included a few survivors of the earliest community—the hope (and warning) that the Kingdom of. God and/or Son of man might come soon" (146). Throughout his gospel writing, "Luke wished to show that the divine plan (and Jesus's understanding of it) did not call for the coming of the Parousia events during the lifetime of Jesus or the earliest community" (148).

75. The earliest New Testament writings are dated at or around AD 50–63. Contextually, this dating corresponds with Nero's ascension to the throne in the Roman Empire (AD 54) and his persecution of the Christian church.

as Israel and the Levitical priesthood.⁷⁶ Given this fact, the writer of the book of Hebrews situates Jesus's high priestly identity as more ancient and greater than the Levitical priesthood, which was still active during Jesus's lifetime and during the early days of the church. Earlier in Heb 1:13, the writer had also situated Jesus in a position of superior authority and power. Quoting Ps 110:1, the writer poetically asserts Jesus's superiority to the angels: "But to which of the angels has he ever said, 'sit at my right hand until I make your enemies a foot-stool for your feet'?"⁷⁷ The angels' purpose, according to the writer of Hebrews, is to participate in Jesus's salvific work until Jesus's enemies become his footstool.

The church's affirmation of Jesus's authority, his eternal priesthood, and superiority to the angels, emboldened the church to live in anticipation of his return. It also signified or became a sign of the church's intent to align their thought and action with Jesus's emphasis upon love during their time of waiting, as is evident in Heb 10:23–25.

> ²³ Let us hold fast to the confession of our hope without wavering, for he who has promised is faithful. ²⁴ And let us consider how to *provoke one another to love and good deeds,* ²⁵ not neglecting to meet together, as is the habit of some, but encouraging one another, and all the more as you see the Day approaching.

The writer urges individual people of faith to consider (Greek: κατανοέω = *katanoeō*) or observe one another so as to provoke (Greek: παραξυσμός = *paroxysmos*) or incite one another to love and good works. Love and good works in the book of Hebrews, as in the Gospels and other New Testament writings, were as cords, binding the community together as they awaited the Day or "day of the Lord."⁷⁸

---

76. The liturgist of Ps 110:4 also speaks of an unidentified "lord" as "a priest forever according to the order of Melchizedek," words echoed in Hebrews in reference to Jesus.

77. Heirs, "The Problem of the Delay," 264; Hiers argues "the preexistent Jewish idea of a future transitional messianic kingdom was combined by many of the earliest Christian with Psalm 110:1 in order to interpret the present time in terms of Jesus's temporary and transitional rule and kingdom." He also notes the frequency with which Psalm 110 is quoted or alluded to in New Testament writings: quoted in Matt 22:24; 26:64; Mark 12:36; 14:62; Luke 20:42–43; 22:69; Acts 2:34–35; Heb 1:13, and alluded to in thirteen to fourteen additional passages of Scripture, making Ps 110:1 the most frequently quoted Old Testament text in the New Testament.

78. The writer of Hebrews does not indicate that the proper noun "Day" in v. 25 refers to the "day of the Lord." Other New Testament writers are more explicit. Paul, in 1 Thessalonians, describes the day of the Lord as coming "like a thief in the night," a disrupting and destructive day from which those who have "obtained salvation through our Lord Jesus Christ" will be spared (1 Thess 5:1–11). Second Peter similarly describes the day of the Lord as coming "like a thief, and then the heavens will pass away with a

Despite the difficulties of life, the church grounded itself in the belief that Jesus was coming soon and that their redemption was sure. In the meantime, church leaders continued to stress mutual love and compassionate care as the church's central praxis. In Heb 13:1–2, the writer accents the importance of this praxis.

> ¹ Let mutual love continue. Do not neglect to show hospitality to strangers, for by doing that some have entertained angels without knowing it. ² Remember those who are in prison, as though you were in prison with them, those who are being tortures, as though you yourself were being tortured.

Not only was the church to extend love to one another. They were to offer the same love and care to their neighbors—to the stranger or foreigner and to those who were imprisoned and tortured.

The apostle Paul, in the First Letter to the Thessalonians, similarly stresses the importance of love as the church awaits the day of the Lord. Referencing Timothy's good report concerning the church at Thessalonica, this writer encourages, "And *may the Lord make you increase and abound in love for one another and for all, just as we abound in love for you.* And may he so strengthen your hearts in holiness that you may be blameless before our God and Father *at the coming of our Lord Jesus with all his saints*" (3:11–13).[79] Again, Paul instructs the church to practice love in the meantime. Echoing Paul's sentiment, James urges his community to desist from grumbling against one another and to wait with patience. As the farmer patiently waits for her crops to push through the earth, James counsels, so must the followers of Jesus strengthen their hearts or wait patiently, for "the coming of the Lord is near" (5:7–11).

The biblical writings that I highlight, and others, sought to help the church make meaning of their lives and of the delay of the Messiah's return. Alexander Stewart, reflecting on 1 Cor 15:23–28, summarizes the early church's response to the delay.

> The resurrection of Jesus was the firstfruits of the much larger harvest: the resurrection of those who belong to the Messiah at his coming (1 Cor 15:23). The end would come following

---

loud noise, and the elements will be dissolved with fire, and the earth and everything that is done on it will be disclosed" (other translations suggest "burnt up") (2 Pet 3:8–10). New Testament references to the "day of the Lord" are also evident in Paul's letters to the church at Corinth and in the two letters to the church at Thessalonica (1 Cor 5:5; 2 Cor 1:14; 1 Thess 5:2; 2 Thess 3:10).

79. See also 1 Thess 5:23–24 and 2 Thess 2:1–12 for additional references to the day of the Lord.

the second coming of the Messiah (1 Cor 15:24). At the end, the Messiah will present his kingdom to God after having destroyed every ruler, authority and power (1 Cor 15:24). The crucial line in verse 25 provides an interpretation of the present time and a reason for the delay—it is necessary (δεῖ) for him to rule (βασιλεύειν) "until [ἄχρι] he has put all his enemies under his feet." It is important to note that Paul replaces the second line of Ps. 110:1 ("sit at my right hand") with the statement that δει γὰρ αυτόν βασιλεύειν. Jesus's exaltation and enthronement is equivalent to his present rule which extends from the resurrection to the *parousia*.[80]

Though the parousia had not materialized, Paul and other New Testament writers were adamant that Jesus's reign had already begun. Jesus reigns from his place of honor at God's right hand—a reign that will continue "until a point of time in the future when everything would be subjected under his feet."[81] The early church's task, therefore, was to hold fast the confession of their faith as they awaited Jesus's ultimate return (Heb 3:1; 4:14), a commitment echoed by many people of faith today.[82]

Navigating the Sociocultural and Theological Terrain

The delay of parousia presented two major difficulties for the church and for individual Christians. The first involved coping with the consequence of their emerging identity as a religious tradition distinctive from Judaism, especially for early Christians who were ethnic Jews. The second difficulty had to do with the church's precarious social location and lack of institutional power, which compounded its vulnerability to persecution by the Jewish religious authorities and increasingly by the Roman Empire.

As to the first difficulty, as time progressed, the church came to identify itself less as a sect of Judaism and more as a distinctive religious tradition. The move towards distinctiveness represented an undeniable and

---

80. Stewart, "The Temporary Messianic Kingdom," 267 (italics, parentheses, and brackets original). Stewart also draws insight from Fee, *The First Epistle to the Corinthians*; Conzelmann, *First Corinthians*; Collins, *First Corinthians*; Thiselton, *The First Epistle to the Corinthians*; Garland, *1 Corinthians*; Lambrecht, "Paul's Christological Use of Scripture."

81. Stewart, "The Temporary Messianic Kingdom," 267.

82. Faith is assumed in Heb 3:1 and 4:14, as the writer does not include this latter phrase. In Heb 10:23, the writer admonishes the church to "hold fast to the confession of our hope without wavering, for he who has promised is faithful"; thus confession could also refer to their anticipation of Jesus's return.

irreparable rift in Judaism between people of faith who believed the Messiah had come in Jesus and those who still awaited the Messiah's advent.[83] The Hebrew people had for millennia anticipated a messiah who would restore the Davidic kingdom. Israel would arise as the seat of peace and salvation, and all nations would be blessed because of their presence. Justo González writes, regarding Israel's eschatological longing, "All, from the Sadducees to the Pharisees, kept the Messianic hope, and firmly believed that the day would come when God would intervene in order to restore Israel and fulfil the promise of a kingdom of peace and justice."[84] While Jesus's followers insisted that he was the Messiah, adherents to traditional Judaism still awaited the Messiah's advent.

The divisions between these two groups of Jewish believers grew stronger as the still-emerging church began expanding its borders. Not only did the church proclaim Jesus as the Messiah. Over time, the church opened wide the borders of its community and welcomed Gentiles, previously prohibited (or unclean) people, as beloved sisters and brothers. The apostle Peter's rooftop visionary experience and his subsequent encounter with Cornelius's household in Acts 10 is emblematic of this expansion of borders.

Peter, while awaiting the noonday meal, goes to the rooftop of the home where he is staying and has a fairly disturbing visionary experience. In it, Peter is presented with a large sheet full of "four-footed creatures and reptiles and birds of the air" (Acts 10:11). A voice tells him, "Get up, Peter; kill and eat," but Peter, aware that some of the animals are ritually unclean, refuses to take from the sheet (vv. 13–16). The voice speaks again, chastising Peter for calling unclean that which God has made, but Peter does not understand. Around the same time, a Roman centurion whose name is Cornelius has an angelic encounter. In response, Cornelius invites Peter to come and speak with his household, and Peter accepts the invitation. Upon meeting Cornelius, Peter awakens to the truth that God welcomes all and shows no partiality.[85] At Cornelius's invitation, Peter proclaims Jesus's life, death, resurrection, and coming judgement to Cornelius's household, and "while Peter was still speaking, the Holy Spirit fell upon all who heard the word" (v. 44). Under ordinary circumstances, Peter and other early Christians of Jewish descent would have summarily rejected the idea that God would have welcomed Gentiles into the household of faith. But Peter's experience with the Divine and with Cornelius and his household

---

83. González, *The Story of Christianity*, 31.

84. González, *The Story of Christianity*, 11.

85. More specifically, Acts 10:34–35 indicates, "Then Peter began to speak to them: 'I truly understand that God shows no partiality. But in every nation anyone who fears [God] and does what is right is acceptable to [God].'"

definitively altered Peter's core beliefs, freeing him to acknowledge the boundarylessness of God's kin(g)dom.

In Acts 11, Peter shares his newfound understanding with the Jerusalem church. Having witnessed the gift of the Holy Spirit poured out upon Cornelius and his household and having baptized all who were in the house, Peter asks the apostles and believers in Jerusalem, "If then God gave them the same gift that he gave us when we believed in the Lord Jesus Christ, who was I that I could hinder God?" (v. 17). On hearing this news, the apostles and believers in Jerusalem "praised God, saying, 'Then God has given even to the Gentiles the repentance that leads to life'" (v. 18). Joyfully, they align their hearts with the heart of God and welcome the Gentiles into the household of faith.

In addition to welcoming Gentiles, the church began to distance itself from the ritual practices of Judaism. The physical sign of covenant relationship that had bound the community together (circumcision by removal of the male foreskin) slowly gave way to the apostle Paul's notion of circumcision of the heart in Rom 2:29.[86] Circumcision of the heart, among Christian believers, affirmed and extended the covenant between God and ancient Israel to include all who would come to God through Jesus the Christ.

Alongside the widening gap between the church and traditional Judaism, the precarious situatedness of the early church within the Roman Empire together with its lack of institutional power created another challenge for the early church. The Roman Empire, writes González, "brought to the Mediterranean basin an unprecedented political unity," which afforded the church certain freedoms while also creating new tensions.[87] On the one hand, Christians could travel throughout the empire without fear of bandits and pirates because the emperor provided cover for the church and other communities that followed religious traditions. On the other hand, two of the means by which the Roman Empire sought to promote unity were "religious syncretism—the indiscriminate mixing of elements from various religions—and emperor worship."[88] While Christians were free to practice their faith, their belief in Jesus as the Christ and in the God of creation as the one God (the only God) entailed a rejection of the Roman Empire's syncretistic religious impulses and its emphasis upon worshiping the emperor.

---

86. Paul's teaching is similar to the heart faith alluded to in Jeremiah's prophetic utterance (Jer 31:31–34) regarding God's decision to write the law upon the hearts of the exiles returning from Babylonian captivity. Circumcision of the heart is also referenced in Heb 10:16.

87. González, *The Story of Christianity*, 13.

88. González, *The Story of Christianity*, 14.

As a result, Christians were regarded as uncooperative outsiders who possessed minimal institutional power to affect the material condition of their lives. This is significant because many of the first Christians were poor and oppressed, and their alignment with the faith of Jesus intensified their plight. Oberey Hendricks, in *The Politics of Jesus,* writes, "the Book of Acts describes the church as beginning with a gathering of peasants, mostly Galileans, who were possibly the most devalued of all first-century Jews, and whose fear of Roman brutality had been heightened by the torture and execution of their beloved leaders (Acts 2.1–42)."[89] Their marginal status in society afforded Christians fewer privileges than other groups, requiring them to respond to the material needs of their community from within their own ranks, as the government did not guarantee their material well-being. Christians, therefore, were initially a rather insular community who held all things common both because of their commitment to mutual love and, I suspect, because of their material dearth and sense of powerlessness in the increasingly hostile environment in which they lived.

These two difficulties—the church's break with Judaism and its precarious social location and lack of institutional power—characterize the transitional years of the Christian church. By the end of the first century, the church understood itself as upholding and developing a distinctive religious tradition, even as its roots remained deeply planted in Judaism, which is also true today. Over the next four hundred years the church worked diligently to clarify its theology and liturgical practices through a robust and oftentimes contentious series of faithful deliberations among the various church leaders. The church's precarious position in the Roman Empire also demanded that the church confront the daunting question of its corporeal survival in the face of persecution by the religious authorities of the time and by the civil government.

Embracing a New Identity

As the years progressed with no sign of the Messiah's return, the church had to adjust to a new normal. This was no simple matter, as adjusting entailed discerning how to live within the tension of its self-understanding as the body of Christ and the demands of life in the shadow of the Roman Empire. How would the church preserve its identity in light of the empire's demand for allegiance and in the face of demands for reverence from the emperor? What measures would the church take to secure the corporeal and spiritual well-being of its members? To what extent would

---

89. Hendricks, *The Politics of Jesus,* 83.

the love ethic that Jesus (and the apostles following him) so passionately proclaimed continue to shape the church's theological praxis? How would the church and Christian people of faith hold fast the confession of their faith when the despairing realities of life gestured toward an ethic of power and domination? How would the church navigate the treacherous contextual terrain of life in the Roman Empire?

Despite challenges to their faith and way of life, in its early years the church persisted in proclaiming love of God and neighbor as its foundational belief and praxis. The Christian community also remained resolute in its expectation that Jesus would return soon. But as the years progressed, the sociopolitical climate and the church's expectations changed. Internally, the Christian community recognized their expectation of the Messiah's soon return would have to sustain them for a considerably longer period of time than they had initially anticipated. The Messiah would return, they believed, but the time of his return became increasingly obscure. Externally, Nero's mid-first-century rise to the throne marked an end to the empire's protective stance toward the church, leaving Christians to *fend for themselves* without support from Roman authorities.[90]

Nero came to power in October of AD 54. Initially, he was well received throughout the empire, including among Christians and other marginal groups. But within ten years, Nero had become a despised ruler, desperate to repair his reputation.[91] On June 18, AD 64, a tragedy struck Rome. A great fire began and burned the city for six days and seven nights, destroying ten of the fourteen sections of the city.[92] Justo González notes, "Two of the areas that had not burned had a very high proportion of Jewish and Christian populations. Therefore, Emperor Nero decided to blame the Christians."[93] At first, officials of the empire persecuted Christians as a response to Nero's charge that Christians started the fire. But as time progressed, Roman officials began persecuting Christians "for the mere fact of being Christians."[94] Throughout this period of persecution, church leaders sought to embolden the Christian community to remain faithful, for Jesus had warned his followers that persecution would come.[95] In AD 68, Nero was deposed and later killed himself, but Nero's death did not quell the empire's persecutory

---

90. González, *The Story of Christianity*, preface to part 1; earlier emperors included Augustus (27 BC—AD 14), Tiberius (14–37), Caligula (37–41), and Claudius (41–54).
91. González, *The Story of Christianity*, 32.
92. González, *The Story of Christianity*, 34.
93. González, *The Story of Christianity*, 34.
94. González, *The Story of Christianity*, 36.
95. See Mark 13:9–13; Luke 12:7–19.

impulse. Though there were brief periods of respite from persecution, the empire's maltreatment of Christians persisted for more than three hundred years and over the reigns of multiple rulers.[96]

Christian persecution as widespread and systemic ended by the fourth century when Diocletian became emperor of Rome and reorganized the empire. The ruling structure included four emperors, two of which bore the title Augustus (Diocletian and Maximian) and two subemperors (Galarius and Constantius Chlorus), who were called Caesar.[97] Diocletian, whose wife and daughter were Christians, was tolerant of his family's religious faith, permitting the church a period of relative peace. Galarius, however, hated Christians and Jews and sought to see them silenced throughout the empire. By AD 303, Galarius had convinced Diocletian to prohibit Christians from military service, expel Christian soldiers who would not renounce their faith, and finally, issue an edict to remove Christians from all positions of governmental authority. Galarius also ordered Christians, under threat of death, to turn over their sacred writings to be burned. And, following Nero's precedent, Galarius accused Jews and Christians of setting fires in the imperial palace. Though Diocletian's reorganization of the imperial structure implied shared authority, the four emperors, and especially Galarius, were in a constant struggle among themselves for ultimate authority. And Christians, in most instances, were but pawns in their quest for power.

---

96. González, *The Story of Christianity*, 2–6; see the chronology. González also notes the difficulties Jews experienced throughout the empire. He notes, "since at times, the distinction between Jews and Christian was not clear in the minds of Roman authorities, imperial functionaries began persecuting any who followed 'Jewish Practices'" (36). Compounding this problem for the Jews was the fact of the temple's destruction in AD 70 and the increased pressure upon them to "remit to the imperial coffers the annual offering they would otherwise have sent to Jerusalem." (36). Jews who refused to comply faced the threat of execution. It is also worth noting that the three hundred years of persecution included the martyrdom of numerous Christian laypeople, bishops, and other leaders who refused to renounce their faith. Known martyrs of the second century include Bishop Ignatius of Antioch; Bishop Polycarp of Smyrna; Felicitas, a consecrated widow who devoted all of her time to the church, and her seven sons; and Justin, a prominent Christian scholar. The best-known martyrs of the third century include the five catechumens and traveling companions in AD 203. The five were new converts in the period of their preparation to receive baptism. Among them were Perpetua, a "well-to-do woman who was nursing her infant child," her slaves, Felicitas (who was pregnant) and Revocatus, and two other young men, Saturninus and Secundulus. After a lengthy judicial process and attempts by the authorities to persuade Perpetua, Felicitas, and their companions to abandon the Christian faith, they were thrown into the arena to be killed by wild beasts.

97. González, *The Story of Christianity*, 103.

Severe infighting, murder, and forced abdication of the throne continued among the various emperors for another nine to ten years.[98] Then, in an odd turn of events in AD 311, Galarius became ill and surmised that the Christian God was punishing him for persecuting Christians. In order to appease the Christian God, Galarius issued an edict on April 30, 311, requiring lapsed Christians to return to their faith and ordering them to pray to God for him and for the empire.[99] Galarius died five days later.

Galarius's death left a vacuum in leadership. Constantine, taking advantage of the situation, waged war against Maxentius, son of Maximian, and assumed the throne as the sole emperor of Rome. In his first act as emperor, Constantine ordered an end to Christian persecution. In AD 313 Constantine issued the Edict of Milan, ordering the restoration of property to Christians throughout the empire and marking the end of Christian persecution for many years to come. Constantine, who came to be known as "defender of Christianity against Licinius the persecutor," reigned until AD 337.[100]

Constantine's rise to the throne marked a turning point in the life of the church, both because he abolished Christian persecution throughout the empire, and because of his relationship vis-à-vis the church. As emperor of Rome, Constantine declared his authority to appoint bishops to the church, designated himself "bishop of bishops," and used the combination of two Greek letters called chi and rho (XP)—a Christian symbol for Jesus—in

---

98. González, *The Story of Christianity*, 103. Eventually, Galarius convinced an ill Diocletian to abdicate his throne, situating himself to become emperor (augustus) of the Eastern Empire. Galarius also threatened to wage war against Maximian, augustus in the West, forcing Maximian to abdicate his throne. As a result, Constantius Chlorus assumed the role of augustus in the West, and he and Galarius appointed Maximinus Daia and Severus respectively to bear the title of caesar. Galarius, hungry to become the sole emperor of Rome, also kidnapped the children of his fellow emperors, Constantine (son of Constantius Chlorus) and Maxentius (son of Maximian), in an effort to make them abdicate their positions. But Constantine escaped capture, and when his father, Constantius Chlorus, died, the people proclaimed Constantine their augustus. Constantine and Maxentius ruled the Western Empire together as augustus and caesar, respectively. Severus committed suicide and Maximinus Daia joined Galarius's enterprise in the East to persecute Christians.

99. González, *The Story of Christianity*, 106.

100. González, *The Story of Christianity*, 117. Licinius had been an emperor in the East alongside Maxentius. Christians, who live free of persecution in Licinius's territory, were "divided over a number of issues, and such divisions led to public disorder," writes González. When Licinius took actions to assure the peace, some among the Christians believed they had been wronged. As a consequence, they "began thinking of Constantine as defender of the true faith, and as 'the emperor whom God loved.'" Licinius viewed their actions as treasonous and took measures against them, affording Constantine an opportunity to present himself as "the defender of Christianity."

battle.[101] But, on what grounds might the church consider Constantine a Christian? As emperor, Constantine refused to submit himself to Christian teachers or to the authority of the church's bishops. He also refused Christian baptism until on his deathbed. Instead, Constantine "reserved the right to determine his own religious practices," which included practices related to Christianity and those of the civil religion of Rome.[102] Solidifying his authority, Constantine also named himself the "*pontifex maximus*, that is, 'chief priest' of the Roman civil religion."[103] By appointing himself *bishop of bishops* and *pontifex maximus*, Constantine assumes ultimate authority over all religious practice in the empire.[104]

Two serious consequences of Constantine's questionable conversion to Christianity resulted. The first, writes Obrey M. Hendricks, is that "Constantine's actions confused militarism and political domination with the cause of Christ," and the church did little to clear up any such confusion.[105] The militaristic impulse has functioned to obscure the church's mission, leading various segments of the church throughout history to abandon Jesus's praxiological emphasis upon love of God and neighbor. Under Constantine this impulse did more than create confusion, however. Equating militarism and political domination with the cause of Christ made and does make living into Jesus's love ethic without partiality unattainable.[106] Constantine's rise to power indeed liberated Christians from centuries of persecution. But it also afforded the church, particularly its leaders, an opportunity to take its place within the larger imperial structure of power and domination.

The second consequence of Constantine's rise to power was its impact upon Christian worship and ecclesial structure. Constantine "introduced a hierarchical structure into Christianity—and fully legitimized it in the eyes of believers."[107] While there already existed hierarchy in the church, Hendricks contends that "the church's hierarchy was a hierarchy of roles and

101. González, *The Story of Christianity*.
102. González, *The Story of Christianity*, 121.
103. Hendricks, *The Politics of Jesus*, 87.
104. González, *The Story of Christianity*, 122. Regarding Constantine's commitment to both authority and Christianity, González writes, "The truth is probably that Constantine was a sincere believer in the power of Christ. But this does not mean that he understood that power in the same way in which it had been experienced by those Christian who had died for it. For him, the Christian God was a very powerful being who would support him as long as he favored the faithful. Therefore, when Constantine enacted laws in favor of Christianity, and when he had churches built, what he sought was not the goodwill of Christians, but rather the goodwill of their God."
105. Hendricks, *The Politics of Jesus*, 87.
106. Hendricks, *The Politics of Jesus*, 87.
107. Hendricks, *The Politics of Jesus*, 88.

functions, not of rank."[108] "In the church's role-based hierarchy," Hendricks continues, "no believer had a higher status than another; all were God's children seeking grace."[109] But after Constantine's claim to Christian authority, Christian worship revealed the influence of imperial protocol both in the accoutrements worn by religious leaders and in the manner of worship.[110] The church also adopted an "official theology," a theology sanctioned by the empire and in turn sanctioning the empire.[111]

What made Constantine's presence and policies so compelling? Many believed that Constantine had been raised up by God to deliver the church from persecution. Eusebius, regarded as the foremost Christian historian of the fourth century, had been elected bishop of Caesarea a few years before Constantine became sole emperor.[112] And though Eusebius was "neither a close friend nor a courtier of Constantine," Eusebius held that Constantine was God's instrument of peace for the church.[113] In Eusebius's view, Christianity and empire were not simply coexistent. Christianity as contextualized in the Roman Empire was rather "the ultimate goal of human history."[114] From the beginning, Eusebius and other such thinkers surmised, the movement of history has been toward the imperial church of Rome.[115] Since God's plan had been fulfilled, Christians had only to hope for their individual attainment of a heavenly home.[116]

Absent from Eusebius's view, however, is any mention of the church's anticipation of Jesus's return. In his theological worldview, the church, alongside the empire, represented the *telos* of human history. González highlights Eusebius's worldview, noting his and "many others of similar theological orientation['s] . . . *tendency to set aside or postpone the hope of the early church, that its Lord would return in the clouds to establish a kingdom of peace and justice.*"[117] By the fourth century, the persecuted church had become the church of the empire and had taken its place in the imperial power structure. The church whose early life had been laced with love for one another and for

---

108. Hendricks, *The Politics of Jesus*, 88.
109. Hendricks, *The Politics of Jesus*, 88.
110. González, *The Story of Christianity*, 125.
111. González, *The Story of Christianity*, 129–35.
112. Eusebius's *Christian History* is one of the few extant church histories that trace the church's early development.
113. González, *The Story of Christianity*, 132.
114. González, *The Story of Christianity*, 132.
115. González, *The Story of Christianity*, 133.
116. González, *The Story of Christianity*, 134.
117. González, *The Story of Christianity*, (italics added).

the neighbor was barely recognizable, and Jesus's emphasis upon good news for the poor was almost inaudible.[118]

The church under Constantine gave birth to a dynamic and oftentimes difficult relationship between church and empire or church and state. This new iteration of church drew people from near and far, as its association with empire raised the church's status. But, as the church relished the growth that was taking place, and adopted the empire's accoutrements, it also lost sight of the foundation upon which it had rested since the first days of its existence: love of God and neighbor. The church had become a powerful symbolic representation of the empire, and membership in the church came to represent one's attachment, if only vicariously, to the symbols of power indicative of empire.[119]

A Fall to Chaos

In the years following Constantine's rise to power, the church sought to clarify its theology, commitments, and practices as well as its relationship to the Roman Empire. In the East, González notes, "the imperial church, which Constantine had inaugurated, continued existing for another thousand years in the Byzantine Empire."[120] But the Western empire fell into disarray, and by the year AD 410 the Roman Empire had crumbled.

Rome was taken by the Visigoths, conquering nations located beyond the Rhine and the Danube Rivers, requiring the Western church to readjust yet again.[121] Under the Visigoths, the church occupied the role of "legislator for the Visigoth Kingdom." In this role, the church sought to maintain order by enacting laws and rulings that were often unjust and inequitable, especially against clergy who defied the bishop's decrees and against the Jews. Over time, the pope of the Roman church assumed authority to crown emperors, reifying the church's relationship with the civil government.[122]

The church's symbiotic relationship with the civil government continued throughout the Middle Ages and under multiple regimes.[123] That relationship was made more complex, however, when in or around AD

---

118. Hendricks, *The Politics of Jesus*, 92.
119. González, *The Story of Christianity*, 136.
120. González, *The Story of Christianity*, 217.
121. González, *The Story of Christianity*, 232.
122. González, *The Story of Christianity*, 234, 243. Pope Leo "the Great" is regarded as the first pope of the imperial church. He was still bishop of Rome in AD 455 and became pope after an encounter with Atilla and his Huns, who were set to invade Rome.
123. González, *The Story of Christianity*, 231–50. The Visigoths were conquered by the Muslim Moors in the eighth century.

622 an unexpected group of conquerors from Arabia led by a deeply religious Arab merchant whose name was Mohammed, came on the scene. Mohammed preached a message that he believed had been revealed to him by the angel Gabriel. He spoke of "a single God, both just and merciful, who rules all things and requires obedience from all."[124] Many in the polytheistic milieu of the old Roman territories that Mohammed and other merchants frequented took issue with his preaching because of his monotheistic leanings. Mohammed, however, "claimed that he was not preaching a new religion, but simply the culmination of what God had revealed in the Hebrew prophets and in Jesus, who was a great prophet, although not divine as Christians claim."[125] Because of opposition to his teachings, Mohammed left Mecca in AD 622 and took refuge in Medina where he founded the first Muslim community.

This series of events initiates the Muslim era. Over the next ten years, Mohammed and his followers embarked upon a political and military campaign that gave them control of Mecca and much of Arabia.[126] They also seized "many of the ancient centers of Christianity, [including] Jerusalem, Antioch, Damascus, Alexandria, and Carthage," placing these regions under Muslim control.[127] In some regions, such as Carthage and surrounding territories, Christianity essentially disappeared.

The Muslim expansion marks a significant turning point in the life of the church. The church, set upon reclaiming territory from the Muslims, become more deeply entrenched in the militaristic impulse that began with the reign of Constantine. On Christmas Day of AD 800, Pope Leo III crowned Charles, king of the Franks, as emperor in the West with the words, "May God grant life to the great and pacific emperor!"[128] King Charles took the name Charlemagne. Initially, Charlemagne was only king of the Franks, but through a series of campaigns against neighboring rulers, some of whom were allies, Charlemagne extended his territory beyond the borders of the ancient Roman Empire.

The Western Church was almost entirely under the control of the emperor during Charlemagne's reign, as the emperor ruled in civil and ecclesial matters, including by appointing bishops and directing ecclesial affairs. But the church's symbiotic relationship with the governance of emperors proved a double-edged sword. One the one hand, the authority to

124. González, *The Story of Christianity*, 249.
125. González, *The Story of Christianity*, 249.
126. González, *The Story of Christianity*, 249.
127. González, *The Story of Christianity*, 250.
128. González, *The Story of Christianity*, 266.

crown emperors afforded the papacy great privilege in Rome and beyond. One the other hand, Rome was in a state of chaos as rulers throughout the region vied for imperial authority, making the "papacy an easy prey for the ambitious, one to be had by bribery, deceit, or even violence."[129] As a result, the papacy also fell into disarray.

Over the next two hundred years the chaos in Rome persisted and popes rose and fell in rapid succession, oftentimes with violence. Yet the church's symbiotic relationship with emperors of what came to be called the Holy Roman Empire continued. One of the most consequential results of this alliance between church and emperor is the medieval Holy Wars of the late eleventh century forward. Not only did the church adopt militarism as essential to its identity, but it did so with no discernible regard for the foundation of love by which the church had come into being. Recall that in AD 622 and going forward, the Muslims had conquered many of the territories in the West. By the eleventh century, the Seljuk Turks, a Muslim nation, were also threatening the Byzantine Empire in the East. Though the territories that had once composed the Western Roman Empire had been in chaos for centuries, the Eastern Empire, namely, the Byzantine Empire, had remained intact. The church in the East also remained viable, but the relationship between the two branches of the church (East and West) was severely strained.[130] The Muslim threat to the Byzantine Empire gave the two branches cause to unite.

Civil authorities in the West, still sour from their losses during the Arab conquest, also sought to unite with the East so as to save the Byzantine Empire from a similar defeat.[131] The joint offensive against the Muslims was that unifying event for the Eastern and Western Churches, and its success depended on Western support in the East.

---

129. González, *The Story of Christianity*, 274.

130. See González, *The Story of Christianity*, 264–65. Though both branches of the church agreed upon the Nicene Creed as their unifying document in AD 325 and again in AD 362, theological fissures between the Eastern and Western Churches persisted for centuries. Arguments regarding the adequacy of the Nicene Creed arose again during Charlemagne's reign as emperor. González writes, "One by-product of this controversy was the resurgence of the Old Roman Creed, now called the Apostles' Creed ... Eventually, through the influence of Rome, the Apostles' Creed supplanted the Nicene Creed as the most commonly used among Western Christians" (265). There were also tensions between the two branches of the church because of clerical celibacy and the use of unleavened bread for communion. González writes, "the Bulgarian archbishop, Leo of Ohrid [Pope Leo IX], accused the West of error because it made clerical celibacy a universal rule, and because it celebrated communion with unleavened bread."

131. González, *The Story of Christianity*, 293.

In 1095 at the Council of Clermont, Pope Urban II proclaimed the offensive against the Muslims, initiating what came to be called the Crusades, with the cry, *Deus vult!* or "God wills it!"[132] Urban's proclamation was received with enthusiasm in many parts of Europe, where crops were failing and disease was rampant. Both poor and nobility relished the opportunity to "go to a foreign land as soldiers of Christ," viewing themselves as players in an apocalyptic drama that would unfold in the not-too-distant future.[133] Some Crusaders, Justo González writes, "had visions of comets, angels, or the Holy City suspended over the eastern horizon," which they understood as confirmation that God indeed willed their actions.[134]

The initial Crusade, known as the People's Crusade, was carried out by what González describes as "a disorganized mob," led by Peter the Hermit, who had been energized by Urban's proclamation and the prospect that they were doing the Lord's bidding. As they set out for Jerusalem, the Crusaders "fed on the land, on which they fell like locusts, and had to fight other Christians who defended their goods and crops. They also practiced their war against the infidel by killing thousands of Jews."[135] Though the campaign failed, the Crusaders' mob mentality construed anyone who tried to stop them as infidels, justifying the persecution and slaughter of Jews and of fellow Christian landowners.

The first formal crusade (called the First Crusade) was led by Urban's personal representative, Adhemar, bishop of Puy.[136] Crusaders from throughout the Western territories, including Peter the Hermit and those who had survived his initial effort, gathered in Constantinople, the designated staging ground. In a joint effort with the Byzantines, the Crusaders took Nicaea (the capital of the Turks), Antioch, and then Jerusalem. The offensives were violent and deadly, as the Crusaders' effort to seize Antioch illustrates.

The Crusaders' first attempt to take Antioch proved more difficult than they had anticipated. Assisted by Armenian Christians, residents of Antioch who opened the city gates to them, the Crusaders entered at the cry of "God wills it." The Turks took refuge in the citadel and held it until a large Turkish army arrived and overwhelmed the Crusaders. The Crusaders' fervor was rekindled, however, "when someone said he had a vision that the Holy Lance with which Christ's side had been pierced lay buried in Antioch."[137]

---

132. González, *The Story of Christianity*, 293.
133. González, *The Story of Christianity*, 293.
134. González, *The Story of Christianity*, 293.
135. González, *The Story of Christianity*, 293.
136. González, *The Story of Christianity*, 293.
137. González, *The Story of Christianity*, 294.

This pronouncement sent the Crusaders into a frenzy, Gonzales notes, and they renewed their efforts to take the city:

> After five days of fasting and prayer, as indicated by the visionary who told them of the Holy Lance, they sallied against the much larger Turkish army. Their standard was the Holy Lance, and they were possessed of such frenzied zeal that the Turks broke and ran, and the crusaders helped themselves to all the provisions that the Turks had brought with them. They also captured many women who had been left behind in the Turkish camp, and an eyewitness boasting of the holiness of the Christian army says: "We did nothing evil to them, but simply speared them through."[138]

Throughout the Crusades, these Christian armies appealed to God for their success and proceeded with the assurance that *God wills it*.

It is helpful to remember the Crusades were initiated in hopes of staving off the seizure of the Byzantine Empire by the Turks. However, once the crusading spirit was kindled, quenching its fire proved almost impossible. The lines between church and empire were significantly blurred such that the empire's priorities became priorities for the church packaged as God's will for church and the state. Thus Christians, intent upon maintaining control of the "Holy Land" and convinced that they were doing God's will, launched repeated offenses and counteroffenses against the Turks and other Muslims. The Crusades heightened the enmity between Christians and Muslims, created new fissures between the various divisions of Christianity, and legitimized a movement in monasticism toward military orders, such as the Order of Saint John of Jerusalem and the Templars.[139] People also became more interested in Jesus's humanity and Christian relics, as the conquest of the Holy Land provided Christians greater access to the geographic region in which Jesus had lived and engaged in ministry.

The Crusades persisted for almost three hundred years, officially ending in AD 1270 after the Eighth Crusade. But the church's entanglement with imperial rule and governments in other forms carries a much longer history. Since the time of Constantine, the church has been torn between, on the one hand, its self-understanding as a religious community with allegiance to the God of creation and the teachings of Jesus, and, on the other hand, its existence as an institution that aims to secure power and authority alongside each era's rulers, empires, and governments. Individual people of faith have also struggled to see ourselves as members of Christ's body and also face challenges to our capacity to love God with our total being and our

---

138. González, *The Story of Christianity*, 294–95.
139. González, *The Story of Christianity*, 199–200.

neighbors as ourselves, especially during times of personal distress, social unrest, and war. Will we again succumb to the deceptive language of despair's distorting messages? Will the church again become perpetrators of negation and dehumanization? Or might we determinedly proclaim Jesus's message of love, as did the prophets before him, the early church after him, and faithful witnesses today who still uphold Jesus's love ethic as the church's central proclamation and as the normative expression of the faith?

The history of the Christian church and the medieval church's fall to chaos serves as a cautionary tale. Whenever the church forgets or suspends adherence to the basic tenets of its faith, such as the command to love God and neighbor or Jesus's emphasis upon living as citizens of God's kin(g)dom, we risk espousing theological and ecclesial distortion. Distortions of this sort concede the deceptive language of despair's assertion that living in loving, just, and life-affirming relationship with one another, the earth, and other living beings is beyond our capacity. The language of despair cajoles us into believing that loving God and neighbor is too difficult a weight to bear, and that embracing our identity as a reflection of divine presence in the earth, *as imago Dei*, is too arduous a task to undertake. Distortion can also convince us that living in anticipation of God's kin(g)dom fully realized is nonsensical, especially at a time when the benevolent God of Jesus the Christ is too often represented as the God of war, division, nation building, and domination. Eventually, theological and ecclesial distortion co-opts our imaginative potential, preventing us from imagining and actualizing new possibilities for our lives together. With such dearth of imagination, we come to believe that while *the way of Christ* is ultimate, the way of greater political clout, money, power, and privilege is the necessary evil to which we must acquiesce in the meantime. Theological and ecclesial distortion, in other words, obscures the voice of Hope and distracts us from living as a nondestructive, nondistorting reflection of God's presence in the earth.

The multiple mediums by which the deceptive language of despair transmits its distorting messages, and the symbolic world such despair creates function to limit our ability to imagine and anticipate the qualitatively better state of existence resonant in Jesus's gospel proclamation. Imaginative dearth, the primary threat to our ability to live with Hope, prevents us from envisaging alternative possibilities for our lives together. In Chapters 2 and 3, we explored nine channels through which the deceptive language of despair propagates its messages: colloquial expressions; idioms of exasperation; cultural assumptions; constituent elements of our known world; and negating and dehumanizing images, myths, ideologies, theologies, and ecclesial commitments. In Chapter 4, we explore the anticipatory language of Hope and the channels by which we shore up our ability to resist the deceptive language of despair and live with Hope.

4

The Anticipatory Language of Hope

[One] of the responsibilities of Christian theology is to be vigilant about the church's tendency to lose the gospel's anti-imperial edge. We should lovingly warn the church when it loses sight of the materially transformative nature of the gospel, when it falls into an easy spiritualization of the message of Jesus that offends no one in power; when it offers no sustaining hope for the weakest and most vulnerable in the world.[1]

—NANCY E. BEDFORD

THE LANGUAGE OF HOPE is anticipatory in nature. It encourages us to imagine our world anew and anticipate its actuality. Notwithstanding the lack of evidentiary support that such a world is possible, the language of Hope emboldens us to reimagine the possible and orient ourselves toward a life of *shalom* as the normative expression of our shared existence. Emboldening new imagination that leads to *shalom* is no easy task. It involves a language, a medium by which we acknowledge and shine a light upon the incomplete and oftentimes chaotic nature of our world while refusing to concede that violence, suffering, oppression, and other forms of dehumanization are natural, normal, or inevitable for our lives. The anticipatory language of Hope is such a medium. It is a metaphor for the multiple means by which we acknowledge and seek to remediate the disordered state of our existence in accordance with God's concern for wholeness, health, and prosperity (*shalom*) and humanity's capacity to live as a nondistorting, nondestructive reflection of divine presence (*imago Dei*). More precisely, the anticipatory language of Hope encompasses patterns

1. Bedford, "Theological Perspective."

of perceiving, thinking, and behaving that evince our identity as *imago Dei* and arc us toward *shalom* as a tangible reality.

The anticipatory language of Hope acknowledges that we and our world are not yet as we should be, not yet a reflection of the Creator's love, not yet purveyors of the just and life-affirming existence that God desires and for which we humans so deeply yearn. Hope's anticipatory language also identifies the disordered state of our existence as ethically and morally opposed to God's just intent for creation, amplifying the necessity of *shalom* as an image of possibility by which we order our lives. In this sense, the anticipatory language of Hope encourages and emboldens us to imagine and live in expectation of a qualitatively better state of existence—one in which all experience wholeness, health, and prosperity as that which is common to our existence and none are devalued or relegated to a life of dearth. The language of Hope also reminds us of God's enduring concern for the well-being of creation, assuring us, writes homiletician Thomas Long, "that whatever the future may hold, God is, in ways often hidden, shaping all human life redemptively and bringing all things to fulfillment in Christ."[2]

God's redemptive work in the world invites human participation, which I characterize as one's decisive yes to God's yes for our lives and for creation. We make our yes known when we stand in solidarity with the most vulnerable and oppressed of our time and engage in practices of love, restoration, justice, compassionate care, peacemaking, repentance, prayerful lament, thanksgiving, and other such spiritual practices as fundamental elements of our everyday existence. Resonances of Hope permeate these practices, bidding us to imagine a world we cannot see, touch, or otherwise experience in the present and to lend our hands, hearts, and resources to the work of bringing that world to fruition. We also make our yes known when we echo Hope's assurance and call through the words we proclaim and speak and as we encourage others to do the same. In word and deed, our yes to God's yes amplifies the anticipatory language of Hope, privileging us to act as catalysts of God's *shalom* for our world today.

Life constituted by God's vision of *shalom* remains obscure in our known world. Globally and domestically, the despairing realities of life—impoverishment, violence, war, overconsumption, repressive attitudes and practices, callous institutional policies, oppressive mechanisms and structures, and the suffering they produce—confront us at every turn, placing us at risk for culturally induced despair. In the previous chapter we identified imaginative dearth as culturally induced despair's primary threat to our ability to live responsive to Hope's assurance and call. Imaginative

---

2. Long, "When Half Spent Was the Night," 13.

dearth fueled by the deceptive language of despair fosters preoccupation with perceived barriers to the just and life-affirming world we desire. It also perpetuates the belief that proposals for a qualitatively better state of existence are nothing more than pipe dreams with no grounding in reality. Alternatively, the language of Hope cultivates imaginative abundance and animates our ability to envisage and live expectantly toward life permeated by God's unifying vision of *shalom*.

Investigating the anticipatory language of Hope's potential for engendering imaginative abundance and purposeful, Hope-filled action is thematic in this chapter. The anticipatory language of Hope embodies Jesus's gospel proclamation and ministerial vision of God's reign upon the earth. It also invites participation in a new ethical domain in expectation of and in service to the new community to which God's reign gives shape. We begin our conversation with attention to Hope's resonance within each of us, *embodied Hope*. Drawing from the apostle Paul's words of encouragement to the Roman church in Rom 8, we explore the Spirit's anticipatory sighs and groans as articulations of Hope. These Hope-filled reverberations trouble our souls and awaken us to our own deep yearning for wholeness and well-being. Hope's resonance, made evident by the Spirit's sighs and groans, also sounds throughout the created order, revealing creation's collective anticipation of God's *shalom*. In this respect, Paul's words remind us humans of the interrelatedness of all creation. That the cry for wholeness, health, and prosperity reverberating throughout creation is also our cry, creation's collective longing for a new reality indicative of God's *shalom*. Jesus's gospel proclamation embodies Hope's anticipatory resonance. Elaborating upon Delores Williams's characterization of Jesus's proclamation of the kin(g)dom as a metaphor of Hope, we explore each element of his now familiar imperative "Repent, for the kingdom of heaven has come near" (Matt 4:17) as an urgent invitation for all who receive his words to live as citizens of the new ethical domain to which the gospel gives shape. Underscoring six qualities evident in Jesus's gospel proclamation, we investigate its significance as an archetypal reservoir from which Hope's anticipatory language flows. Finally, we highlight several mediums through which we encounter the anticipatory language of Hope and the significance of such articulations for cultivating imaginative abundance and purposeful, Hope-filled action.

Anticipatory Sighs and Groans

Throughout our conversation, I have described *embodied Hope* as a conceptual metaphor for that which creates within human persons yearning for wholeness and well-being, the always-speaking voice of God's Spirit assuring us of God's faithfulness, power, and redemptive presence and calling us toward loving, just, and restorative action.[3] As the apostle Paul reveals in Rom 8, we experience Hope's presence as the spiritual tug we sense, the holy indignation we feel, that yearning for justice and well-being that confronts us as truth. Hope is a *something within* continually reminding us of our identity as *imago Dei* and of God's concern for the well-being of creation. Hope, we might say, is a gift God gives to humanity to remind us of our identity as *imago Dei* and to assure us that the God who faithfully called women, men, and children of the past to partnership remains faithful in the present and into the future.

In a nod to *embodied Hope*, the apostle Paul's mid-first-century letter to the Roman church (from AD 56 or 57) reminds us, "in [or by] hope we are saved" (8:24a). Through this letter, Paul seeks to buoy the faith of those within Rome who have committed themselves to the way of Christ. Nearing the conclusion of a rather extensive argument about the meaning of God's righteousness and human salvation, Paul makes clear the distinction between legalistically following the law and the embodiment of God's Spirit as a source for living the Christian life. Living according to the Spirit enables us to concentrate on the things of the Spirit, which for Paul includes living the law intuitively and not by legalistically following a set of rules. Echoing the Old Testament prophet Jeremiah's postexilic prophecy to the houses of Israel and Judah of a day when God would put the law within them and "write it on their hearts" (Jer 31:33), Paul emphasizes the necessity of remaining attentive and responsive to the Spirit's presence within despite the material conditions of our lives.

Aware that Christians experiencing persecution in Rome could likely abandon the faith, the apostle Paul assures them they already embody "the first fruits of the Spirit" (Rom 8:23). The Spirit groans within us, he declares, filling us with anticipation of God's redemptive presence. Therefore, Paul encourages his audience to remain faithful to the way of Christ, as suffering with Christ will ultimately lead to deliverance.

> I consider the suffering of this present time are not worth comparison with the glory about to be revealed to us, for the creation waits with eager longing for the revealing of the children of God; for the creation was subjected to futility, not of its own will but by the will of the one who subjected it, in hope that the

---

3. Though not the subject of the current publication, I might also suggest the Spirit manifests herself as Love or Charity and Faith, as hinted in Rom 13:13. Moral theology identifies Faith, Hope, and Charity (Love) as theological virtues, and I am inclined to agree.

creation itself will be set free from its bondage to decay and will obtain the freedom of the glory of the children of God. (Rom 8:18–21)

Paul is not condoning or recommending indiscriminate suffering. Nor is he proposing human suffering or any created element's suffering as redemptive in nature, as suffering possesses no redemptive quality of itself. Paul is speaking more precisely about suffering that results when one remains faithful to the way of Christ, suffering *with* Christ, especially in hostile conditions. Christians in Rome experienced such suffering—persecution, expulsion, false accusation, death. People of faith and good conscience today also suffer with Christ. We suffer with Christ when we live our faith by standing alongside or advocating for asylum seekers; for racial, ethnic, and gender minorities; for those affected by war; for those who are impoverished or otherwise vulnerable; or for the vulnerable natural world. Christly acts such as these invite suffering, as they rock the proverbial boats of social, political, and religious acceptability; but such acts are not futile. Paul assures the church at Rome and all who suffer with Christ today that *the sufferings of this present time* will ultimately give way to deliverance for those who suffer and ultimately for all creation.

Following his words of assurance and attention to the groans of the Spirit in Rom 8:18–25, Paul names the Spirit's efficacy as the power behind our ability to remain faithful to God's will. In v. 26, he introduces what biblical scholar Emerson Powery describes as a *functional pneumatology*.

> Here in a chapter where Spirit language dominates, Paul now provides a *functional pneumatology*. First the Spirit is one who assists humans in their weakness. She accomplishes this task by making intercession on their behalf (note the γὰρ). Second, and directly related, the Spirit benefits "the children of God" because her intercession is always compatible with the will of God.[4]

The Spirit in Rom 8 is no ghostly figure that ignores the plight of God's creation. Nor does she counsel us to assent to the deceptive language of despair's distorted claim that salvaging our world is futile and nonsensical. Instead, the Spirit actively intercedes on our behalf, countering assertions regarding the incomplete and chaotic nature of our world with images of God's *shalom* for all creation.

As helper and intercessor, the Spirit enlivens our imaginative potential. She evokes restless intolerance with the chaotic state of our existence,

---

4. Powery, "The Groans of 'Brother Saul,'" 320 (italics original).

which we experience as intense anticipation of a new or renewed creation. Paul writes, in vv. 22–23,

> We know that the whole creation has been groaning in labor pains until now; and not only the creation, but we ourselves, who have the first fruits of the Spirit, groan inwardly while we wait for adoption, the redemption of our bodies."

God's vivifying breath, God's *ruach*, fills all creation with sighs and groans of anticipation, signaling that we are about to give birth to something new. All creation groans, the earth and all her inhabitants, groaning and sighing together so as to call into question the too often individualized conception of God's Spirit in our world today. The practice of breathing together compels us to sync our collective breathing with the Spirit's distinctive inhale and exhale. Thereby, we experience together the Spirit's vivifying presence, helping us in our weakness so that we do not lose heart amid the myriad manifestations of despair competing for our imaginative potential.

Breathing together also reveals the redemptive possibility of new life and empowers us to collectively live toward and anticipate God's *shalom*: "For in [by] hope we are saved. Now hope that is seen is not hope. For who hopes for what is seen? But if we hope for what we do not see, we wait for it with patience" (Rom. 8:24–25). We are redeemed or saved by adopting patterns of perceiving, thinking, and behaving that reflect Hope's presence in our lives; by eagerly and with fortitude (δι' ὑπομονῆς ἀπεκδεχόμεθα = *di hypomonēs apekdechometha*) living in expectation (ελπίς = *elpis*) of the yet unrealized redemption of all creation. For we do not anticipate that which is already evident. The Spirit's sighs and groans within fuel anticipation of that which remains obscure, a reality concretized in the imagination though intangible to our corporeal existence.

The Spirit's soulish (Hebrew: *nepes*) groans and sighs evince Hope's presence within. They trouble our souls and awaken us to our own deep yearning for wholeness and well-being. Religious educator Anne Wimberly describes this "deep inner yearning" as the impetus for humanity's desire "to move beyond external and internal barriers that block their experiences of positive relationships with God, self, others, and all things."[5] These deep inner vibrations animated by Hope awaken those who attend Hope's assurance and call to the possibility of new life. They disclose the dissonance between the world as it currently exists, and the world God intends. Awareness of such dissonance makes us restless, preventing us from conceding, except with great difficulty, to the deceptive language of

---

5. Wimberly, *Soul Stories*, 20.

despair's divisive and destructive construal of reality as fractured beyond repair.[6] Restlessness provoked by Hope's anticipatory impulse invites us to dream our world through the prism of God's *shalom,* even in the most chaotic of times. Even more, it beckons us to embrace our role as fitting participants in bringing that world to fruition.

Rubem Alves's theological assertion that God's Spirit impregnates us with intense anticipation of wholeness and well-being for all creation accentuates this yearning.

> "Every situation is pregnant with ultimate possibility; every moment is made explosive by the presence of an infinite power."
> . . . [Humans] and creation are thus pregnant, having within themselves a new life, a new tomorrow, engendered by the Spirit which, in the words of Paul, dwells in you (Rom. 8:11). It is because the Spirit is present that the reality of the presence of the future, the groaning of travail and the reality of hope are created. We hope, we are determined for the future because we are pregnant. We are "infected" with the presence of the future.[7]

Our impregnation with the Spirit determines us for the future. It awakens us to the voice of Hope resonant within each of us, that *something within* assuring us of God's enduring concern for the well-being of creation. Hope calls us toward the future, both imminent and eschatological, urging us to acknowledge our identity as *imago Dei* and to participate in God's ongoing work in the world. By Hope we are rescued from a life of perpetual despair so that we with all creation might experience "the glory of the children of God" (Rom 8:21). As recipients of Hope's salvific work and as *imago Dei*, we courageously and expectantly anticipate a future in which all creation receives the dignity, respect, and honor God intends.

I am convinced the Spirit continues to groan and sigh within us and throughout creation. I am also compelled by the idea that "we are

---

6. See Moltmann, *Theology of Hope*, 229. While Moltmann agrees that Christians groan with all creation, the groaning for Moltmann is motivated by the dissonance between the unredeemed state of the world and "the fulfilment of the resurrection of the dead that is promised in his resurrection." While I do not reject the idea of Christian expectation of Christ's ultimate return, I am also not convinced the groaning we sense within is primarily in anticipation of the eschaton. The groaning we sense within—the Spirit groaning within—is also a signal that ought to awaken us to the role we can play toward creating the qualitatively better state of existence Jesus's proclamation of the kin(g)dom and teachings reveal and invite us to anticipate.

7. Alves, *A Theology of Human Hope*, 96. Alves is reflecting upon and quoting Paul S. Minear's *Eyes of Faith*, 16. Contrary to Moltmann, Alves argues it is not hope that creates the pregnancy but humanity's impregnation with the Spirit that creates hope. See Alves, *A Theology of Human Hope*, 179n25.

'infected' with the presence of the future."[8] The Spirit's anticipatory sighs and groans at once create restlessness and call us toward a future that is gloriously new. If we set our minds upon or surrender our imaginative potential to the deceptive language of despair's distorting assertions, restlessness becomes hopelessness, and culturally induced despair wins the day. Or paraphrasing Paul's words in Rom 8:7–9a in light of culturally induced despair's persistent lure, "For this reason the mind that focuses too exclusively on the despairing realities of life risks becoming hostile to God; it finds difficulty submitting to God's just intent for creation—indeed it cannot, and those who are so subsumed cannot please God. But you are not and do not have to be subsumed by the despairing realities of life; you are in the Spirit, since the Spirit of God dwells in you." When people of faith and good conscience attend the voice of Hope and live responsively, we evince our inherent identity as those in whom God's Spirit dwells, *imago Dei*.[9] For by the Spirit's sighs and groans, and because we with all creation have within ourselves a new tomorrow, we are able to sense Hope's anticipatory impulse within and dream a new world into existence.

Hope and Jesus's Gospel Proclamation

Hope's anticipatory impulse resonates in and throughout Jesus's life and ministry, most evidently in his proclamation of God's unfolding reign, the "kingdom of heaven" or "kingdom of God."[10] Such resonance did not always sound as clearly in the now familiar proclamation of God's kin(g)dom, especially as we initially encounter it in the biblical text. We first hear "Repent, for the kingdom of heaven has come near" in the mouth of Jesus's cousin John, whom we know affectionately as John the Baptist (Matt 3:2). The Synoptic Gospel writers portray John as a rather eccentric prophetic figure who clothed himself in camel's hair, wore a leather belt around his waist, sustained himself on locusts and wild honey, and preached repentance for the forgiveness of sins.[11] Paraphrasing Isa 40:3, Mark and Matthew's Gospels

---

8. Alves, *A Theology of Human Hope*, 96.

9. While I contend the Spirit dwells within each human being, humans also bear responsibility for making the Spirit's presence evident. The Spirit speaks, assures, and compels but does not force us to align our patterns of perceiving, thinking, and behaving with her assurance and call.

10. The Gospel of Matthew includes "kingdom of heaven" and "kingdom of God" to describe the reality to which Jesus refers. The Gospels of Mark and Luke prefer "kingdom of God."

11. See Matt 3:1–12; Mark 1:1–8; and Luke 3:1–20 for descriptions of John's life and ministry.

identify John as the Messiah's forerunner, the one who has come to "prepare the way of the Lord" (Mark 2:3) and "make his paths straight" (Matt 3:3).[12] Self-identifying as such, John unhesitatingly (presumably at each baptismal gathering) announces, "I baptize you with water for repentance, but one who is more powerful than I is coming after me; I am not worthy to carry his sandals. He will baptize you with the Holy Spirit" (Matt 3:11; Mark 1:7-8).[13] Despite his brief tenure, John's prophetic proclamation attracted people from throughout the Judean countryside and Jerusalem who, confessing their sins, went out to him to be baptized in the Jordan River.

In John's way of thinking, his proclamation of the kingdom of heaven paralleled warnings of the day of the Lord in the mouths of Old Testament prophets, Isaiah and Amos among them. Their prophecies made known God's dissatisfaction with the chaotic state of the world and forewarned kings and everyday people alike of God's retributive justice.[14] Isaiah warns of God's impending punishment of Babylon and other nations when he writes,

> Wail, for the day of the Lord is near;
>   it will come like destruction from the Almighty! (Isa 13:6)

In v. 11 of the same chapter Isaiah continues,

> I will punish the world for its evil,
>   and the wicked for their iniquity;
> I will put an end to the pride of the arrogant,
>   and lay low the insolence of tyrants.

Amos likewise characterizes the day of the Lord as a dreadful day, especially for those who misrepresent what it means to live faithful to God:

> Alas for you who desire the day of the Lord!
>   Why do you want the day of the Lord?
> It is darkness, not light;
>   as if someone fled from a lion,
>   and was met by a bear;
> or went into the house and rested a hand against the wall,

---

12. The NRSV translates Isa 40:3, "A voice cries out: / 'In the wilderness prepare the way of the Lord, / make straight in the desert a highway for our God.'"

13. Matthew expands Mark's assertion by indicating that the one who comes after John will baptize with "the Holy Spirit and fire." In addition, John includes a stark warning: "His winnowing fork is in his hand, and he will clear his threshing floor and will gather his wheat into the granary; but the chaff he will burn with unquenchable fire."

14. Highlighting the disciple John's understanding of the coming kingdom as judgment, Charles Aaron writes, "He may have expected a full-blown purging of evil that no one could miss. In [Matthew] chapter 11 he seems disappointed that such cleaning did not take place." See Aaron, "Exegetical Perspective."

and was bitten by a snake.
Is not the day of the LORD darkness, not light,
and gloom with no brightness in it? (Amos 5:18–20)

Amos and Isaiah's warnings sound clearly in John the Baptist's prophetic assertions and especially in his encounters with Pharisees and Sadducees who came to him to be baptized.

In Matthew's Gospel, some Pharisees and Sadducees come to be baptized, but John is not convinced of their sincerity.[15] Concerned that they are trying to avoid God's coming wrath by relying upon their ancestral connection with Abraham, John exclaims, "You brood of vipers! Who warned you to flee from the wrath to come? Bear fruit worthy of repentance" (Matt 3:7b–8).[16] Whether John baptized the Pharisees and Sadducees or sent them away remains unclear. What is evident, at least from John's perspective, is that avoiding the wrath to come demanded something more of the Pharisees and Sadducees. Both knew well the way of the Lord and professed faith in God. The Sadducees were preservers of the Mosaic law as written and rejected any form of interpretation. The Pharisees prided themselves on interpreting the law in light of the challenges each era presented, including through midrash (rabbinic interpretation), and were equally insistent that their approach to Scripture was right. But avoiding God's wrath required more than their expert knowledge of Scripture could provide. Avoiding God's wrath demanded concrete action indicative of faith in God—something that (according to John the Baptist) was certainly missing from the daily practices of these Pharisees and Sadducees listening to him.

John's prophetic warning and call to repentance creates the backdrop for Jesus's ministerial journey and gospel proclamation. As so many others do, Jesus comes out to the wilderness to be baptized by John, and though initially hesitant, John consents to baptizing Jesus. As John immerses Jesus's surrendered body into the baptismal waters of the Jordan River, John senses the gravity of the moment. This is no ordinary baptism or confessional act, John intuits, for Jesus is indeed the one greater than himself. As John lifts

15. See Herzog, "Exegetical Perspective," 49. The NRSV translates Matt 3:7a as "But when he saw many Pharisees and Sadducees *coming for* baptism, he said to them, 'you brood of vipers! Who warned you to flee from the wrath to come?'" However, Herzog, in *Feasting on the Word*, suggest the Greek ἐρχομένους ἐπὶ (= *erchomenous epi*) might be better translated "coming *against*" rather than "coming *for*" baptism. Coming *against*, writes Herzog, "fits the context better," as it acknowledges the adversarial relationship between John the Baptist and the religious elites of the time.

16. Luke also records John's "brood of vipers" comment but identifies the larger crowd as the audience to which John directs these comments. Whether John addresses Pharisees and Sadducees or a larger crowd, his response emphasizes the connection he perceives between confession and godly thought and action.

Jesus from the waters, the heavens open, the Holy Spirit descends upon Jesus like a dove, and a definitive word of affirmation resounds from the heavens: *"You are my Son, the Beloved with whom I am well pleased!"*[17]

Still dripping wet with the waters of baptism, Jesus is led by the Holy Spirit into the wilderness to be tempted by the devil. And after forty days of fasting, praying, and resisting the deceiver's attempts to dissuade him from his ministerial call, Jesus leaves the wilderness and embarks upon a ministerial journey that will change the world forever. He travels to Galilee, some thirty miles from his hometown of Nazareth. After hearing of John's incarceration, Jesus picks up John's proclamation and gives it new meaning: "Repent, for the kingdom of heaven has come near" (Matt 4:17). Or, "The time is fulfilled, and the kingdom of God has come near; repent, and believe in the good news" (Mark 1:15).[18]

From the day Jesus initiates his ministerial journey until his death, he punctuates his healing, delivering, and miracle-working ministry by proclaiming the nearness God's kin(g)dom or commonwealth. He also shifts its meaning away from John's emphasis upon the wrath to come, inviting all to adopt patterns of thinking, imagining, perceiving, and behaving indicative of citizenship in God's new community. In an eloquent reflection on Jesus's ministerial vision, ethicist Larry Rasmussen says, "Jesus sees what others do not yet see. Jesus's faith in God is constitutionally restless. He has an incurable eschatological itch. He lives from a dream, the Kingdom, or world, of God, and he is committed to the discipline of seeing that dream become a fact."[19] Jesus proclaims and epitomizes life in God's kin(g)dom not because the sociopolitical and religious evidence suggests its feasibility but because he dares to imagine and invites others to imagine life constituted by God's reign. Theologian Karen Baker-Fletcher writes that the reign of God "has to do with the fulfillment of God's vision for the entire cosmos. All of creation is redeemed—delivered from evil, oppressive, and corrupting forces—and brought into healing and wholeness by that which is the strength of life and

---

17. Matt 3:13–17; Mark 1:9–11; and Luke 3:21–22 provide virtually identical accounts. Matthew expands the story by adding an exchange between Jesus and John in which Jesus persuades John to agree to the baptism: "Let it be so now; for it is proper for us in this way to fulfill all righteousness" (Matt 3:15).

18. Luke 4:14–15 indicates that Jesus begins teaching in synagogues throughout Galilee after his experience in the wilderness. The synagogue in his hometown of Nazareth is among the synagogues he visits.

19. Rasmussen, as quoted in Lundblad, *Transforming the Stone*, 98. See also, Rasmussen, "Jesus and Power." In this lecture Rasmussen paraphrases a statement by Rabbi Irving Greenberg: "Hope is a dream committed to the discipline of becoming a fact." (Public forum of the Rainbow Coalition, Jewish-Christian Dialog group, autumn, 1986).

transforms fear of evil into faith and hope."[20] Jesus embodies this ministerial vision, making evident God's fidelity to the well-being of creation and God's power to interrupt human history for the sake of a qualitatively better state of existence.

As though creating a major musical chord, one from which all others derive, Jesus makes three basic assertions. The first involves the imperative "repent" (μετανοεῖτε = *metanoeite*), an invitation to turn away from an ethical domain in which bifurcated systems of valuation, oppression, and exploitation are not just permissible but considered normal and necessary. The second, his use of γὰρ, translated "for" or "because," as indicative of the need for repentance, as it highlights the inconsistency and incompatibility of the existing ethic for life in the kin(g)dom of heaven or kin(g)dom of God. Finally, his assertion that "the kingdom of heaven has come near," which announces and invites our participation in a new ethical domain indicative of the reign of God. The three notes of this chord reveal Hope's anticipatory impulse, as they together and individually invite us to lean into Hope's assurance and call. God is indeed faithful, powerful, and redemptively present in our world today, both acting as God chooses and inviting us as *imago Dei* to live into our potential as a nondistorting, nondestructive reflection of God's presence.

Repent

The word "repent" is difficult for many of us to hear today. It evokes memories of fiery preachers spewing words of condemnation, demanding that we repent or spend eternity in hell. For some, the word also conjures feeling of unworthiness and perpetual guilt, the sense that we are not and will never become sufficiently moral or ethical enough to stand in God's presence. But Jesus is not making a statement about our eternal home or individual infractions or missteps we consider sinful. He is not issuing an edict or an apocalyptic warning regarding the wrath of God. Instead, Jesus urges his followers to embrace a new spiritual practice: to repent or remorsefully turn away from the ethic that had ordered their lives, and toward a radically new way of being in which love of God and neighbor are the normative expression of human existence. Repentance in Jesus's kin(g)dom proclamation is a spiritual practice with ethical implications, the fruit of which becomes evident in the just quality of our relationship with God and the many others with whom we share our lives.

20. Baker-Fletcher, "The Strength of My Life," 128–29.

Repentance as a spiritual practice implies communal well-being or *shalom*. Jesus's call for repentance invites his followers then and now to shift our sociopolitical and theological worldviews from the reign of empire (the reign of the Roman Empire in Jesus's day) to God's reign upon the earth. Jesus is far more concerned, that is, with theological and sociopolitical transformation than with indicting and punishing individual people for sin. That Jesus begins his ministerial journey in Capernaum of Galilee sheds light on the communal implications of his message. Matthew's geographic reference to Capernaum, the location of the ancient territories of Zebulun and Naphtali, and Isaiah's assertion "The people who walked in darkness have seen a great light," which Matthew virtually quotes, set the stage for Jesus's proclamation (Matt 4:12–17; see also Isa 9:2). These territories have "a long history of experience with empire and oppression," writes Nancy Bedford, "but also a deep narrative of hope for transformation by the grace of God."[21] Jesus is God's agent of transformation in Matthew's Gospel. He is not only Israel's messianic deliverer. He is "the Messiah who some seven centuries after Isaiah's words has come to give light to the Gentile darkness."[22] He is, in other words, Messiah for all people.

The location of Jesus's proclamation also highlights the sociopolitical implications of his message. New Testament scholar Stephanie B. Crowder writes,

> The *basileia* (kingdom) follows Matthew's narrative involving King Herod and Archelaus as key figures in the Roman Empire (chap.2). The author does not discount the kingdom of the *Pax Romana* (Peace of Rome). However, the writer from the onset wants the readers to know that there is another kingdom present—a kingdom that is not of this world. It is a kingdom from heaven that will triumph over the political prowess of the earth.[23]

Nancy E. Bedford similarly declares,

> The nearing of God's commonweal or reign, a theme woven throughout this time of ministry, is rightly understood as a challenge to the imperial governmental structure. The proclamation and actions of Jesus reflect his conviction that God desires to

---

21. Bedford, "Theological Perspective," Kindle. Regarding Capernaum and the territories of Zebulun and Naphtali, Bedford notes, "Zebulun and Naphtali were two of the ancient Hebrew tribes that had colonized northern Palestine. These territories fell to the Assyrian empire in 722 BCE and by the time of Jesus had come in turn under Roman domination."

22. Crowder, "Exegetical Perspective," Kindle.

23. Crowder, "Exegetical Perspective," Kindle.

establish a reign of justice in the world in a way that contradicts the logic of empire. God's reign therefore has not only an individual dimension but also a wider structural one. The implications of the gospel should not, in other words, be privatized.[24]

Jesus's call for repentance is an invitation to reconsider our lives in light of God's reign—to turn away from distraction and distortion and toward a new community in which love and justice are the cords that bind us together.

The communal implications of Jesus's gospel proclamation are also evident in his emphasis upon love of God and neighbor as foundational for the faith. As we discussed in Chapter 3, Jesus and the early church affirmed the commands to love God and neighbor (Lev 19:18; Deut 6:4–5) as the ethical code by which we live as citizens of God's new community. Repentance rooted in agapic love, therefore, is crucial to the realization of God's kin(g)dom. Emilie Townes writes, "The agapic dimension of . . . care is that which is unselfish and seeks the good for all—not just the common good. Therefore, it is concerned for self *and* for others."[25] Repentance shines a light upon institutional and societal practices that fail to consider the *good for all*, revealing our communal need for corrective action. Remediating such conditions begins, not with right speaking or sentimental expressions, but with a genuine change of heart about the inadequacies of our world with action following. Jesus's call to repent, therefore, urges us to shift our orientation away from negating and oppressive attitudes and practices. To turn away from social and religious ideologies that promote violence and dehumanization. To turn away from the numerous isms that prompt us to deny the inherent dignity and worth of all people. To turn away from systemic oppression and forced impoverishment. To turn away from xenophobic rhetoric and mean-spirited and callous policies so that we can turn toward a new theological worldview in which love of God and neighbor are foundational for our shared existence.

Despite Jesus's relational emphasis, many people still conceive of repentance as an archaic, punitive measure rather than a spiritual practice. Punitive conceptions of repentance pose several concerns. Repentance so construed suggests humans are "bad," negating the core of our identity as *imago Dei* and consequently our potential for living as a nondistorting, nondestructive reflection of God's presence. Punitive conceptions of repentance also emphasize expressions of individual guilt over systemic sin, resulting in feelings of personal worthlessness, which minimize attention to the institutional nature of violence, suffering, oppression, and other forms of

---

24. Bedford, "Theological Perspective," Kindle.
25. Townes, *Breaking the Fine Rain of Death*, 175 (italics original).

dehumanization. Additionally, repentance as "feeling bad" can mask itself as concrete action, suggesting that if we feel bad enough, we have indeed acted. But Jesus is not asking his followers to feel bad about the quality of their relationship with God and others or about the suffering and oppression of their time. Jesus urges his disciples to genuinely repent—to reject attitudes and practices that inhibit our ability to love God and neighbor, and to embrace a radically new orientation whose ethical core is love.

Because

The spiritual practice repentance is the first step toward ordering our lives in light of God's reign, but it is not the final one. The subordinating conjunction γὰρ (= *gar*) in Greek, translated "for" or "because," gives meaning to repentance in Jesus's gospel proclamation. The word "because" anticipates God's kin(g)dom as a concrete reality. It also creates an indelible connection between humanity's affirmative response to Jesus's call to repent and the ongoing emergence or formation of God's kin(g)dom. The expansion of God's kin(g)dom and ultimately its fullness is conditioned upon humanity's willingness to repent or change course, especially when we conceive of repentance as ethical reorientation rather than avoidance of punitive judgment. This condition does not negate the possibility that God as Creative Force by which the universe came into existence could simply re-create and impose greater restriction upon human freedom. Nor does it negate or seek to minimize the importance of God's redemptive presence in the world and in our lives. Quite the opposite, the *becauseness* and thus meaningfulness of Jesus's call for repentance underscores our potential as *imago Dei*.

Confident in our ability to choose rightly and righteously, God in infinite wisdom and grace permits us freedom to discover and live into our identity as *imago Dei*. For better or worse, God continually affords us the opportunity to turn away from self- and other-destructive attitudes and practices and toward God's just intent for our individual and communal lives. Jesus's gospel proclamation is yet another invitation to do that—to hold in heart and mind the reality to which repentance directs us. Repentance made meaningful by *because* reminds us that citizenship in God's new community is incompatible with worldviews that legitimize violence, suffering, oppression, and other dehumanizing conditions. And it leans us toward the loving and just world God intends.

Highlighting the *becauseness* of Jesus's gospel proclamation, Bedford cautions against an overly spiritualized reading of the gospel: "If it is not good and transformative news for those most marginalized by the empires and powers of the prevalent economic and political systems, then it has little to do with the reign or commonweal of God that Jesus begins to announce in Galilee."[26] Jesus delivers a message of Hope to those who have been marginalized and oppressed far too long, beginning in Capernaum and extending into the present moment. He also delivers a similar message to those who escaped or never occupied the sociopolitical and religious margins, inviting reflection upon the role each of us must play in actualizing God's new reality.

Such reflection is significant, as it confronts us with the uncomfortable but necessary choices we must make as citizens of God's commonwealth. Uncomfortable because Jesus's gospel proclamation touches every aspect of our individual and communal existence—economic, social, political, religious, and familial. Equally uncomfortable because the gospel will not permit us the benign benediction of feeling bad or simply acknowledging the inadequacy of our known world. The gospel offers us a reminder that we and our world are not yet what God intends—a reminder that throughout time and as we mature in faith, invites progressively tougher decisions about our readiness to embody the ethical demands of Jesus's proclamation. The *becauseness* of the gospel gives meaning to such decisions; gives us a reason to grapple with difficult economic, social, political, religious, and familial concerns and their impact upon our lives. Hence, the gospel provides a lens for discerning what it means to live as citizens of God's commonwealth alongside the many others with whom we share our lives.

The Kingdom of Heaven Has Come Near

Jesus's gospel proclamation provokes anticipation of the reign of God fully realized. In *Sisters in the Wilderness*, Delores Williams highlights this anticipatory quality when she describes the kin(g)dom of God as "a *metaphor of hope* God gives those attempting to right relations between self and self, between self and others, between self and God as prescribed in the Sermon on the Mount, in the golden rule and in the commandment to show love above all else."[27] Though the loving and just quality of relationship God intends remains wanting, Jesus's proclamation and demonstration of life in God's kin(g)dom exposes "the ethical thought and practice upon which to build positive productive quality of life," or life indicative of God's vision of *shalom*.[28] In *Hope Within History*, Walter Brueggemann similarly highlights the

---

26. Bedford, "Theological Perspective," Kindle.
27. Williams, *Sisters in the Wilderness*, 165–66 (italics added).
28. Williams, *Sisters in the Wilderness*, 166.

kin(g)dom of God's significance for Jesus's life and ministry. He writes, "the metaphor, 'kingdom of God,' stands at the center of the social imagination of Jesus."[29] This new orientation judges all other constructions of reality inadequate, including the imperial government and religious establishment of Jesus's time and of the present. Brueggemann continues, "His parables are articulations of the kingdom clearly in metaphorical modes. His miracles are enactments of the kingdom which are rightly perceived by his opposition as subversive assaults on the rulers of this age."[30] Jesus proclaimed, advocated, and demonstrated life in God's kin(g)dom and invited others to do the same. To shift their imaginative potential away from empire as the dominate understanding of reality and toward patterns of perceiving, thinking, imagining, and behaving indicative of life under God's reign. Unlike the Roman Empire, the reign of God's implies a commonwealth, a just and life-affirming domain of existence that calls us to right relationship with self, others, and God and to partnership in God's redemptive work in the world.

Each Synoptic Gospel writer reveals the good news of God's kin(g)dom or commonwealth as central to Jesus's ministerial vision and proclamation. In Mark's Gospel Jesus proclaims, "The time [has been] fulfilled," (Greek: ὅτι πεπλήρωται ὁ καιρός = *hoti peplērōtai ho kairos*), "and the kingdom of God has come near; repent and believe in the good news" (Mark 1:15). The Greek word καιρὸς (= *kairos*) establishes Jesus's proclamation as more than a revolutionary assertion that the kingdom of God had come during his historical period or calendar year (Greek: χρόνος = *chronos*). "The kingdom of God has come near," Jesus proclaims, because this moment is the *kairos*, the favorable and right time for the emergence of God's commonwealth. Also compelling is Jesus's assertion that "the *kairos* has been fulfilled." The Greek πληρόω (= *plēroō*), translated "fulfilled," implies a divine promise about to be realized in the present, a promise that beckons an active human response and forecasts a fundamental shift in the order of things.[31] Not only does God promise to do something new, but God's new thing exerts a claim upon our lives, enlisting us in the work of drawing the kin(g)dom near. Viewed in this light, Jesus invites us to shift our core commitments away from fearfully perpetuating or enduring the inadequacies of the present and toward God's redemptive vision of reality. Thereby,

---

29. Brueggemann, *Hope Within History*, 221.
30. Brueggemann, *Hope Within History*, 221.
31. Bauer, *A Greek-English Lexicon*. This lexicon describes the Gr. πληρόω (fulfilled): "of fulfillment of divine prediction or promise." "The active bringing to fulfillment, partly of God who brings his prophecies to fulfillment . . . partly of men who, by what they do, help to bring the divine prophecies to realization."

we evince faith in God and situate ourselves as fitting participants in the continuous formation of God's commonwealth.

Matthew's and Luke's Gospels also reveal the good news of the kin(g)dom as the central message of Jesus's proclamation. In Matt 4, Jesus returns from the wilderness of temptation and begins his ministerial journey by proclaiming, "Repent, for the kingdom of heaven has come near" (v. 17).[32] Then, employing a midrashic interpretation of the law and prophets (chapters 5–7), Jesus lays an ethical foundation for life in God's commonwealth. Setting the stage for this teaching, Jesus declares, "Do not think that I have come to abolish the law or the prophets; I have come not to abolish but to fulfill" (5:17). He also warns, "Whoever breaks one of the least of these commandments, and teaches others to do the same, will be called least in the kingdom of heaven; but whoever does them and teaches them will be called great in the kingdom of heaven" (5:19). The challenge then and now, of course, is that Jesus's midrashic exposition demands more than legalistic adherence to a set of rules. It requires renewed ethical commitment to God's just intent for creation (see Matt 5–7).[33] In God's commonwealth, unresolved anger and discord are tantamount to murder. Adultery is no longer confined to physical acts, as it encompasses the imagination. Husbands are no longer permitted to divorce their wives arbitrarily, even as permitted by law.[34] Unabashed truthfulness replaces oaths of all forms. Retaliation and judgment are prohibited; love of enemies becomes requirement; acts of piety are to be performed in secret; and self-reflection is given utmost importance. Jesus's teaching exposes a new ethic and paradigm for human relationship, which he summarizes in Matt 7:12: "In everything do to other as you would have them do to you; for this is the law and the prophets." He also highlights the challenge and possibility of following this teaching. The gate through which Jesus directs us is narrow and the road is difficult, but embracing and embodying an ethical foundation indicative of God's commonwealth situates us upon solid ground (Matt 7:13–14, 24–28). Storms will come, but we shall not be moved.

In Luke's Gospel as in Matthew and Mark, Jesus leaves the wilderness of temptation and, full of the Holy Spirit, begins his teaching ministry in

---

32. Matthew uses "kingdom of God" and "kingdom of heaven" interchangeably.

33. I am compelled by Jesus's attentiveness to the contextual significance of his proclamation and ethical mandates. I advocate adopting Jesus's contextualizing, midrashic practice in light of our current era so that faithful proclaimers today might discern the implications of these teachings for life in the twenty-first century. Like Jesus, I propose a hermeneutic of expansion and reinterpretation rather than one of rejection.

34. The emphasis of this prohibition is on the behavior of husbands, as women had no legal recourse in the matter in first-century Palestine.

synagogues throughout Galilee. Among his many stops is his hometown synagogue in Nazareth where he reveals the good news of the kin(g)dom of God during his one-sentence homily on a Sabbath day. In preparation for the reading, Jesus stands. The attendant gives him the scroll of the prophet Isaiah and Jesus selects a reading from chapter 61: "The Spirit of the Lord is upon me, because he has anointed me to bring good news to the poor. He has sent me to proclaim release to the captives and recovery of sight to the blind, to let the oppressed go free, to proclaim the year of the Lord's favor" (Luke 4:18–19; see Isa 61:1–2). After completing the reading, Jesus rolls up the scroll and returns it to the attendant. Attentive listeners will know that Jesus has offered a variation of Isaiah's words for contextual relevancy, but the sentiment remains the same—God is preferentially concerned for the most vulnerable among us. Sitting down to teach, Jesus proclaims, "Today this scripture has been *fulfilled* in your hearing" (4:21). This assertion implies a divine promise or prediction about to be realized in the present, as was also true in Mark 1:15. But because of its brevity and disruptive implications, Jesus's message proved particularly challenging for the people gathered in the synagogue that day. They had heard about his healing and delivering miracles throughout Galilee, but Jesus performed no miracles in Nazareth. And absent additional commentary on Isa 61, Jesus's teaching seems to reiterate Isaiah's message—the promise or fulfillment of *the year of the Lord's favor*.

The *year of the Lord's favor* or *year of Jubilee* would have sounded notes of familiarity among Jesus's Jewish listeners. Lev 25 describes the Year of Jubilee as a year of restoration for ancient Israel and for the land on which they resided. Every seventh year was a Sabbatical Year, during which there was to be no sowing, and the land was to lay fallow. In the fiftieth year, one year after the seventh Sabbatical Year, the land was to again lie fallow. This was the Year of Jubilee, a year hallowed or set aside to the Lord. During the Year of Jubilee, everyone was to return to his or her ancestral property, and ownership would be restored. Enslaved Israelites would be released from servitude, and all sales and trade agreements were to be equitable. People experiencing difficulty were to receive support from their kin (typically males) with no requirement to pay interest on loans or compensate family members for providing food and shelter during their time of trouble. Liturgical scholar J. Frank Henderson identifies the basic principles involved in the Year of Jubilee: "that God, as creator, is the true owner of the land; individuals, therefore, are only tenants, and they cannot permanently transfer ownership to others. Additionally, in the exodus event God has already released the people from slavery; they must not be re-enslaved in any way."[35] The Priestly writers of Leviticus punctuate these principles in Lev 25:38: "I am the LORD your God, who brought you out of the land of Egypt, to give you the land of Canaan, to be your God."

The reasonableness of the Sabbatical laws in Lev 25 has been much debated, as have the particulars of their implementation and the implications of these laws for the other nations in the region. For example, these laws do not universally prohibit slavery, as Israelites could enslave people from neighboring countries (Lev 25:44–46), an area of tension for modern-day readers.[36] This tension is especially pronounced for those of us who bear the legacy of US chattel slavery. Provisions regarding the return of property also vary. There are time limits on the sale of certain properties and special provisions for houses within walled cities (Lev 25:29–32). In addition, questions abound about whether or not ancient Israel actually observed the Year of Jubilee every fiftieth year, citing the potential economic impact of such a cycle and its inconsistency with the ecological conditions of the time.[37] Yet in the Nazareth synagogue Jesus chooses a Scripture reading that evokes the Year of Jubilee as the textual foundation for his sermonic teaching.

One possibility for why Jesus chooses this reading could be that he is concerned only about people within the house of Israel. A revolution for insiders only which he affirms without need for alteration. Of course, this reading of Jesus's proclamation would negate his praxis of welcoming those whom his tradition relegated to the margins, including bleeding women, lepers, and the people with whom Jews of his time were in fiercest contention, namely, Samaritans. Comparative literature scholar Calum Carmichael discloses another possible reason for Jesus choice of Isa 61. The aim of the Sabbatical/Jubilee cycle, he suggests, was "to trigger historical memory" of ancient Israel's sojourn in Egypt and God's deliverance of them from captivity.[38] Isaiah proclaimed the Year of Jubilee to those returning from exile in Babylon as well as those who had endured the Babylonian occupation of their homeland. Isaiah's words helped the people imagine new possibilities for their lives, awakening them to the voice of Hope by promising that the God who delivered them from Egypt would release them from Babylonian captivity and restore their homeland. Jesus, following this prophetic

---

35. Henderson, "Justice and the Jubilee," 191.
36. Carmichael, "The Sabbatical/Jubilee Cycle," 224–25. Carmichael notes, "Unlike the equivalent Exodus and Deuteronomic rules, which have slaves released after six years' service, the Levitical law could have a slave serve for forty-nine years. In effect, those who became slaves just after a Jubilee year would never experience freedom."
37. Carmichael, "The Sabbatical/Jubilee Cycle," 225.
38. Carmichael, "The Sabbatical/Jubilee Cycle," 227.

tradition, proclaims the Year of Jubilee to those who had been persecuted or relegated to the margins in the Roman Empire and by the religious establishment of his day, *triggering historical memory*. His proclamation, in effect, reminds his followers of God's just intent and establishes an ethical foundation upon which to imagine life anew.

Jubilee is more than a promise of restoration and new life. In addition to giving "life by releasing individuals and community from all that diminishes life," Jesus's proclamation of the Year of Jubilee requires something of his followers, as was also true of the Levitical code and Isa 61.[39] The Levitical code required those who prospered during the years of sowing and reaping to assume responsibility for impoverished family members during the Year of Jubilee. Also, as we celebrate God's promise of liberation and restoration in Isa 61, we should note the nuanced manner by which Isaiah announces restoration:

> *They shall* build up the ancient ruins,
>   *they shall* raise up the former devastations,
> *they shall* repair the ruined cities,
>   the devastation of many generations" (v. 4).

It is the people's task, with God's blessing, to restore the city and rebuild its walls.

These images, I suspect, would have been very present with the people to whom Jesus preached in Luke 4. Their initial response is joyful reception of their kinsman who had proven himself such a powerful teacher. But joy soon gives way to anger, and some in the town seek to throw Jesus off a cliff. At first glance, their response seems odd. However, when the audience response is viewed in light of Jesus's word "fulfilled" spoken as a divine summons, what becomes clear is that the audience is unwilling to consider what the Scripture's fulfillment might mean for them, what it might require of them. "The Scripture is being fulfilled in your hearing" demands an active human response to divine intent and is no less troubling today than when Jesus first spoke those words.

If we are among the privileged of our time, "fulfilled" necessitates a decision regarding those privileges afforded some because of familial inheritance, social standing, race, class, gender, sexual orientation, geographic location, and the like—privileges that are simultaneously denied others on the same grounds. Living into Jesus's word "fulfilled" necessitates, in many instances, redistribution or renegotiation of privilege, power, and wealth so that those whom the system disprivileges might rise to a place

---

39. Henderson, "Justice and the Jubilee," 191.

of parity. Jesus's suggestion that the Scripture has been "fulfilled" is also disturbing for the powerful of his and our time because of its emphasis upon restoration, justice, and well-being for those who daily experience the sting of suffering and oppression—for fulfilment requires remediation of such ills. Jesus's words concerning "fulfilment" are similarly disturbing for those who suffer. For rather than suggesting that we sit back and wait for God or some benevolent entity to relieve our oppression, Jesus calls us all to the ministry of restoration, enlisting us in the service of rebuilding what has been ruined in our own lives and locales so that we might lift up as ourselves our sisters and brothers in other locales. Jesus's proclamation that the year of the Lord's favor *is being fulfilled in our hearing* exerts a claim upon our lives. It requires us to imagine and live toward a new reality, buoyed by Hope's assurance of God's power, fidelity, and redemptive presence among us, and a call to partnership with God.

Throughout Luke's Gospel, Jesus devotes himself to proclaiming, demonstrating, and advocating the changes necessary for life in God's kin(g)dom or commonwealth. That Jesus proclaims *and* demonstrates the good news is particularly significant among those who are relegated to the margins, people for whom the possibility of a healthy, whole, and prosperous life remains a theological abstraction. Rather than abstraction, Jesus makes God's commonwealth tangible with each healing, delivering, and miracle-working act. Not only does he disrupt the disparate systems of valuation constituting his known world—Jews over Gentiles, males over females, adults over children, wealthy over all others, physically and mentally "abled" over those with varying degrees of physical and mental ability and wellness. Jesus also proposes a new construction in which all are welcomed and regarded as vital members of God's commonwealth. Furthermore, Jesus entrusts his followers then and now to do likewise, to proclaim and demonstrate the good news of God's commonwealth as metaphor of Hope's assurance and call. For Jesus came to proclaim the good news, the Hope-infused gospel to which he devoted his life, as he makes evident to the people of Galilee upon his departure: "I must proclaim the good news of the kingdom of God to the other cities also; for I was sent for this purpose" (Luke 4:43).

Jesus's gospel proclamation echoes Hope's assurance of God's unassailable power, intractable faithfulness, and emancipatory presence. As a metaphor of Hope, the gospel makes evident the dissonance between the world God intends and our own, accentuating the restless yearning within for a more loving, just, and God-infused existence for all creation. With accent upon Jesus's proclamation and demonstrative practice of life in God's commonwealth, the gospel is an invitation to envisage our world through the prism of God's *shalom* and live as if that reality is already discernible in our midst. For not only does Jesus announce the good news. He creates (proclaims, advocates, demonstrates) the conditions by which marginalized individuals and communities can live with dignity and respect in the sociopolitical and religious milieu of the time. Through his gospel proclamation in word and deed, Jesus lived and invites other to live in anticipation of God's commonwealth fully realized.

Imaginative Abundance and Purposeful, Hope-filled Action

Jesus's gospel proclamation is the archetypal reservoir from which Hope's anticipatory language flows. The gospel echoes Hope's assurance and call and invites anticipation of and participation in a new ethical domain indicative of God's reign upon the earth.[40] Six qualities evince the gospel's efficacy in this respect: (1) the gospel acknowledges, shines a light upon, and seeks to remediate the disordered state of our existence in accordance with God's vision of *shalom*; (2) the gospel negates the deceptive language of despair's proposals regarding dehumanization's necessity, inevitability, and normalcy, characterizing them as ethically and morally opposed to God's just intent for creation; (3) the gospel fosters ethical reorientation and gives form to a new ethical domain grounded upon love of God, neighbor, and self; (4) the gospel nurtures new imagination and evokes patterns of perceiving, thinking, and behaving indicative of life in God's commonwealth; (5) the gospel invites commitment to God's vision of *shalom* as a realizable possibility, and (6) the gospel equips us as fitting participants in God's redemptive work, implicating our inherent identity as *imago Dei*.

The gospel as archetype for Hope's anticipatory language functions as a standard by which to judge all other anticipatory articulations so as to assess their efficacy as expressions of Hope and not as distortions thereof. We encounter Hope's anticipatory resonance in multiple forms, including in the life-affirming images, myths, ideologies, theologies, and cultural mores that give shape to our known world and beyond as well as in the attitudes, practices, and expressions they promote. These Hope-infused articulations embody in total or in part the qualities to which the gospel invites us. Consider, for example, the Reverend Dr. Martin Luther King Jr.'s theological and sociological conception of the "beloved community" or "God's kingdom on

---

40. See also Bedford, "Theological Perspective" (Kindle) regarding the anti-imperial emphasis of Jesus's proclamation and actions. She writes, "the proclamation and actions of Jesus reflect his conviction that God desires to establish a reign of justice in the world, in a way that contradicts the logic of empire."

earth" and its significance to the African American struggle for civil and voting rights. Also consider Gustavo Gutiérrez's conception of "Utopia" in the Latin American freedom movement, and Archbishop Desmond Tutu's emphasis upon the "Rainbow People of God" as a natural outgrowth of Black South Africans' liberation from apartheid. The anticipatory language of Hope resonates in and through these and other forms, leaning us toward wholeness, health, and prosperity for all creation. From stained-glass images of Jesus in churches such as the Sixteenth Street Baptist Church in Birmingham, Alabama; to the many congregations publicly declaring "Black Lives Matter"; to clergy in collar and stole marching in support of the Poor People's Campaign, climate justice, LGBTQAI rights, and other such movements; the anticipatory language of Hope resounds.[41] The anticipatory language of Hope resounds among mothers marching against gun violence or for the return of their disappeared children; it resounds in online protests against the abduction of Nigerian schoolgirls under #Bring Back Our Girls. Among activists fighting for clean energy and in countless other life-affirming efforts throughout the world, Hope's anticipatory language resounds. These and other life-affirming assertions, attitudes, and practices shine a light upon the sociocultural and religious ills of our time. They are articulations of Hope that intentionally and in some instances inadvertently (i.e., with no explicit religious intent) propagate God's vision of *shalom*, inviting people everywhere to adopt Jesus's practice of proclaiming, advocating, and demonstrating the changes necessary for life in God's commonwealth.

Resounding amid the chaos, the anticipatory language of Hope gives public expression to discontent.[42] It makes known our collective yearning for *shalom*, a theological repudiation of the deceptive language of despair's misrepresentation of reality as broken and impervious to transformation. In *Hope in the Holler*, A. Elaine Brown Crawford describes Black women's "refusal to be silenced, ignored or dismissed" as the "Holler." It is Black women's expression of Hope, the "unquenchable passion and undauntable power that connects black women across the centuries" in calling out the violence, suffering, oppression, and sexualized characterizations we (Black women) have endured and survived.[43] The Holler, in my way of thinking, also discloses possibilities for other marginalized and oppressed communities to renounce inadequacies and make known their unique ways of propagating the anticipatory language of Hope.

41. See Sixteenth Street Baptist Church, *Sixteenth Street Baptist Church* (website).

42. See Walter Brueggemann on lament, in Brueggemann, "The Formfulness of Grief"; Brueggemann, "The Costly Loss of Lament"; and Bruegemann, *The Prophetic Imagination*.

43. Crawford, *Holler*, 82.

In addition to its potential for repudiating the deceptive language of despair, the anticipatory language of Hope invites new imagination and renewed commitment to patterns of perceiving, thinking, and behaving indicative of *shalom*. Maxine Greene's wise counsel is apropos here: "When people cannot name alternatives, imagine a better state of things, share with others a project of change, they are likely to remain anchored or submerged, even as they proudly assert their autonomy."[44] The inability to name alternatives or image a better state of things makes us vulnerable to the deceptive language of despair. Articulations of Hope guard against such vulnerability and awaken us to the possibility of new or alternative constructions of reality. Rather than imaginative dearth, Hope's anticipatory language invites imaginative abundance in anticipation of God's *shalom*. Rather than complacency and lassitude, the anticipatory language of Hope evokes *purposeful, Hope-filled action*, the capacity to live with Hope even in the most chaotic of times. The anticipatory language of Hope, that is, marshals our imaginative potential and emboldens us to live in anticipation of a new reality indicative of God's vision of *shalom*.

Imaginative abundance and purposeful, Hope-filled action are vital for the realization of *shalom*. Imaginative abundance in anticipation of God's *shalom* is a dream worth pursuing no matter the cost, an intentional dream in response to the numerous sociopolitical and religious maladies threatening to plunge us into the depths of despair. Despite or perhaps because of these maladies, imaginative abundance fuels our ability to create new futures, to imagine a world of wholeness, peace, and prosperity so viscerally it sets us in motion even as its actuality remains obscure. Simply put, imaginative abundance gives rise to purposeful, Hope-filled action.

Purposeful, Hope-filled action, or the practice of living with Hope, occupies the space between dream and actuality. It evinces our considered commitment to and praxis of living in the present as though that which we anticipate were already actual. We sense this praxis in Jesus's life and ministry, in his commitment to proclaiming, advocating, and demonstrating the contours of life in God's commonwealth even as its fullness remains in the not-yet. We sense this praxis among enslaved Africans in the US who acted out freedom through Sorrow Songs, hushed tones, coded phrases, concealed gatherings, revolts, and escapes under threat of severe physical punishment or death, even as the freedom and dignity they sought remained elusive. We sense this praxis among the numerous scared, scarred, impoverished, marginalized, oppressed, unwell, and fragmented people today who seek a life of wholeness, health, and prosperity for themselves and all creation. Among

---

44. Greene, *The Dialectic*, 9.

families, friends, and allies who stand alongside another and champion their causes. Among preachers, prophets, pastors, teachers, activists, and numerous others who, despite or because of the deceptive language of despair's contention that social, political, and ecclesial disorder is impervious to transformation, choose to proclaim, demonstrate, and advocate a qualitatively better state of existence indicative of God's *shalom*. Purposeful, Hope-filled action makes tangible our response to Hope's presence within—our praxis of living with Hope and our commitment to the continual formation of God's commonwealth despite all efforts to deny its feasibility. Therefore, we pray, "Thy kingdom come, thy will be done, on earth as it is in heaven," confident in our identity as *imago Dei* and devoted to the work of imagining and living in anticipation of God's kin(g)dom fully realized. For thereby our lives become an articulation of the anticipatory language of Hope and our commitment to live responsive to Hope's assurance and call.

— 5 —

The Disruptive and Energizing Power of Proclamation

> It is of the nature of the gospel itself to be a 'genuine' stumbling block to hearers . . . That is, any message that has at its center a crucified messiah, requires its adherents to love their enemies, and pronounces it easier for a camel to get through the eye of a needle than for a rich person to enter the realm of heaven is intrinsically offensive. While such stumbling blocks may indeed lead to a rejection of the gospel message, they are obstacles the preacher dare not remove in proclamation. To remove them is to disfigure the gospel itself.[1]
>
> —Leonora Tubbs Tisdale

PROCLAMATION OF THE GOSPEL is, by its very nature, disruptive yet energizing. The gospel's energizing potential is in its invitation to imagine a new reality, the kin(g)dom of God, and to live toward its actualization. It is an offer of freedom *from* and freedom *for*. Freedom from patterns of perceiving, thinking, imagining, and behaving that explicitly or tacitly enable dehumanizing and violating systems of oppression to persist, and freedom for new patterns of living powered by the ethic of love, justice, and peace to which the gospel invites us. Over and against the deceptive language of despair's characterization of dehumanizing social, cultural, political, and ecclesial arrangements as intractable, the gospel announces a new reality. And in opposition to the despairing assertion that imagining alternative possibilities is a pointless endeavor, the gospel invites imaginative abun-

---

1. Tisdale, *Preaching as Local Theology*, 34.

dance and purposeful, Hope-filled action toward a qualitatively better state of existence constituted by love, justice, and peace.

Therein we also discover the gospel's disruptive potential. Encountering the good news of God's unfolding reign and the ethic to which it beckons us is like finding pure gold at the water's edge. In some instances, we leap with joy in anticipation of participating in God's new reality, at times leaping right past the ethical thought and practice necessary to live daily as followers of Christ. At other times, we find ourselves standing alongside Jesus's disciples and the inquisitive young man in Matt 19:16–30, arrested by the sober realization that as gold the gospel must be tested with fire or some other caustic substance to reveal its transformative potential. Testing the gospel means trying it, surrendering to it, courageously and audaciously living it even as the deceptive language of despair denies its feasibility. It means standing in that fearful place and coming face-to-face with our tendency to hold two or perhaps more competing commitments at the same time. Testing the gospel involves scrutinizing our own unexamined practice of on the one hand acknowledging the dangerous potential of sinful, bifurcated systems of valuation, access, and power and on the other hand simultaneous acquiescing to such systems as purveyors of meaning. Testing the gospel, that is, entails becoming uncomfortable with the comfortable spaces in which we stand so as to disrupt the synchronicity between competing systems of meaning—and to do so for the sake of God's new reality and its ongoing emergence among us.

Preaching participates in this energizing and disruptive cycle. When we proclaim the gospel in word, we bear witness to the possibility and efficacy of a new reality made evident in Jesus's proclamation of God's emerging kin(g)dom. Bearing witness disrupts the deceptive language of despair's insidious assertions and bolsters our potential for imagining health, wholeness, and prosperity for all creation as viable and realizable possibilities. Imagining such possibilities sets us upon a new course with the blessed assurance that God's faithfulness, power, and redemptive presence are as certain today as in times past. The good news of God's enduring concern for the well-being of creation also invites a human response, urging and welcoming our participation as colaborers with God, which is our reasonable or logical service as *imago Dei* (see Rom 12:1 KJV). When we reply affirmatively, we evince our readiness to proclaim, advocate, and demonstrate the gospel—our readiness to live with Hope.

Recall that in the previous chapter we described Jesus's gospel proclamation as the archetypal reservoir through which Hope's anticipatory language flows. In Matthew's and Mark's Gospels, Jesus announces the nearness of God's kin(g)dom, affirming Hope's assurance of God's unassailable power, intractable faithfulness, and emancipatory presence. Jesus amplifies his gospel proclamation in Luke 4 (vv. 16–30) with a midrashic reading of Isa 61:1–2. Through a short yet powerful sermonic assertion about the contextual significance of Isaiah's words, Jesus encourages his followers to embody Isaiah's prophecy as ethical praxis—to envisage our world through the prism of God's *shalom* and live as if that reality were already discernible in our midst. But the people who gathered that day sacrificed faithful embrace of the gospel on the altar of apathy, choosing homicidal outrage instead.[2] Despite this and other such experiences, Jesus persisted in proclaiming, demonstrating, and advocating the gospel and the ethical thought and practice necessary for life in God's kin(g)dom. Not only did Jesus proclaim good news to the poor, but he lived the good news throughout his life and ministry. And while there were people who rejected his message, even more welcomed his invitation to become citizens of God's kin(g)dom. By both proclaiming and living the good news, Jesus demonstrated its power to energize even as it disrupts.

There is a definitive link between Jesus's commitment to the gospel and the church's ministry today. In keeping with Jesus's ministerial vision, churches throughout the world continue to proclaim the news of God's unfolding reign and thereby propagate the anticipatory language of Hope. And they do so, in many instances, in the face of unimaginable violation and dehumanization. This chapter explores preaching as an essential channel through which the church embodies Jesus's practice of proclaiming the good news as well as the significance of preaching for enriching our sensitivity to Hope's assurance and call and our self-understanding as *imago Dei*. As an entrée to the conversation, we explore the church's role in promoting the ethical commitments to which the gospel invites us with emphasis upon the formative, transformative, and sustaining work of the church. We continue our conversation by exploring four homiletical values that aid faithful proclaimers in disrupting the deceptive language of despair and so heighten congregations' sensitivity to Hope's assurance and call. Translating these values into preaching practice can also enhance proclaimers' ability to create transformative experiences that energize individuals and communities to live as citizens of God's kin(g)dom. These values and practices include: (1) embracing empathy proofed by compassion, (2) eliminating distortion, (3) amplifying Hope's assurance and call, and (4) cultivating imaginative abundance and purposeful, Hope-filled action.

---

2. See a detailed discussion of Jesus's sermon at Nazareth in Chapter 4, above. See also Luke 4:16–30.

The Forming, Transforming, and Sustaining Work of the Church

Anyone who has spent time with me in a preaching course will recognize this statement as a mantra they hear throughout the semester.

> *The central task of the church and thus the task of preaching is to proclaim the gospel with the intent of evoking the imagination and creating experiential encounters that form, transform, and sustain individuals and communities in the Christian faith.*

The church does not proclaim the gospel in a vacuum as though no one is listening. Nor does it proclaim without purpose as though its proclamation is *of no effect* or is powerless to stimulate change. The church proclaims the gospel because it must. The gospel is the theo-ethical construct that grounds the church's self-understanding as body of Christ and its ethical practice of proclaiming, advocating, and demonstrating the good news of God's unfolding reign. The gospel is also the reservoir through which Hope's anticipatory language flows, and its proclamation in word and deed is the means by which the church cultivates dispositions of heart and mind indicative of life in God's kin(g)dom. Therefore, the church proclaims the gospel with intentionality, purposely concerned with evoking the imagination and creating formative experiences that enable us to embody the ethic of love, justice, and peace to which the gospel invites us.

Holding these commitments sacrosanct, the church at its best refuses to occupy itself with promoting random or fanciful visions of reality, as not all tantalizing visions properly enable us to live as citizens of God's kin(g)dom. Instead, the church seeks to transform the "human capacity to imagine—to form mental pictures of the self, the neighbor, the world, the future, to envision new realities" which resonance emanates from the gospel.[3] In order to enhance its imaginative and formative potential, the church creates a broad range of experiential encounters that evokes the imagination and nurtures our ability to embody the ethical thought and practice to which the gospel invites us. Through preaching, teaching, liturgy, and concrete practices of faith, the church invites us to imagine as a realizable possibility a world in which all are well nourished; possess clothing sufficient to their environs; have access to affordable healthcare and life-sustaining medicines; and are able to live, work, and play in a nonexploitative, safe, and comfortable environment in which each person affords all others the dignity and respect each one deserves. And this without discrimination or marginalization based

---

3. Taylor, *The Preaching Life*, 40. Taylor places greater stress upon cultivating the imagination as the central task of the church.

upon race, class, gender, ethnicity, sexual orientation, nationality, religious beliefs, or any other identifying characteristic.

The gospel is not the only imaginative or formative construct vying for our allegiance. The church's invitation to order our lives in light of the gospel is always juxtaposed with other systems and constructs similarly infused with imaginative and formative potential—many of which substantively oppose the gospel. In *Branded: Adolescents Converting from Consumer Faith*, for example, religious educator Katherine Turpin identifies consumer capitalism as a faith system from which ongoing conversion is needed. "More than a system of economic engagement in the world," she writes, "consumer culture offers a story of meaning and purpose to define human existence."[4] When understood as a system of faith, the human relationship to consumer culture "runs much deeper than intellectual assent to an economic system or even the mindless mimetic behavior of consumption. It implies a faithful dependency that orders the self at a primary level."[5] Breaking our dependency upon consumerism demands "ongoing conversion," Turpin contends, as what must be transformed is our faith in consumer culture.[6]

Consumer culture is but one among many imaginative and formative constructs competing for our allegiance and from which we need transformation. I am writing this chapter during the COVID-19 global pandemic of 2020 and was struck recently by a group of armed protesters in Michigan demanding that governor Gretchen Whitmer ease social distancing requirements so they could return to normal activities.[7] Similar protest quickly sprang up in other parts of the nation. As someone who had observed my own state's stay-at-home orders for over two months at the time, I understand the frustration. What struck me as odd, however, were the numbers of people who amplified their frustration by brandishing assault-style weapons, wearing clothes bearing anti-Semitic logos or language, holding derogatory signs, waving American flags, and in some instances also waving Confederate flags. There appears no discernible relationship between the governor's decisions regarding COVID-19 and protesters' apparent expressions of patriotism or concern regarding their constitutional freedoms. The relationship between COVID-19 and the US Civil War, which the Confederacy lost in 1865, is equally indiscernible, as is the potentially dangerous practice of donning assault rifles and other

---

4. Turpin, *Branded*, 4.
5. Turpin, *Branded*, 40.
6. Turpin, *Branded*, 44.
7. Smith, "'Lock Her Up.'" The COVID-19 global pandemic has extended well into 2021.

firearms during protests. The crisis at hand is related to health. We are not at war. The US and numerous nations throughout the world are experiencing the ravages of a global pandemic that cannot be resolved by verbal assaults and pseudopatriotic gestures.

Why is this important? Reflexive responses such as those identified above reveal a familiar pattern in the US among individuals with White supremacist leanings. While it is impossible to know with absolute certainty a protester's heart, the accouterments and actions associated with such protests suggest faith-like attachment to norms that oppose the gospel. Three gospel-opposing norms come to mind. First, the demand upon the government to make decisions that betray the public health reveals indifference or apathy toward the gospel's emphasis upon health, wholeness, and well-being for all. Second, former president Donald Trump's, his administration's, and many in the news media's characterizations of the pandemic as a war nurtures a war-like mentality. As a result, some citizens have come to consider those exposed to the virus or those who die as a result of COVID-19 as casualties of war—as people whose exposure, death, or both, are unfortunate but to be expected. Lack of mindfulness about such interpretive filters can lead to callousness about increasing numbers of COVID-19 infections at home and abroad. This too is inconsistent with the gospel's emphasis upon communal well-being.

On Sunday, May 24, 2020, the front page of the *New York Times* and several pages following revealed the names of the almost one hundred thousand people who had died from COVID-19 in the US, a milestone at the time.[8] By Saturday, November 28, 2020, infection in the US had reached 12.9 million, and deaths were approaching three hundred thousand (263,956).[9] Globally, as of December 22, 2020, the pandemic had killed approximately 1.6 million with 75 million infections.[10] The pandemic has also led to widespread unemployment, food insecurity, economic distress, and psychic unrest—all of which underscore the need for the gospel's emphasis upon compassionate care and communal well-being.

Finally, the symbolic and communicative potency of the Confederate flag opposes the gospel's mandate to love God and neighbor. The Confederacy sought to concretize Black people's enslavement, disenfranchisement, and violation while upholding White racial dominance as the national

---

8. *New York Times*, "U.S. Deaths Near 100,000."

9. United States Center for Disease Control and Prevention, "CDC COVID Data Tracker."

10. World Health Organization, "Weekly Epidemiological Update—22 December 2020."

norm.[11] Bearing the confederate flag implies attachment to the ideals that the Confederacy espoused, especially from the perspective of those who continue to experience the harmful impact of racism's hardy persistence in American culture. Reflexive attachment to racist ideologies and other negating formative constructs distorts the gospel.

As the church leans into its call to proclaim the gospel, two complexities come into view about the gospel's collocation with constructs that oppose its ethical orientation. The first involves the church's readiness and enthusiasm about acknowledging the socially nonconforming nature of the gospel. The gospel seeks transformation in the direction of the kin(g)dom of God, a reality already emergent but not yet fully formed among us. This reality, in its obscurity, exerts a definitive claim upon our lives, compelling us to live as though that which we cannot see, touch, or otherwise situate is already an actuality. As an act of courage, the church resolutely proclaims the gospel with a determination to live in anticipation of God's kin(g)dom, no matter the gospel's socially nonconforming nature.

Lenora Tisdale highlights the necessity of such courage in *Preaching as Local Theology and Folk Art* when she writes, "It is of the nature of the gospel itself to be a 'genuine' stumbling block to hearers."[12] Rehearsing some of the absurd-seeming elements of the gospel, including the centrality of the crucifixion and the gospel's mandate to love our enemies as ourselves, Tisdale warns, "while such stumbling blocks may indeed lead to a rejection of the gospel message, they are obstacles the preacher dare not remove in proclamation. To remove them is to disfigure the gospel itself."[13] At its most courageous moments, the church refuses to disfigure the gospel: At its best the church refuses to mitigate the gospel's offensiveness, mute its condemnation of dehumanization and injustice, or name violence, suffering, and oppression necessary evils—after all, the gospel affords the church no such latitude. At its most courageous moments, the church follows in the footsteps of a crucified Messiah, fully aware that following his teachings invites persecution today as surely as in the past. At its most courageous moments, the church remains resolute in its commitment to advocating right relationship with God, self, and others and invites us to do the same, to love God and love our neighbor as ourselves.

A second complexity arises as we consider the broader formative environments in which we develop and discern meaning for our lives. Neither

---

11. More specifically, they sought to concretize the notion that people who identify as White Anglo-Saxon Protestant are superior to everyone else.

12. Tisdale, *Preaching as Local Theology*, 34.

13. Tisdale, *Preaching as Local Theology*, 34.

you nor I, nor the numerous others with whom we share the Christian faith, begins our faith journey or comes to an awareness of our graftedness into the faith (i.e., baptism, christening, blessing) *tabula rasa*. Whether through confirmation, soul salvation, or conscious assent, most if not all of us come to such awareness already armed with durable patterns of perceiving, thinking, behaving, and imagining by which we discern meaning for our lives. For this reason, churches most often focus upon the need for transformation rather than on initial faith formation. The church would do well to acknowledge and reflect upon the broad range of formative experiences by which congregants give meaning to their lives, with particular attention to the consistency or not of such experiences with Jesus's gospel proclamation. What existing formative experiences might Christian communities of faith build upon? And what formative experiences might such communities seek to remediate?

Katherine Turpin prefers the language of conversion when speaking about Christian formation and transformation. Reflecting upon Paulo Freire and others who stress the importance of critical awareness as a pathway to transformation, Turpin perceptively notes, "conversion . . . refers to not just a change in awareness and understanding, but to a change in both our intuitive sense of the way the world is (imagination) and our capacity to act in light of that intuitive sense (agency)."[14] Conversion, however, is not something that happens in a single moment or because of a single encounter. Drawing on James Fowler's characterization of conversion as "an *ongoing process*—with, of course, a series of important moments of perspective-altering convictions and illuminations—*through which people (or a group) gradually bring the lived story of their lives in congruence with the core story of the Christian faith*," Turpin also proposes a process of "ongoing conversion."[15] Ongoing conversion implies a progressive shift toward ways of imagining and patterns of perceiving, thinking, and behaving indicative of the Christian faith's reliance upon Jesus's gospel proclamation. And, while conversion may begin in one moment, such as in my own Missionary Baptist tradition's emphasis upon a moment of decision, the process continues for a lifetime.

---

14. Turpin, *Branded*, 59. See also Freire, *Pedagogy of the Oppressed*; James, *The Varieties of Religious Experience*; Anderson, "Liturgical Catechesis"; Fowler, *Becoming Adult*; Ricœur, *History and Truth*; Mahan, *Forgetting Ourselves on Purpose*; Williams, *Seeing a Color-blind Future*.

15. Fowler, *Becoming Adult*, 115; Turpin, *Branded*, 74. Fowler, *Becoming Adult*, 114–15 distinguishes between conversion and development, characterizing conversion as one's transformation toward religious vocation. Development, on the other hand, implies a "more single-minded pursuit of one's group or personal destiny."

Augmenting her emphasis upon conversion as it relates to awareness and imagination, Turpin highlights the necessity of a corresponding shift or process of conversion as regards our sense of agency.

> Agency refers to the capacity to make choices and to act in light of one's sense of what is meaningful. Agency values both the intentionality and the power to assert oneself actively in the world, often expressed as being the subject of one's own life and not the object of others' control.[16]

Turpin's emphasis upon agency has implications for our ability to live the gospel and participate as coworkers in bringing God's vision of *shalom* to fruition. Agency also speaks to our readiness to acknowledge our identity as *imago Dei* and to live as a nondistorting, nondestructive reflection of God's presence in the earth—*to assert ourselves actively in the world.*[17]

Creating experiential encounters that form, transform, and sustain us in the faith is an essential aspect of the church's ministry. Formative experiential encounters remind us of our identity as *imago Dei* and our potential as colaborers with God. They assure us of God's presence, power, and fidelity, and empower and energize us to live as an expression of God's presence in the earth. For not only is the church concerned with individual transformation; its ultimate goal is to expand the borders of God's kin(g)dom to whosoever will come, so as to create the conditions necessary for a more loving, just, and God-infused existence for all creation. When we, the church, commit ourselves to the task of proclaiming the gospel in word and deed no matter the risk, we reveal ourselves, as the apostle Paul indicates in his commendation to the church at Corinth, as "a letter of Christ ... written not with ink but with the Spirit of the living God, not on tablets of stone but on tablets of human hearts" (2 Cor 3:3).

Preaching Jesus's Hope-Filled Gospel Proclamation

The church's persistence in proclaiming the gospel signals the "life of [Jesus's] *ministerial* vision gaining victory over the evil attempts to kill it."[18]

---

16. Turpin, *Branded*, 66.
17. Turpin, *Branded*, 66.
18. Williams, *Sisters in the Wilderness*, 165 (italics original). Williams critiques substitutionary or surrogacy characterizations of Jesus's crucifixion, highlighting the danger of such theologies for black women and others who have experienced surrogacy oppression. She continues her thought regarding Jesus's ministerial vision and the resurrection thusly: "Thus, to respond meaningfully to black women's historic experience of surrogacy oppression, the womanist theologian must show that redemption of

The church is a signal initiated by Jesus's resurrection, according to Delores Williams, and which echo we sense in the present moment. In word and deed, the church endeavors to amplify this Hope-filled resonance, to announce the kin(g)dom of God's ascendancy over evil (over violence, suffering, oppression, and other forms of dehumanization) as well as its vision of a qualitatively better state of existence for all creation. Through its multiple ministerial endeavors, the church makes known the good news of God's unfolding reign and the ethical and moral responsibility to which the gospel calls us. In the same way, the church nurtures our ability to confidently anticipate the fullness of God's reign and embrace our role as colaborers in its actualization.

Preaching is one of the mediums through which the church proclaims the gospel and nurtures our ability to live as citizens of God's kin(g)dom. Preaching in the tradition of Jesus evokes anticipation of a new reality in which love of God, self, and neighbor are paramount. Anticipation of this reality involves more than the mental act of imagining a better state of things. It also entails concrete acts of turning or ethical reorientation in light of God's still-emerging kin(g)dom. In this light, those of us who preach pray that our sermons will so stir the soulish desire for connection, so open hearts and minds to the inadequacies of the present, so cultivate a sense of yearning and imaginative abundance that we and our congregations begin to live toward God's vision of *shalom* even as its actuality remains obscure. Preaching, that is, disrupts and energizes.

Simon Peter's Disruptive and Energizing Experience of the Gospel

Simon Peter's encounter with the Roman centurion Cornelius exemplifies well the disruptive and energizing power of gospel proclamation. Simon, affectionately known as Peter, is one of Jesus's most devoted disciples. Peter is the one who boldly walks out on the water to Jesus in the middle of a windstorm and calls out to him for salvation when it seems certain he will drown (Matt 14:28–33). He is the one who without hesitation responds to Jesus's query "But, who do you say that I am?" with the bold assertion "You are the Messiah the son of the living God" when everyone else remained silent (Matt 16:15–16; see also Mark 8:29; Luke 9:20). In the Gospel of John, Peter is the fearless and impassioned friend who cuts off

---

humans can have nothing to do with any kind of surrogate or substitute role Jesus was reputed to have played in a bloody act that supposedly gained victory over sin and/or evil."

Malchus's ear when temple police and Roman soldiers arrest Jesus in the Garden of Gethsemane, and then Peter follows Jesus into the high priest's courtyard, intent upon rescuing him from this death-dealing situation, at least as I imagine it (18:1–18).[19] And though he denies knowing Jesus when he is faced with the possibility of exposure and death, Peter's position in the courtyard permits him to witness Jesus's interrogation before Annas, Caiaphas's father-in-law and the former high priest (18:13). On the first weekday following Jesus's crucifixion and after hearing a report of his resurrection from "Mary Magdalene, Joanna, Mary the mother of James, and the other women," Peter gets up and runs to the tomb to witness for himself that Jesus is not there (Luke 24:10–12). Later that day, Peter is among those gathered in Jerusalem as two travelers (Cleopas and his companion) testify to their experience with Jesus during their journey from Jerusalem to Emmaus. The hearts of these travelers burned within as Jesus expounded upon the Scriptures along the way and revealed himself during their communal breaking of bread (Luke 24:13–35). Yet later, Jesus appears to Peter and the other disciples in Jerusalem, revealing himself as the crucified Savior and instructing them to remain in the city "until you have been clothed with power from on high" (Luke 24:36–49).

On the day of Pentecost, the Holy Spirit makes her presence known, and the disciples are indeed clothed with power from on high. Peter, under the Spirit's influence, echoes the prophet Joel's disruptive and energizing declaration: "God will pour out the Spirit upon all flesh equitably, with no disparity based upon gender, socioeconomic status, race, ethnicity, legal status or other such demarcations of difference" (Acts 2:17–18, paraphrased). So Peter disrupts existing structures of power and privilege while also energizing and urging those who had gathered to embrace a new ethical orientation—one that seeks parity in church and society for all who live on the margins. Highlighting Jesus's Davidic lineage, Peter boldly proclaims Jesus the long-awaited Messiah for all people, concluding his sermonic reflection by issuing a call to repentance and an invitation to discipleship (Acts 2:38). In response, three thousand new converts are baptized in Jesus's name, joining themselves with other disciples, who give thanks and praise to God and sell their possession so that distribution can be made to all "as any [have] need" (Acts 2:44–45).

The most significant illustration of the gospel's disruptive and energizing potential, however, does not happen when Peter initiates the disruption. Rather, Peter himself is claimed by the very gospel he proclaims

---

19. Another disciple who was known by the high priest spoke to the woman guarding the gate and secured Peter's access to the courtyard.

and experiences its disruptive and energizing potential. In Acts 10, Peter finds himself at the intersection of that which had become familiar and comfortable and the new thing Jesus set in motion through his kin(g)dom proclamation—and this intersection requires Peter to assess his own readiness to live as a citizen of God's new reality.

We meet Peter in the city of Joppa at Simon the tanner's house. Peter has earned quite a reputation as a teacher, healer, and miracle-worker, especially after calling Tabitha, a faithful disciple, back to life (Acts 9:36–40). News of his power spreads far and wide, and many believe in Jesus because of Peter's ministry.

As a follower of Jesus and an observant Jew, Peter prays three times per day—morning, noon, and evening. On the day in question, Peter climbs the steep ladder to the roof of Simon's house with the intent of keeping the midday prayers while his host prepares the meal. But hungry and drained by the noonday sun, Peter falls into a trance. The heavens open before him and he sees "something like a large sheet coming down, being lowered to the ground by its four corners" (Acts 10:12). The sheet is covered with numerous beasts, fish, reptiles and birds, all of which the Levitical law considers unclean. A voice Peter identifies as God's speaks to him, instructing Peter to kill and eat. Shocked and amazed that God would instruct him to defile himself by eating what is unclean, Peter refuses. "By no means Lord; for I have never eaten anything that is profane or unclean," he exclaims, to which the voice responds, "What God has made clean, you must not call profane" or unclean (v. 15). Three times the voice instructs Peter to kill and eat, and three times Peter refuses, becoming more impassioned each time as he endeavors to keep the deeply formative practices upon which his religious identity is grounded. God's admonishment grows more insistent as well, cautioning Peter repeatedly, "What God has made clean, you must not call profane" (vv. 15–16). And then as suddenly as it had begun, "the thing" is taken up and the vision ends.

Sitting there on the rooftop, Peter tries to make sense of what he has seen and heard, pondering its implications for his identity as a follower of Jesus and an observant Jew. While the church no longer advocated participation in ancient Judaism's major festivals or the sacrificial system, some teachers still stressed the necessity of circumcision as a sign of covenant relationship with God as well as the importance of the dietary and purity regulations. These practices constituted their faith and linked their identity as Christian definitively with that of their ancestors. Eating from the visionary sheet, in Peter's way of thinking, would have severed that connection and made him unclean in the presence of God. Yet, Peter also senses that

God is trying to tell him something through this banquet of unclean things on the rooftop of Simon the tanner's house.

That something begins to reveal itself when we meet Cornelius, a centurion of the Roman military. Cornelius lives about nine hours away from Joppa, on the coast of the Mediterranean Sea, in the city of Caesarea, and is a person of considerable wealth and authority. Cornelius is "an upright and God-fearing man" who gives generously, prays the hours in accordance with the Hebrew Scriptures, and is "well spoken of by the whole Jewish nation" (Acts 10:22, 30–31). One afternoon at about three o'clock, while Cornelius is praying, an angel of God also appears to him in a vision. The angel assured him the sweet aroma of his prayers and alms had ascended to God, lingering there in God's presence as a reminder of Cornelius's faithfulness. Startled, yet deeply affirmed, Cornelius leans in to listen as the angel instructs him: "Send men to Joppa for a certain Simon who is called Peter; he is lodging with Simon, a tanner, whose house is by the seaside" (v. 32). Without question or hesitation, Cornelius gathers two of his servants and a devout soldier and sends them to Joppa.

Cornelius's delegation arrives while Peter is still on the rooftop, calling him from the gate and recounting the events that prompted their journey. And at the Spirit's leading, Peter and six companions make the coastal journey with them as they return to Cornelius's home in Caesarea.

When they arrive, Peter transgresses the boundaries of religious tradition and common decency among Jews and enters the home of a Gentile. Fully aware that this decision could garner dire consequences if others in the church were to find out, Peter announces, "You yourselves know that it is unlawful for a Jew to associate with or to visit a Gentile" (v. 28). Then, in a moment of confessional grace and divine clarity, Peter continues, "but God has shown me that I should not call *anyone* profane or unclean" (v. 28).

Peter risks it all! And that *is* what God was asking of Peter that day on the rooftop of Simon the tanner's house—to risk it all, to challenge the practices and regulation that had constituted his faith and identity, to reconsider deeply held beliefs and stand upon the shifting sands of God's new word of truth for the sake of the gospel.

Peter's first confession takes place during the greeting and may have involved a smaller and more intimate gathering (v. 24). But Cornelius believes Peter has come with a message for his entire household, so Cornelius invites Peter to deliver the message the Lord has given him. Peter stands, and rather than sounding a sectarian note pitting his Jewish identity against their designation as Gentiles, Peter makes another confession. "I truly understand," says Peter, "that God shows no partiality, but in every nation anyone who fears God and does what is right [lives righteously] is acceptable to God" (v. 34).

Through this confessional act, Peter surrenders himself and permits God to shift his core beliefs away from a bifurcated system of faith fueled by dichotomous thinking along lines of acceptability—clean over unclean, profane over holy, Jews over Gentiles, insiders over outsiders, an able body over disabling conditions. Instead, Peter acknowledges God's expansive love and radical hospitality, which leads him to affirm Cornelius and his household as citizens of God's kin(g)dom. And "while Peter was still speaking, the Holy Spirit fell upon all who heard the word. The circumcised believers who had come with Peter were astounded that the gift of the Holy Spirit had been poured out even on the Gentiles, for they heard them speaking in tongues and extolling God" (v. 44).

Peter not only discovers the disruptive and energizing potential of the gospel during his journey with Jesus and on the day of Pentecost. He also discovers its potential to disrupt the comfortable synchronicity he and others in the early church sought to maintain between their bifurcated understanding of faith and God's just intent as revealed in Jesus's gospel proclamation.

Peter would have to defend his decision to eat at Cornelius's home and baptize his household on two occasions. In Acts 11, he recounts his experience to leaders in the Jerusalem church, declaring "the Holy Spirit fell upon them just as it had upon us at the beginning" (v. 15). Then he convincingly asserts, "If then God gave them the same gift that he gave us when we believed in the Lord Jesus Christ; *who was I that I could hinder God?*" (11:17). With this statement the church agreed. In Acts 15, in response to teachers who insisted upon requiring Gentile Christians to be circumcised, Peter stands with Paul and Barnabas before the Jerusalem Council and again recounts his experience. He explains how "God, who knows the human heart, testified to them by giving them the Holy Spirit, just as he did to us," and how "in cleansing their hearts by faith God has made no distinction between them and us" (vv. 8–9). James, then leader of the council, receives their report and reaches the decision to "not trouble those Gentiles who are turning to God" regarding circumcision (v. 19), though the requirement to keep the law in other respects remains. Peter's as well as Paul's and Barnabas's witness to the Holy Spirit's presence among the Gentiles disrupt what had become comfortable, for the sake of the continual emergence of God's kin(g)dom.

Peter experiences the disruptive and energizing potential of the gospel in his vision on the rooftop of Simon the tanner's house and in the subsequent encounter with Cornelius's household. Though Peter had witnessed the Holy Spirit's outpouring on the day of Pentecost and had echoed the prophet Joel's powerful vision of the Spirit's expansive reach, he had not considered the challenge this proclamation would pose for his own core beliefs and religious understandings. The visionary experience on Simon's rooftop and the Holy Spirit's outpouring upon Cornelius and his household disrupted Peter's bifurcated understand of faith and transformed his religious and ethical orientation. No longer could he view God's grace through the lens of partiality or Gentiles as marginalized *others*, for he had discovered beyond any shadow of doubting that God indeed shows no partiality, a truth that endures even today.

The persistence of bifurcated systems of valuation in church and society today affords preachers an opportunity to learn from Peter's disruptive and energizing experience and follow his lead. For the sake of the gospel and with courage and humility, Peter bore witness to his own experience of transformation, first to Cornelius and his household and then in advocacy for the Gentiles before the Jerusalem Council and the Jerusalem church. Peter's experience challenges those of us who preach today to examine our own theological and ethical commitments in the light of the gospel and where necessary surrender to God's transforming grace. For when we courageously and humbly acknowledge our own experiences of transformation, we free ourselves to witness the Spirit's impartial presence and activity among unacknowledged peoples and in unimagined spaces in our world today, which also frees us to advocate on their behalf among those with whom we possess influence. Sprit-born transformation enables us to disrupt structures of power and privilege operational in our world today and to energize those with whom we preach to likewise lend their hands to God's restorative work. Spirit-born transformation empowers us to proclaim the boundarylessness of God's kin(g)dom and God's boundless extension of grace made evident in Jesus's gospel proclamation in Matt 4:17 and Mark 1:15 and in Jesus's self-identification as the one who came to proclaim the year of the Lord's favor (Luke 4:18–19). Spirit-born transformation prepares us to demonstrate and advocate the ethical thought and practice to which the gospel calls us in tangible and observable ways, to *fulfil* it in our lives and ministries as a divine promise to which we offer a human response. Transformation in the light of the gospel, that is, enables us to live with Hope so that our proclamation will embolden others to do the same.

Approaching sermon preparation and delivery with four homiletical values in mind can enrich the faithful proclaimer's ability to do just that: to preach sermons that disrupt the deceptive language of despair's seductive lure, that heighten our sensitivity to Hope's assurance and call, and that energize us to live as citizens of God's kin(g)dom. To that end, faithful proclaimers might approach sermon preparation and delivery with these four homiletical values and practices in mind: embracing empathy proofed by compassion, eliminating distortion, amplifying Hope's assurance and call, and cultivating imaginative abundance and purposeful, Hope-filled action.

Embracing Empathy Proofed by Compassion

Cultivating empathy as a practice for preaching gives credence to the Spirit's sighs and groans throughout the created order. Empathy heightens our sensitivity to the heuristic interrelatedness of our own deep yearning for wholeness and well-being and the soulish troubling that people within our congregations and throughout the world similarly experience. Attentiveness to the congregation's troubled cries makes us aware of our own deep yearning for wholeness and well-being. Likewise, the troubling we sense within can make us more sensitive to the anguished cries of others. Attentiveness invites empathy, the human capacity to stand in the shoes of another and imagine life from their vantage point without losing sight of our own distinctiveness.[20] Empathy also holds potential as a gateway to compassion, conditions applying.

Celia Deane-Drummond, a scholar in science and religion, notes the connection between empathy and compassion: "Empathy requires an *accurate imagining* of what the other person/creature is feeling and is a prelude to compassion where those feelings are associated with a bad state."[21] But, she continues, "empathy . . . just as easily can result in a lack of compassion, as when enemies read the intentions of their foes and manipulate them for their own purposes."[22] As faithful gospel proclaimers, we pray that our sermons will indeed awaken the people with whom we preach, as well as ourselves, to the necessity of empathy proofed by compassion. As dough must be proofed for yeast to have its desired effect, compassion proofs empathy, prioritizing compassionate care for the vulnerable among us. Empathy proofed by compassion awakens us to opportunities for solidarity and connection, reminding us that no one should have to make this Hope-filled journey alone. We journey alongside and in the company of people far and near who yearn for the qualitatively better state of existence to which Jesus's gospel proclamation invites us.

20. See also Nussbaum, *Upheavals of Thought*, 327–28.
21. Deane-Drummond, "Empathy and the Evolution of Compassion," 262 (italics added). See also Peterson, "Is My Feeling Your Pain Bad for Others?"
22. Deane-Drummond, "Empathy and the Evolution of Compassion," 262.

Dorothee Soelle's reflection upon the importance of *compassio* in *The Silent Cry* further amplifies the necessity of empathy proofed by compassion. *Compassio*, she writes, "arises in the immediacy of innocent suffering and from solidarity with those who have to bear it."[23] Soelle distinguishes *compassio* from religious asceticism and other forms of suffering "people bring upon themselves."[24] As a Christian concept, *compassio* implies "suffering with Christ and all who suffer."[25] Regarding *compassio*'s transformational potential, Soelle writes, "Mystical love for God makes us open to God's absence: the senseless, spiritless suffering that separates humans from all that makes for life."[26] To suffer with Christ is to immerse ourselves into the mystical love of God and, as an expression of that love, stand with those to whom God appears to be absent. Suffering with Christ also entails acknowledging personal experiences of suffering as well as advocating for and co-suffering with people within our own identity or affinity groups. For no sufferer should be denied the gift of *compassio* or empathy from another.

Numerous individuals and communities cry out for empathy proofed with compassion today. On the macro level, the COVID-19 global pandemic discussed earlier has impacted the lives of more than sixty-two million people worldwide and more than twelve million in the US. Many never imagined their voices would be included in the global lament that sounds so distinctively throughout the cosmos. Yet numerous people are experiencing levels of economic distress, material lack, food insecurity, joblessness, homelessness, and impoverishment alongside physical, psychic, and spiritual distress they thought inconceivable prior to 2020. The pandemic has also intensified the suffering of communities already experiencing such challenges as well as those communities in which violence, suffering, oppression, and other forms of dehumanization remain daily realities. Even more, the 2020 crisis shined a light upon deeply entrenched systemic maladies that have long constituted America's socioeconomic, political, and religious milieus—maladies that many believed were political talking points or hyperbolic assertions supporting the agendas of a few disgruntled individuals or racial and ethnic groups. Most devastating in 2020 and quite likely beyond, the maladies of systemic racism, sexism, and classism appear to have intensified. Despite efforts on the

---

23. Soelle, *The Silent Cry*, 139; see also, Soelle, *Suffering*.
24. Soelle, *The Silent Cry*, 139.
25. Soelle, *The Silent Cry*, 140.
26. Soelle, *The Silent Cry*, 140. Highlighting the necessity of *compassio*, Soelle vividly writes, "the nausea caused by this world of injustice and violence ought at least to be perceptible; it ought to increase to the point of physical vomiting, as is told about so many highly gifted women from Catherine of Siena to Simone Weil. That kind of nausea is an experience of compassio."

part of some to recoil from them, unsee them, or claim they are fallacious, these maladies cannot be ignored.

A Pew Research Center study tracked income in the US from 1968 to 2018 and found significant income disparity. According to the study, among those with recorded household incomes, the highest-earning 20 percent of earners possessed more than half of all US income in 2018.[27] Four other findings are also worth noting: (1) When compared to other G7 nations, the US shows the highest percentage of income inequality.[28] (2) Among medium-income households in the US, the income of Black households was 61 percent of White household income in 2018. (3) The wealth gap between the richest and poorest families in the US more than doubled between 1989 and 2016. (4) While the US economic recession of 2007–2008 impacted everyone, the richest families were the only ones to have gained wealth during and following the recession (between 2007 and 2016).[29] I identify these statistics for two reasons. First, they provide an example of the ways a bifurcated system of power, privilege, and access impacts the lives of everyday people. Second, they help us contextualize the cry for empathy proofed by compassion from individuals and communities who bear the sting of oppression and economic dearth as a daily reality both within our nation and abroad.

The yearning for empathy proofed with compassion resounds even the more as we draw closer to our everyday existence and individual lives. Many among us experience crises in multiple domains of life—familial unrest, sickness, disease, death, loss, grief, or loneliness—all of which leave us crying out for empathy proofed with compassion. When experiencing a dearth of self-esteem; when constrained by guilt, shame, and fear; when consumed by anger, resentment, insecurity, or other life-denying affective conditions; our souls long for someone who will hear us, acknowledge us, stand with us. We long for empathy proofed by compassion. Suffering confronts us with a tone of inevitability or as that which seems normal. But the gospel negates such claims. The gospel invites us to demonstrate empathy proofed by compassion for the vulnerable with the blessed assurance that when we face crises of myriad forms, someone will offer us the same. Suffering is in no wise normal or inevitable, and we should by no means dismiss it as such.

Is empathy proofed by compassion always advisable as a value and practice in preaching? If compassion for the vulnerable among us is the

---

27. Schaeffer, "6 Facts about Economic Inequality."

28. The Group of Seven (G7) nations include the United States, Great Britain, Italy, Japan, Canada, Germany, and France.

29. Schaeffer, "6 Facts about Economic Inequality."

ultimate goal of empathy in preaching, then the answer is yes. The qualifier "for the vulnerable among us" is necessary because of individuals and entities who characterize as suffering discontentment over constraints preventing them from misusing their privileged positions in church and society. The social construct of privilege connotes inordinate access to power, money, influence, and control based upon one's gender, race, sex, class, education, familial ties, social location, and other privileging identities. Privilege also implies the simultaneous denial of such position to people outside of or in binary relationships to privileged identity groups. My own pastoral experience illumines this point.

In 2003, a local pastor asked me to serve in his stead as interim pastor for a year, as he was called to active military duty in Iraq. I was at the time one of four ordained ministers, the only female among seven associates, and a fairly recent member of the congregation. During our first worship gathering with me as the interim, one of the male ministers stood and openly contested my appointment as interim pastor, exclaiming, "The pastor made a terrible mistake in asking this woman to serve as pastor!" He was prepared to say more, but the deacons were not amused and swiftly ushered him from the pulpit and out of the building. He never returned. In his way of thinking, the role and privilege of pastor should be reserved for men. Permitting a woman to fill that role was both inappropriate and potentially disastrous.

My response in the moment was less than empathic. I offered words of assurance that God would see the congregation through the transitional moment we were experiencing, then prayerfully prepared for the morning message. The chairperson of the deacons' board offered similar assurances and pledged their support for my leadership. Later, the man's misogynistic outburst evoked a range of emotions—anger, disappointment, outrage, disgust, and fatigue. Yet, I also felt grateful for the congregation and its leaders' support as we continued our journey of worshiping, serving, and growing together.

As I reflect today upon the man's comments, I view them through the lens of empathy. I am reminded of how deeply de-forming and dangerous misogynistic and androcentric (not to mention other negating) ideologies can become if faithful proclaimers do not persist in reminding ourselves and the congregations with whom we preach of our shared identity as *imago Dei*. Therefore, faithful proclaimers would do well to respond to those who bristle at limitations to assumed privilege by seeking to understand their perspective (to respond with empathy). This is especially necessary when associated actions threaten to exploit, harm, disenfranchise, oppress, constrain, or otherwise dehumanize others. The preacher's response begins with empathy, standing in the shoes of the aggrieved so as to understand their grievances. Understanding, however, does not legitimize the perspective, license inappropriate behavior, or necessitate solidarity with the aggrieved. To the contrary, understanding the grievance provides faithful proclaimers insight into how they might compel the aggrieved one to acknowledge and experience the harm their actions cause for others. Corrective or restorative consequences may also apply.[30] Additionally, faithful proclaimers might shepherd such ones toward repentance, ethical reorientation, and ongoing formation in the light of the gospel. Empathy proofed by compassion, in other words, both names the conditions that prevent us from living fully into our identity as *imago Dei* and reveals possibilities for overcoming such obstacles.

As a homiletic value and practice, embracing empathy proofed by compassion entails viewing life from the vantage point of another, prioritizing compassion for the vulnerable among us, advocating on their behalf and on their terms, offering tangible expressions of love and care, and acknowledging our shared identity as *imago Dei*. The excerpt below comes from a sermon I initially preached for a Women's Day observance in 2007 at Greater Bethany Baptist Church, a predominately African American congregation in Atlanta, Georgia.[31] The sermon title, "Mercy Suits Our Case" (John 7:53—8:11), forecasts the sermon's emphasis upon empathy proofed by compassion. It also echoes the African American prayer tradition in which the repetitive refrain "Mercy suits our case" punctuates the petitioners prayer.

Framing Text

³ The scribes and the Pharisees brought a woman who had been caught in adultery; and making her stand before all of them, ⁴ they said to him, "Teacher, this woman was caught in the very act of committing adultery. ⁵ Now in the law Moses commanded us to stone such women. Now what do you say?"

Sermon Excerpt

Jessica's story reveals something of Jesus's love and compassion, pressing us toward embracing the compassionate love of Jesus for the many sisters and brothers in our lives who are in Jessica-like

---

30. In situations requiring a legal response or ecclesial corrective action, congregational leaders, victims, or both should pursue such actions with support of the church.

31. Two additional texts, Ps 51:1–14 and Eph 2:19–22, compliment the preaching text.

situations: situations in which a snapshot of our lives, in which one transgression, mars our image for all times.

They bring Jessica before Jesus. As we look into her eyes and search the details of her face, we are caught a little off guard. We realize we've seen her, we know her, perhaps we've been her.

She is the outsider looked down upon by the Scribes and Pharisees of our time.

She is the one trembling and fearful, very careful to put on just the right front, lest she be caught. *For if anyone really knew her, knew what she'd done, knew where she'd been, knew about "It," she would no longer be welcomed among the beloved.*

He is the one who drinks in hiding, cries in silence, and covers his brokenness behind a façade of strength, because real men are never vulnerable.

She gives herself as an act of repentance to the church, to her family, at the job, and she gives until there's none of her left to give.

They never feel quite good enough, quite worthy enough to be one of them, so they live their lives outside the walls of the holy temple we call church.

They never feel quite good enough, quite worthy enough to be one of them, but they wear the façade and live their lives within the walls of the holy temple we call church—their secrets remain hidden in this place.

She is the woman, the man, who cannot find her voice, who cannot breathe, who cannot find his song.

The one who has been hiding for so long that she, that he, cannot risk . . . does not dare come forward, because *"nobody knows the trouble I've seen, nobody knows my struggle."*

But, late at night he repents time and time again because he could, at any moment, be dragged before the crowd, exposed and sentenced to death.

She is many of us. All of us. She is our sister and our brother, exposed and laid bare for the world to see![32]

Through the rhetorical use of experiential touchstones, the excerpt invites the congregation to embrace empathy proofed with compassion for people whose secrets are at risk of public exposure. Experiential touchstones, unlike an extended story, invite the congregation to view the problem through a variety of lenses as well as to reflect upon the hidden-things in our own lives that evoke a desire for mercy. Sermons that embrace empathy proofed by compassion as a homiletical value and practice also invite congregations

---

32. This sermon excerpt has been significantly redacted for illustrative purposes.

to stand in Jessica's shoes and in the shoes of numerous other individuals and communities whose cries join the global lament emanating from myriad spaces and places throughout the earth.

Eliminating Distortion

Eliminating distortion as a value and practice for preaching highlights the necessity of attentiveness to that which prevents us from responding to Hope's assurance and call. Hope's resonance within assures us of God's power, faithfulness, and redemptive presence even in the most difficult and devastating of times. Hope also invites our participation as colaborers in God's loving, just, and restorative work in the world, which we have characterized as living with Hope. Hope speaks always over and against despairing assertions resonant through multiple channels in various sectors of our known world. These distorting and distracting assertions incessantly declare that we and our world are irreparable flawed and fallen; that the loving, just, and God-infused existence for which we yearn is an absurdity; and that our efforts toward its actualization is futile. We have described this distorting mechanism as the deceptive language of despair. Left to run its course, the deceptive language of despair promotes a view of reality that numbs us to the disordered state of our existence. The deceptive language of despair characterizes negating and oppressive realities as normal and expected aspects of our shared existence to which we should simply adjust.

Acquiescence to the deceptive language of despair's distorting images of reality as truth diminishes our imaginative potential, placing us at risk for culturally induced despair. Our task as preachers, therefore, is to nurture imaginative abundance. It is to fuel the human capacity to imagine or envisage a new reality and live toward its actualization. To cultivate anticipation so visceral we feel as though the world for which we long is already taking shape in our midst, even as chaos swirls around us. That work, the work of nurturing imaginative abundance and eliminating imaginative dearth, does not begin by simply telling people to imagine something new. It begins with nurturing an alternative vision of reality as a realizable possibility while also eliminating the distortions that deem such imaginings absurdities.

Here we explore the task of eliminating distortion as a homiletical value and practice and will return to cultivating imaginative abundance later in our discussion. As a value for preaching, eliminating distortion is concerned with identifying or naming both the messages that distort our ability to live with Hope and the means by which the deceptive language of despair conveys those messages. Naming the messages and the means acknowledges, unveils, and seeks to remediate disordered social, political, and ecclesial arrangements in accordance with God's vision of *shalom* made evident in Jesus's gospel proclamation. Naming the messages and means of despair also exposes such arrangements as fallacious misrepresentations of what might be possible for our shared existence. Rather than a recalcitrant system impervious to change, naming reveals the world as open for transformation.

Transformation begins with exposing and analyzing the problem. Alongside an alternative vision of possibility (i.e., the continual emergence of God's kin(g)dom), faithful proclaimers seek to uncover the mechanistic interworking of the problems to which sermons respond as well as the impact of such maladies upon our ability to sense and live responsive to Hope's assurance and call. Critical analysis can aid that process. As an element of sermon preparation, critical analysis exposes the deceptive language of despair's resonance within disordered sociocultural, political, and ecclesial arrangements. It also aids preachers in identifying negating images, myths, ideologies, theologies, attitudes, and practices that undergird such arrangements. Critical analysis renders distortion even the more evident, as it supports the preacher's quest to identify the problem, expose and analyze its parts, and discern a faithful response.

I propose A Critical Analysis for Preaching (ACAP) as a tool to aid such an investigation.[33] With specificity to a particular malady or problem and attention to the congregation with which we preach, the investigative process I have developed consists of three interrelated elements.[34] The first element, *Exposing Distortion*, affords preachers an opportunity to investigate the mechanistic interworking of the problem. What is it? How do we identify it? From what source does it arise? How is it sustained? A second element, *Analyzing the Impact*, invites preachers to consider implications of the problem for the congregation and its members' quality of life—physically, spiritually, emotionally, and relationally. We might also consider the implications of the problem for our ability to live as a nondistorting, nondestructive expression of God presence in the earth. Additionally, the step of analyzing the impact highlights the implications of the problem for the welfare of the larger community, state, nation, and world. Who benefits most from the preservation of the mechanism of despair? To whom does its persistence pose the greatest degree of harm? Because exposing mechanisms of despair to the light of the gospel can trigger intense opposition

---

33. See Appendix A, below.

34. I intend this tool to augment the exegetical process. Therefore, I recommend it under the assumption the preacher has already completed a thorough exegesis of the biblical text.

from entities and individuals who wish to preserve the privileges or harmful effects that the mechanism of despair keeps in place, the step of analyzing the impact encourages preachers to reflect upon risks related to exposing harmful mechanisms of despair to the light of the gospel.

The final element, *Discerning a Faithful Response*, derives from the previous. In dialogue with a variety of preaching resources—biblical, exegetical, theological, rhetorical, demonstrative, ecclesial, sociocultural, and the like—preachers begin the difficult yet grace-filled work of discerning a faithful response illustrative of the gospel. As preachers and coworshipers, faithful proclaimers listen for the voice of Hope in the midst of the chaos, prayerfully committed to emboldening individuals and communities to acknowledge our shared identity as *imago Dei* and as fitting participants in God's redemptive work. With specificity to the problem and attentiveness to the preaching context, the preacher ascertains attitudes and practices that can aid congregants' ability to resist the seductive lure of despair and live responsive to Hope's assurance and call.

The sermon excerpt below is from a sermon I preached in 2016 at Wesley Theological Seminary, Washington, DC, titled "Dare to Dream," based on Mic 6:6-8. The congregation consisted of students preparing for ministry in church and society and the faculty, staff, and administrators who guide their journey. The mechanism of concern here is silence and its potential for preventing people of faith from living and speaking prophetically in our world today. Silence, though often inadvertent, perpetuates the notion that violence, suffering, oppression, and other forms of dehumanization are permissible and tolerable constructions of reality. Consequently, silence undermines prophetic vigor.

Framing Text

[6] "With what shall I come before the LORD,
  and bow myself before God on high?
Shall I come before him with burnt offerings,
  with calves a year old?
[7] Will the LORD be pleased with thousands of rams,
  with ten thousands of rivers of oil?
Shall I give my firstborn for my transgression,
  the fruit of my body for the sin of my soul?"
[8] He has told you, O mortal, what is good;
  and what does the LORD require of you
but to do justice, and to love kindness,
  and to walk humbly with your God?

Sermon Excerpt

How can we live into our deepest commitment to a just and life-affirming world for all people at a time in human history when so much instability and brokenness exists? What does it mean to believe in reconciliation in a world so deeply divided? To become coworkers of justice and peace in a world to which terror is no stranger? And, of what use are dreamers at a time when pragmatic solutions appear more needful than imaginative possibilities?

. . . Suffering abounds in the lives of people throughout the world . . . Even those of us in the Western world—people who never imagined our voices would join the chorus of global lament—cry out for wholeness. For lack and instability are no longer socioeconomic descriptors reserved for individuals and communities, nations and peoples identifiable by rubrics like the have-nots, the powerless, the poor, or the colorful ones. No, these descriptors speak to the present reality of many in our nation and throughout the world who are weeping and wailing, moaning and groaning, grieving and mourning, praying and lamenting for wholeness, wholeness, wholeness . . .

We read Micah 6:6–8 and hear it as a corrective for what we have done wrong *or* as a reminder that we should do more. And while this is a perfectly valid reading, it is not the only alternative. We might also consider what it means to stand in the shoes of the prophet—to be the speaker and not the receiver of these words. To hear the lamenting cries and sense the pain of a world praying and sighing and groaning for wholeness and, rather than silence, respond to God's divine summons, a summons that even today urges us to speak truth about oppressive ideologies and practices prevalent in our own ministry contexts and throughout the world . . .

What if we, like Micah, synced our hearts with the heart of God, permitting our heartbeat to pick up the divine pulse that has been beating throughout creation from the very beginning and has never stopped beating, not even for a moment? What if we let something of God's hopeful expectation and fidelity to the well-being of creation take up residence in our lives, so much so that our own hearts begin to beat in sync with that Divine pulse?[35]

The invitation to stand in Micah's shoes is augmented by a series of *what if* questions as well as a protracted invitation intended to invite prophetic

---

35. This sermon excerpt has been significantly redacted for illustrative purposes.

vigor. The sermon concludes with a final invitation to say yes to God's yes for creation. I ask listeners to reflect upon why we say yes and about the implications of our yes for our individual and communal well-being. "We say yes," I surmise along with Teresa Fry Brown, "because, as exhausting and exhilarating as ministry may become, we have learned to dance to the rhythm of G.O.D., the pulsating rhythm of the One whose heart has never stopped beating in creation, not even for moment."[36]

Amplifying Hope's Assurance and Call

As a homiletical value and practice, amplifying Hope's assurance and call evinces the preacher's commitment to repeatedly and through multiple means reminding those with whom we preach of God's enduring concern for the well-being of creation. Chapter 8 of the apostle Paul's Letter to the Romans highlights the necessity of this fourth value and practice. Speaking to the reality of suffering in the church and noting the entire creation's deep yearning for redemption, Paul assures the church at Rome that the Spirit's inward groans are salvific in nature. By way of the Spirit's presence, humanity and creation groan in anticipation of ultimate deliverance and restoration, for even creation "will be set free from bondage and decay and will obtain the freedom of the glory of the children of God" (v. 21). Reflecting upon the Spirit's inward groan, New Testament scholar Luke Timothy Johnson writes, "the Spirit, then, is a 'pledge' of their future redemption. Their human suffering is not eliminated by the resurrection life, but it is transformed, since they are sustained in it by the Spirit (8:17–21)."[37] Hope calls us as to labor with God in God's redemptive work, which also includes soberly acknowledging the suffering that exists in the present even as the Spirit sustains us. Confident in the Spirit's power to sustain, Paul declares, "For in hope we were saved. Now hope that is seen is not hope. For who hopes for what is seen? But if we hope for what we do not see, we wait for it with patience" (vv. 24–25). Waiting, in Paul's way of thinking, does not imply lassitude or sluggishness. To wait is to live in anticipation of, to expect, to knowingly await the fulfillment of God's redemptive work. Therefore, Paul encourages the church to wait, assuring us of the Spirit's presence within and intercession on our behalf.

So confident is Paul in the salvific efficacy of Hope that he makes the bold assertion, "All things work together for good for those who love God,

---

36. See Brown's description of call as "singing in the key of G-O-D" in Brown, *Weary Throats and New Songs*, 53.
37. Johnson, *The Writings of the New Testament*, 356.

who are called according to God's purpose" (v. 28). This is not a pie-in-the-sky promise of good things, as though suffering does not exist. Rather, these words reflect Paul's effort to remind the church at Rome and us today of the radical love of God for all creation and of the necessity to remain resilient despite the despairing realities of life. As though anticipating a rebuttal to his claims, Paul continues by posing a series of rhetorical questions about God's love and commitment to the well-being of creation followed by a definitive response: "For I am convinced that neither death, nor life, nor angels, nor rulers, nor things present, nor things to come, nor power, nor heights, nor depth, nor anything else in all creation will be able to separate us from the love of God in Christ Jesus our Lord" (vv. 38–39). With these words, Paul assures the congregation at Rome that the God who has been faithful, powerful, and redemptively present in the past remains so in the present and toward the future.

Paul's words to the Roman church serve as a model for amplifying Hope's assurance and call. He begins by inviting ethical reorientation, distinguishing between "life according to the Spirit" and "life according to the flesh" (Rom 8:1–17). Life consistent with the ethical demands of the gospel connotes "life according to the Spirit." Conversely, "life according to the flesh," signifies life driven by impulse, desire, and need without regard for the implications of our decisions and actions for the well-being of others. Second, Paul acknowledges the problem to which he is responding: the suffering of this present moment (v. 18). The letter does not specify the type of suffering, affording readers an opportunity to reflect upon experiences in our own lives that thwart our ability to live with Hope. Third, Paul proposes living with Hope as an adequate response, amplifying Hope's salvific efficacy (vv. 19–30). God, he declares, remains faithful, present, and powerful, warranting the church's fidelity in return. Finally, reiterating the necessity of Hope as a response to "these things" (v. 31), Paul makes the definitive claim that nothing, no thing or person, can separate us from the "love of God in Christ Jesus our Lord" (v. 39). Faithful proclaimers today might also adopt these practices.

The sermon excerpt below illustrates the power of Hope's assurance and call to compel risk-taking action on behalf of another. Drawn from Exod 1:15–17 and titled "Girl, Call the Midwife, I'm About to Give Birth," this sermon was first preached at a women's retreat for Emmanuel Baptist Church in Winston Salem, North Carolina, in 2012. The sermon reveals the radical possibility of our responsive yes to God's yes to change the world. That is, when we respond to Hope's assurance of God's presence, power and fidelity by lending our hands to God's redemptive work, our actions may very well produce life-changing, even world-changing consequences.

Framing Text

[15] The king of Egypt said to the Hebrew midwives, one of whom was named Shiphrah and the other Puah, [16] "When you act as midwives to the Hebrew women, and see them on the birthstool, if it is a boy, kill him; but if it is a girl, she shall live." [17] But the midwives feared God; they did not do as the king of Egypt commanded them, but they let the boys live.

Sermon Excerpt

Shiphrah and Puah are midwives by profession, women committed to the well-being of other women and their children. They are so identified with the role of midwife that some might even describe it as their calling, because the names Puah (meaning "to twist the umbilical cord") and Shiphrah (meaning "brilliance") reveal the essence of being a midwife. Not only do they assist in the birthing process, but their lives also reveal something of the loving grace of God in their willingness to secure the life of a child born of another woman's womb . . .

In many respects, they are just ordinary working women doing their jobs as best they can. On the other hand, it seems their ordinary work has placed them in the precarious position of becoming God's partners—strategically located at the intersection of life and death, nationhood and genocide, and with the power to either secure the future or facilitate its untimely demise . . .

Partnering with God is complicated for Shiphrah and Puah. They perform their duties at the behest of the pharaoh, a frightened and uncertain pharaoh who believed securing his nation's well-being necessitated annihilating any perceived threat. And in his mind, the Hebrew people were a threat . . . Shiphrah and Puah come into view at this precise moment in history. They were to become the pharaoh's "weapons of mass destruction."

Midwives and *killing*—two contradictory and incompatible concepts. Midwives are Life-Givers and Life-Preservers. To be a midwife means we are willing to sit with another sister as she struggles to give birth to her hopes and dreams, to breathe with her as she pushes the baby out, to bend our back to the floor and place our hands in the blood and gore, to cut the cord and discard the afterbirth of fear and doubt so the baby can live outside of the womb . . . Midwives walk with their sisters during the most dangerous and exciting times of life, doing all they can to ensure a live birth. And if the baby should die, the midwife stands with her just the same . . .

As Shiphrah and Puah receive the pharaoh's instructions, they are conflicted. As much as they want to remain loyal citizens of Egypt, they also want to remain faithful to their oath to preserve life. Even more, a bond of sisterhood has begun to develop between Shiphrah and Puah and the Hebrew women as they share their hopes and dreams and their common struggle as women in cultures that refuse to call them worthy . . . Over time, Shiphrah and Puah come to fear the God of their Hebrew sisters, to reverence this Mighty and Powerful One more than they feared the pharaoh . . . So, they do what midwives do . . . they give life!

. . . That's our challenge today, to acknowledge the power for life that God has placed within us and refuse to give in to the demand we do otherwise. To create new histories and defy the death-dealing power of the pharaohs of this age . . . For new life and a new reality become possible when those who give birth and life-preserving midwives unite.[38]

This sermon sought to amplify Hope's assurance and call by inviting reflection upon the ways our ordinary gifts, vocations, and avocations might be used in service of God's redemptive work in the world. To most people of Shiphrah and Puah's time, including the pharaoh himself, it would have been inconceivable for anyone, and most especially women, to defy the pharaoh's orders. But the midwives knew themselves as life-givers and life-preservers. Perhaps they even sensed the Spirit's groans within or felt called by the Hebrew women's fearful cries. Whatever the motivation, the midwives were so claimed by an alternative vision of possibility that they defied the pharaoh's orders and created bonds of solidarity with childbearing Hebrew women. This sermon invites us to consider the power and potential of boundary crossing as indicative of our responsive yes to Hope's assurance and call and as an expression of the gospel. For if the gospel is indeed concerned with participating in a new ethical domain of love, justice, and peace, then boundary-crossing for the well-being of others situates us at the heart of the gospel. For, who knows? The boundaries we cross today and the everyday tasks we perform may very well change the world.

---

38. This sermon excerpt has been significantly redacted for illustrative purposes.

Cultivating Imaginative Abundance and Purposeful, Hope-Filled Action

As a homiletical value and practice, cultivating imaginative abundance and purposeful, Hope-filled action begins with nurturing anticipatory imagination of a qualitatively better state of existence indicative of Jesus's kin(g)dom proclamation. Advancing this vision involves more than rhetorically announcing the kin(g)dom's continuous expansion. It also entails our considered response to the question, What are we asking people to imagine? How do we proclaim the good news of the kin(g)dom of God in a language that makes Jesus's gospel proclamation accessible, intelligible, and inspirational for modern-day worshipers? Jesus's use of kingdom imagery is somewhat foreign to those of us born in the US, as most of our referents in this regard are based upon media representations rather than lived experiences. People more accustomed to monarchical forms of governance may experience ambivalence about the use of kingdom imagery, given its potential for connoting benevolent as well as repressive governance. Alternative images, such as commonwealth, reign, kin-dom, kin(g)dom, or kinship community are often more accessible, as they evoke relational paradigms common to our lived experiences. Yet even these modernized images necessitate discernment with regard to a congregation or community's context and experiential encounters. The phrase "reign of God," for example, retains the imperial connotations evident in kingdom imagery.

Throughout our conversation, I have referred to Jesus's proclamation of the kin(g)dom of God as the archetypal reservoir through which Hope's anticipatory language flows. In an effort to more thickly describe the reality Jesus's proclamation connotes, I have characterized the kin(g)dom of God as a new ethical domain constituted by love, justice, and peace—a kinship community or kin-dom in which all are well, and none are relegated to the margins or to a life of dearth.[39] My desire is to make gospel proclamation intelligible, accessible, and a source of inspiration for those of us who receive it today, and to make known its implications for our ability to live toward a qualitative better state of existence for ourselves and for all with whom we share our lives. As a homiletical value and practice, cultivating imaginative abundance and purposeful, Hope-filled

---

39. See Geertz, *The Interpretation of Cultures*, chapter 1. In ethnographic research, thick description involves investigating and interpreting, at the most elemental level, the "what?" "when?" "how?" "what for?," and "so what" of an action, ritual, idea, or concept.

action begins with identifying or naming the reality to which the gospel invites us through the use of "thick description."[40]

In his now famous "I Have a Dream" speech, the Reverend Dr. Martin Luther King Jr. employs thick description to articulate the social change necessary to further the nation's journey toward becoming a beloved community.[41] King's theological conception of the beloved community, though not the full realization of God's kin(g)dom, reflects the kin(g)dom's ethical orientation in microcosm. With attention to the problem of racial injustice, the speech also invites ethical reorientation. After extensive reflection upon racial injustice's deep stain upon America's social fabric, King articulates confidence in the nation's ability to distance itself from ethical lassitude and respond to the "fierce urgency of now."[42] Seeking to awaken that same confidence in his audience, he concludes his speech by announcing, "I say to you today, my friends, though, even though we face the difficulties of today and tomorrow, I still have a dream."[43] Throughout the conclusion, King repeatedly declares, "I have a dream . . . ," augmenting the phrase with an aspect of his dream for the nation at each rhetorical turn. In this manner, King not only articulates his dream, but he also nurtures imaginative abundance by inviting hearers to adopt the dream as their own. King's use of "thick description" transforms his dream into an unambiguous articulation of that which characterizes a qualitatively better state of existence. It invites the audience to reimagine their lives and world through the lens of God's just intent for all.

Thick description can similarly support faithful proclaimers' efforts to articulate characteristics of a qualitatively better state of existence today. Rather than an abstract idea of the *better*, insights arising from thick description equip preachers to speak concretely and succinctly about attitudes and practices necessary for life in God's kin(g)dom. Equipped with such insights, preachers aid congregations in imagining tangible, embodiable, practical possibilities for embracing the ethic to which the gospel invites us. In other words, thick description fuels a preacher's ability to nurture imaginative abundance and purposeful, Hope-filled action.

Imaginative abundance refers to the act of intentionally dreaming or imagining a qualitatively better state of existence that is ethically and morally indicative of Jesus's gospel proclamation. Intentional dreams are meaning-full dreams, images, and representations that give meaning to

---

40. Geertz, *The Interpretation of Cultures*, chapter 1.
41. King, *The Autobiography*, 223.
42. King, *The Autobiography*, 223.
43. King, *The Autobiography*, 223.

our lives. As an intentional or meaning-full dream, imaginative abundance will not permit us to rest in or remain content with the givenness of life. Our search for meaning will not allow it. Instead, imaginative abundance in light of the gospel makes us hungry and thirsty for a more loving, just, and God-infused existence for all creation, feeding our desire to reimagine and re-story our lives. This hunger and thirst for right relationship with God and others set us in motion toward God's vision of *shalom*, even as its actuality remains obscure. Imaginative abundance, in other words, gives rise to purposeful, Hope-filled action.

The practice of singing among enslaved Africans in the US reveals the power of imaginative abundance to provoke or generate purposeful, Hope-filled action. Though enslaved women, men, and children surrendered their bodies to the ferocity of chattel slavery, the singing of spirituals like "Down by the Riverside" and others evinced their deep longing for and determination toward freedom.[44]

> I'm goin' to lay down my burdens,
>   down by the riverside
>   down by the riverside
>   down by the riverside
> I'm goin' to lay down my burdens,
>   down by the riverside
> Ain't goin' to study war no more
> Well I ain't goin' to study war no more,
> ain't goin' to study war no more,
> study war no more, study war no more . . .

Drawing upon biblical imagery from the prophets Micah and Isaiah, the people who first sang this song *hoped against hope* that they would cross the river that led to freedom. For some, crossing the river meant traveling to the city of God where they could put on clean and fresh clothing, freely stroll through the city, and take a leaf from the tree in the middle of the city to heal their physical and psychic wounds.[45] Others imagined themselves traveling up the river that ran through their communities to a place of freedom in the North, a this-worldly liberation sanctioned by God. In either case, they anticipated a place where the battle would be over; where swords, shields, and slave garments would be discarded and they would learn or study a

---

44. See also Smith, *Reclaiming the Spirituals*; Cone, *The Spirituals and the Blues*; Thurman, *Deep River*; Guenter, *In Their Own Words*.

45. See Rev 22:1–2 for city-of-God imagery.

way of being alternative to the embattled existence that encompassed their lives.[46] By way of anticipatory imagination, they found sustenance for their souls. They determined themselves for freedom, imagined it so completely that it mobilized many to not only sing about freedom, but also take the steps necessary to secure the freedom they so deeply desired.

Imaginative abundance emboldens us to actively resist the deceptive language of despair's negating and dehumanizing view of reality. It also powers our ability to engage in purposeful, Hope-filled action, making us conspirators in God's redemptive work. Our actions implicate us as *imago Dei* and disclose our potential for living as a nondistorting, nondestructive reflection of God's presence in the world. And we do so, not as solo actors, but by breathing together or con-spiring with God and alongside the many others who align themselves with and give their resources to support God's redemptive work in the world.

I preached the sermon excerpt with a group of aspiring seminarians attending a recruitment event at Wesley Theological Seminary during the 2018 Lenten season. The sermon, titled "Bearing the Cross," is drawn from Mark 8:31–36. It reveals the dissonance between Jesus's characterization of himself and his followers as cross-bearers and the image of a conquering Messiah that Peter and the other disciples wished Jesus to embrace. The sermon begins with a reflection on "Must Jesus Bear the Cross Alone?," hymn number 404 in the *Baptist Standard Hymnal*, and its effectiveness as an expression of faith.[47] Given the redemptive intent of Jesus's death and resurrection and the immensity of human suffering, the introduction queries, "if we must bear crosses today . . . , what are we bearing and why is it important?" The sermon responds to this query, inviting the gathered community to live toward the *better* by wrapping our ministerial endeavors in Jesus's ministerial vision.

---

46. The specific references include Mic 4:3, "He shall judge between many peoples, / and shall arbitrate between strong nations far away; / they shall beat their swords into ploughshares, / and their spears into pruning hooks; / nation shall not lift up sword against nation, / neither shall they *learn war* any more" (italics added), and is similarly stated in Isa 2:4 (NRSV). The Hebrew לָמַד (= *lāmad*]) is translated "learn" in the NRSV and KJV, "train" in the NIV, and "know" in the New Jewish Publication Society of America (NJPS) translation. In each case, the suggestion is that war has been a course of study which of necessity would be eliminated and replaced by universal peace.

47. G. N. Allen, "Must Jesus Bear the Cross Alone?"

Framing Text

[34] He called the crowd with his disciples, and said to them, "If any want to become my followers, let them deny themselves and take up their cross and follow me. [35] For those who want to save their life will lose it, and those who lose their life for my sake, and for the sake of the gospel, will save it. [36] For what will it profit them to gain the whole world and forfeit their life? (Mark 8:34–36)

Sermon Excerpt

In Mark 8:31–36, Jesus reveals an aspect of his identity the twelve had scarcely imagined . . . He tells them his-story: that he is the Son of Man or Son of Humanity, the One come from God who will be rejected by the religious leaders, killed, and in three days rise again . . . More than the kingly Messiah Peter imagined, more than an unconquerable military leader or new monarch sent to destroy the Roman Empire, Jesus identifies himself as the One who stands with and among humanity—the suffering Messiah who, with resurrection power, came to bring redemption to a world sorely needing and deeply longing for God's presence among us . . .

Peter would hear none of that! He is stunned, angry, afraid, disappointed. Peter, like many of us today, wanted a conquering king, a military Messiah who can annihilate the enemy and take care of all our problems . . .

Peter missed the mark, it seems . . . Or perhaps Peter understood. Perhaps this got all too real for Peter and he realized if Jesus the Healing/Teaching/Preaching/Delivering Messiah and Son of Humanity could be killed, his follower could meet the same fate, and Peter was not at all sure he wanted to lose his life for the sake of the gospel . . .

And that is what Jesus was asking them to do, *asking of us, you know*; that those who follow him must risk their lives for his sake and for the sake of the gospel; that we *are* to take up his gospel proclamation and carry it like a cross and follow him; that we *are* to unashamedly and boldly proclaim the good news of God's unfolding reign and then live as though the reality for which we hope is already present. That we are to go ahead and begin loving without constraint, hoping beyond boundaries, and lending our hands to God's restorative work in the world.

> For what would it profit us to gain the whole world and lose the moral integrity that defines us as Jesus's disciples.
>
> That's what Jesus tells us just six days before that mountaintop experience we call the Transfiguration; that the gospel just might cost our lives, and if we are not willing to take that risk, if we are ashamed to own him and carry forward his clarion call, then he will be ashamed to own us—and we have to make a decision because this thing is happening now! The kingdom of God is taking shape right in the midst of human history, expanding itself as women, men, and children join this great work, and it is coming with power!
>
> Jesus is calling us in this moment to wrap our ministries in the ministerial vision that gave shape to his gospel proclamation more than two thousand years ago!
>
> So, what about it, preachers, teachers, pastors, prophets, seers, and seekers? Dare we take up the gospel like a cross and follow Jesus? Dare we proclaim and live the gospel in this present age? Dare we bind the wounds of the broken and the torn, speak hope where despair has created a void, stand for that which is just and right, and negate that which destroys? . . . Dare we, can we, will we proclaim the good news of the gospel, confident in its ability to reveal truth in the midst of chaos, life in the midst of death, joy in the midst of sorrow, and Hope in the midst of the seemingly impossible?[48]

Jesus's persistence in proclaiming the gospel and the ethic to which it invites us makes a definitive claim upon the lives of Christian people of faith today and upon the life and ministry of the Christian church. The sermon brings us face-to-face with that challenge. It confronts us with difficult yet necessary questions about our willingness to take up the gospel as a cross and follow Jesus wherever he may lead us. The questions are difficult because of the gospel's power and potential for disrupting the systems and structures that undergird our known world; difficult because the gospel calls us beyond our comfort zones and positions of privilege and power into a reality that seeks parity for all, beginning with the most vulnerable in our world; difficult because as surely as the gospel affords opportunities for flourishing and right relationship, it also presents occasions for stumbling should we cling too tightly to the way things are in the present.[49] Despite these difficulties, the

---

48. This sermon excerpt has been significantly redacted for illustrative purposes.

49. See Tisdale, *Preaching as Local Theology*, 34. Tisdale, drawing upon Paul Tillich's distinction between "genuine" and "wrong" stumbling blocks in proclamation, describes "genuine stumbling blocks" as aspects of the gospel message that demand more of us regarding ethical thought and action than we are willing to give. This is distinctive

gospel and the ethic it invites claims us as surely today as in the past. For as we follow in Jesus's footsteps, we also advance the emergence of God's kin(g)dom and the realization of *shalom*.

Preaching is one of the means by which faithful proclaimers endeavor to follow in Jesus's footsteps. The four homiletic values and practices we have explored—embracing empathy proofed by compassion, eliminating distortion, amplifying Hope's assurance and call, and cultivating imaginative abundance and purposeful, Hope-filled action—can nurture our ability to do just that: to follow in Jesus's footsteps by proclaiming the good news of the kin(g)dom of God and unambiguously advocating and demonstrating the ethical orientation to which Jesus's gospel proclamation invites us. Each preaching moment affords us an opportunity to disrupt the deceptive language of despair's distorting and distracting messages and to heighten congregations' sensitivity to Hope's assurance and call. Preaching also enables us to create transformative experiential encounters that energize congregants to live with Hope.

Living with Hope entails aligning our patterns of perceiving, thinking, and behaving with Hope's assurance of God's enduring concern for the well-being of creation. Living with Hope also encompasses embracing our inherent identity as *imago Dei* and acknowledging our role as fitting participants in God's redemptive work in the world. Preaching, this monologue with dialogical intent, joins other ministries of the church in promoting the church's ministry of eliminating distortion and nurturing imaginative abundance and purposeful, Hope-filled action. Those of us who preach pray that our words of proclamation will nurture congregations' ability to embody ways of being and relating that arc the world more intently toward God's vision of *shalom* made evident in Jesus's gospel proclamation.

---

from "wrong stumbling blocks," which impede practices in proclamation that result from the "humanness of the preaching event and inadequacies of communication on the part of the preacher" (34).

— 6 —

The Courageously Audacious Practice of Hope

> There is a deeper reason to fight for causes that may not succeed. The world would be worse off if no one did . . . Imagine a world without troublemakers and you have defined a WASP paradise. Imagine a world without dissenters, revolutionaries, jesters, or dreamers and you have imagined a world that is not human. The existence of evil requires the consciousness of good.[1]
>
> —Thomas Hayden

> Moral imagination is the ability of the preacher, intuitive or otherwise, in the midst of the chaotic experience of human life and existence, to grasp and share God's abiding wisdom and ethical truth in order to benefit the individual and common humanity.[2]
>
> —Frank Thomas

LIVING RESPONSIVE TO HOPE's assurance and call is a courageously audacious act. Audacious because it signifies acknowledgment of our inherent identity as *imago Dei* and potential as colaborers in God's restorative and redemptive work. All the more audacious because we make these acknowledgments in a social and religious milieu that places greater emphasis upon human frailty and failure than upon our capacity to live as a nondistorting, nondestructive reflection of God's presence in the earth. This is not to say human frailty and failure does not exist; we are indeed fallible creatures, as

---

1. Hayden, *Irish on the Inside*, 66.
2. Thomas, *How to Preach a Dangerous Sermon*, xxii–xxiii.

the condition of our world attests. But fallibility and frailty are but one aspect of the human condition and should "never be our last and only word about the nature of humanity and the ways in which the divine works in our lives," as Emilie Towns so adeptly notes.[3] As bearers of God's image and beings through whom God's divine breath (Hebrew: *ruach*) flows, we humans possess the capacity to imagine and fashion a world in which love, justice, and peace are the normative expression of our shared existence.

Fashioning such a world necessitates the audacity to imagine the possibility of a new reality and the courage to act upon that which we imagine. We perceive such audacious imagining in Jesus's ministerial vision of God's kin(g)dom on earth, a metaphor of Hope through which Christian people of faith and others can discern the ethical thought and practice necessary to live toward a new reality. Grounded in a biblical ethic of love, this vision anticipates God's *shalom* for all people and, by implication, all creation. For, the entire "creation has been groaning in labor pains until now," as we together, with eager expectation, await God's ultimate redemption (Rom 8:23).

Preaching that embodies Jesus's ministerial vision of the kin(g)dom of God empowers the faithful to both anticipate and live toward a qualitatively better state of existence. Gustavo Gutiérrez highlights this point when he writes, "The life and preaching of Jesus postulate the unceasing search for a new kind of humanity in a qualitatively different society."[4] When considered in light of the gospel, "qualitatively different" or, as I have suggested, *qualitatively better* signifies a world in which the earth and all her inhabitants experience wholeness, health, and prosperity as that which is common to our lives: a loving and just world sustained by courageous and audacious people of faith and good conscience who boldly live with Hope despite the numerous obstacles we encounter. And while the realization of God's kin(g)dom is neither synonymous with nor dependent upon the establishment of a just society (Gutiérrez emphasizes this point), "the announcement of the Kingdom reveals to society itself the aspiration for a just society and leads it to discover unsuspected dimension and unexplored paths."[5] Thereby, writes Gutiérrez, "the political is grafted into the eternal."[6] When preachers actively proclaim, demonstrate, and advocate the ethical thought and practice to which the gospel invites us, we reveal possibilities and make known the gospel's implications for a qualitatively better state of existence for all.

3. Townes, "Introduction," xi.
4. Gutiérrez, *A Theology of Liberation*, 134–35.
5. Gutiérrez, *A Theology of Liberation*, 134–35.
6. Gutiérrez, *A Theology of Liberation*, 134–35.

The preacher's efforts toward proclaiming, demonstrating, and advocating the gospel also include a comparable commitment to disrupting and eliminating obstacles that inhibit our ability to live responsive to Hope's assurance and call. Our primary obstacle is imaginative dearth. Fueled by the deceptive language of despair's assertion that inadequate social realities are fixed and ineradicable, imaginative dearth impedes our ability to envisage and work toward a more loving, just, and life-affirming world for all. Inadequate social realities, as we have discussed throughout this conversation, are various and extensive. Among them are oppressive mechanisms, suppressive structures, and repressive attitudes and practices that promote material, physical, and psychic impoverishment; dehumanizing and negating images, myths, ideologies, and theologies; violence and militaristic practices; materialism and hedonistic consumption; callous institutional policies rife with all manner of negating isms and the suffering they produce. Fatalistic preoccupation with such conditions diminishes our capacity to live responsive to Hope's assurance and call. Courage, on the other hand, promotes imaginative abundance and buoys our ability to engage in purposeful, Hope-filled action, even in the most difficult and chaotic of times.

Responding to Hope's Assurance and Call

Through the audacious and courageous practice of Hope, we say yes to God's yes for creation and for our lives. Our yes evinces confidence that though evil persists, God remains faithful, loving, and just as surely today as in the past. Proclamation of the gospel in word and deed fuels our ability to say yes. Gospel proclamation cultivates both the ethical thought and ethical practice to which the gospel invites us, which together give birth to imaginative abundance and purposeful, Hope-filled action. Ethical ideas must necessarily precipitate ethical practice. Or, paraphrasing the New Testament's Epistle of James (2:14–17), verbal articulations of faith or belief without tangible expressions of love for one another are indeed dead. In this sense, proclamation of the gospel cultivates what homiletician Frank Thomas characterizes as "moral imagination."[7]

In preaching, writes Thomas, "moral imagination is the ability of the preacher, intuitive or otherwise, in the midst of the chaotic experience of human life and existence, to grasp and share God's abiding wisdom and ethical truth in order to benefit the individual and common humanity."[8] In the face of despair, preaching invites and emboldens us to imagine and actualize a

---

7. Thomas, *How to Preach a Dangerous Sermon*, xxiii–xxiv.
8. Thomas, *How to Preach a Dangerous Sermon*, xxiii–xxiv.

new reality which foundation is love, justice, and peace. But this is not the work of preaching alone. The Hope-filled message of the gospel also invites Christian people of faith to cultivate moral imagination among the individuals and communities within our sphere of influence—to let our light shine by proclaiming, demonstrating, and advocating the gospel.

In this final phase of the conversation, I invite us to celebrate individuals and communities who exemplify the courage and audacity to live with Hope in seemingly impossible situations, to celebrate those who survive in the face of horrific and dehumanizing conditions too painful to express and still believe in the possibility of a qualitative better state of existence for themselves and for future generations. Hope resounds and so is celebrated in those determined to "fight for causes that may not succeed."[9] Nevertheless they fight, says Thomas Hayden, because "the world would be worse off if no one did."[10] To these ambassadors of Hope and doers of love, justice, and peace we owe a debt of gratitude for the legacy of imaginative abundance and purposeful, Hope-filled action they bequeath to us, and we in turn to future generations.

In US history, the African American journey toward racial justice and equality gifts us with such a legacy. Its roots extend more than four hundred years to the children, women, and men whom Europeans captured from their homelands in Africa or purchased from rival tribal leaders and transported to North America under a system of forced servitude called chattel slavery. Their story and stories—my ancestral story—present a case study in Hope. My ancestral story bears witness to the courage and audacity necessary to live responsive to Hope's assurance and call when the circumstances suggest our efforts are in vain. So, with this story in mind and Rev. Dr. Martin Luther King's dream of the beloved community as a heuristic backdrop, we take a brief trek through history to highlight the African American journey toward racial justice and equality. For, they dared to dream in a society where dreaming was prohibited for people of African descent.

Journey toward the Beloved Community: A Practice of Hope

Of the many expressions of Hope in the twentieth and twenty-first centuries, the Reverend Dr. Martin Luther King Jr.'s anticipation of and purposeful, Hope-filled action toward the beloved community is among the most compelling. Diana L. Hayes, in her contribution to *Revives Our*

---

9. Hayden, *Irish on the Inside*, 66.
10. Hayden, *Irish on the Inside*, 66.

Souls Again, explores King's spirituality "within the history, traditions, and ongoing activism of the black church and the spirituality of African Americans."[11] She identifies three coalescing spiritual strands that give rise to King's vision of The Beloved Community and purposeful, Hope-filled action toward its realization.

The first strand involves the spirituality of the Black church. The beloved community, which King understood as indicative of God's kin(g)dom on earth, is rooted in sensibilities evident in "the Christian religion in which he had been immersed from birth."[12] Namely, the preaching and teaching of the Missionary Baptist Church. Regarding the beloved community's relationship to the kin(g)dom of God, Lewis V. Baldwin and Victor Anderson, also contributors to *Revives Our Souls Again*, write, "King advocated employing the spiritual means of nonviolence to achieve the spiritual ends of 'The kingdom of God on earth,' which he viewed as the theological equivalent of the ethical ideal of the beloved community."[13] Though not the full realization of the God's kin(g)dom on earth, King's vision of the beloved community elucidates the ethical necessity of justice and equality for the kin(g)dom's ongoing emergence. King's and others' insistence upon nonviolence as the modus operandi for social change is also grounded in the preaching and teaching of the Black church. The Black church, Hayes insightfully notes, not only gave King and other leaders "a foundational basis upon which to launch their sit-in, pray-in, and marches, it also gave them the theological and spiritual language in which they could ground their calls for civil, social, and economic liberation for persons of African descent."[14] They translated the language of the church into the sociopolitical language necessary to effect the change they wished to realize.

As a second strand, Hayes reveals the rootedness of King's emphasis upon *community* in African spirituality. In African spirituality, community, family, and religion coalesce to give meaning to life. Without these three, writes Hayes, "there can be no viable life."[15] Also important is the African concept of *Ubuntu* (full humanity), which "lies at the heart of King's effort to develop the Beloved Community, which he saw as that 'period of social harmony and universal brotherhood that would follow the current social

---

11. Hayes, "A Great Cloud of Witnesses," Kindle ed.
12. Hayes, "A Great Cloud of Witnesses," Kindle ed.
13. Baldwin and Anderson, "The Promptings," Kindle ed.
14. Hayes, "A Great Cloud of Witnesses," Kindle ed. Hayes is quoting Julius Lester, "God and Social Change."
15. Hayes, "A Great Cloud of Witnesses," Kindle ed.

struggle.'"[16] These understandings reveal King's attentiveness to the contextual realities and structures of power that so stridently sought to deny African Americans the right to live with dignity and respect.

King's attention to context highlights a third strand in his spirituality. His desire for the beloved community grew out of "the struggle for liberation from injustice, prejudice, and discrimination, and for equal rights and citizenship" that had been a part of Black people's experience in North America for more than four hundred years.[17] King as well as his predecessors and colaborers in the movement knew all too well the depth and breadth of the horrific sociocultural, political, and ecclesial realities that necessitated perseverance on the journey toward justice and equality.

In this respect, King's vision and purposeful, Hope-filled action toward the beloved community's actualization serve as a lens for contextualizing the practice of living with Hope over an extended period of time in anticipation of a qualitatively better state of existence. As a heuristic device, the journey toward the beloved community makes the struggle and those who share in the struggle more visible. It also sheds light upon the historical and present-day challenges of many other marginalized communities as well as our individual struggles for wholeness and well-being in multiple domains of life. Ultimately, reflecting upon the journey toward the beloved community and other such journeys as praxes of Hope remind us of our soulish connection with each other and our shared inheritance as *imago Dei*. So, let us journey together.

From Genocide and Enslavement to Reconstruction

Enslaved Africans were not America's first racial victims. The nomadic ancestors of modern-day indigenous peoples, often referred to as Native Americans, American Indians, or First Nation Peoples, were North America's first recorded inhabitants. Fifteen thousand years ago, millions migrated across the Bering Strait to Alaska and spread across the North American continent.[18] When Europeans arrived in the fifteenth century there were an estimated fifty million indigenous peoples already living in North America, including as many as twelve million in the land that became the United States of America.[19] The European migration to North America was disrup-

---

16. Hayes, "A Great Cloud of Witnesses," Kindle ed. See also Lischer, *The Preacher King*, 234.
   17. Hayes, "A Great Cloud of Witnesses," Kindle ed.
   18. Dulik et al., "Mitochondrial DNA."
   19. Jobe, "Native Americans."

tive and tragic. Not only did diseases such as bubonic plague, chickenpox, cholera, malaria, measles, typhoid, and other deadly viruses and infections previously unknown in the Americas decimate their populations. Wars, land treaties, local conflicts with European settlers, and state-sanctioned violence and violation effectively stripped away their freedoms and displaced millions from their homelands.[20]

The arrival of Europeans to North America was equally devastating for peoples throughout the African continent, especially nations on Africa's west coast. European migration to North America coincided with the start of the transatlantic slave trade and American colonists' embrace of chattel slavery, one of the most brutal and dehumanizing forms of slavery to date. While slavery was not a new phenomenon in Europe or in other parts of the world, the association between slavery and ethnicity or race—specifically, Black racial and ethnic groups—became a distinctive feature of chattel slavery in what became the US.

Joy DeGruy Leary, in *Post Traumatic Slave Syndrome*, describes the connection between race-based chattel slavery and the brutality and dehumanization that characterized slavery in what would become the US.

> According to Thomas D. Morris in *Southern Slavery and the Law, 1619–1860*, Africans were considered to be "presumed" or "natural slaves" based on their skin color. They were also referred to as "thinking property" and inherently "rightless persons." In few societies, if any, was so large a group of people considered to be less than human based upon physical appearance. Yet Europeans concluded that black Africans were fitted by a natural act of God to the position of permanent bondage. It was this relegation to lesser humanity that allowed the institution of slavery to be intrinsically linked with violence, and it was through violence, aggression, and dehumanization that the institution of slavery was enacted, legislated, and perpetuated by Europeans.[21]

Race-based chattel slavery is inherently dehumanizing. Its grounding in the binary notion of Black racial inferiority and White racial superiority allows for and legitimizes the treatment of Black people as less than human. Binary thinking of this sort also has a double-edged effect. In general, it sanctions dehumanizing perceptions of others. But those who perceive themselves as possessing the preferable quality in the binary (in this case Whiteness) consent to becoming lesser human beings themselves.

20. Strauss, "Columbus Day."
21. Leary, *Post Traumatic Slave Syndrome*, 35.

Referencing King on this point, Baldwin and Anderson note, "He felt that all too many white people had become victims of 'mental' and 'spiritual slavery' through their own enslaving and oppressive routines."[22] Adherence to such notions, in other words, diminishes one's capacity to embrace humanity's shared identity as *imago Dei*. It promotes a diminished sense of self, which also prevents one from living as a nondistorting, nondestructive reflection of God's presence.

Notwithstanding the horror and dehumanizing effects of mass slaughter and enslavement, European settlers persisted in building a nation whose economy, infrastructure, and system of governance relied upon the near genocide of Indigenous peoples and the importation and enslavement of Black Africans. Dutch traders brought the first African slaves to the colony of Jamestown, Virginia, in 1619. In 1662 the General Assembly of the Commonwealth of Virginia defined slavery as a hereditary, lifelong condition, designating any child born of an enslaved woman as a slave without regard to fatherhood.[23] Slave colonies and states throughout what became the US enacted similar laws, quashing any prospect that children born into slavery would ever taste freedom. They also initiated strict miscegenation laws prohibiting free English and other European men and women from marrying a "negroe, mulatto, or Indian man or woman bond or free" under threat of banishment or other forms of punishment.[24]

The institutionalization of chattel slavery also presented a dilemma for the Christian church. The pressing question became, Does baptism alter one's legal status? To resolve the dilemma, the Virginia Assembly determined baptism had no bearing upon the physical condition of slaves.

> WHEREAS some doubts have risen whether children that are slaves by birth, and by the charity and piety of their owners made pertakers of the blessed sacrament of baptisme, should by vertue of their baptisme be made ffree; It is enacted and declared by this grand assembly, and the authority thereof, that the conferring of baptisme doth not alter the condition of the person as to his bondage or freedome; that diverse masters, ffreed from

---

22. Baldwin and Anderson, "The Promptings," Kindle ed.

23. Act XII (1662): "Negro womens children to serve according to the condition of the mother. WHEREAS some doubts have arrisen whether children got by any Englishman upon a negro woman should be slave or [free,] Be it therefore enacted and declared by this present grand assembly, that all children borne in this country shal be held bond or free only according to the condition of the mother, And that if any christian shall committ [fornication] with a negro man or woman, hee or shee so offending shall pay double the [fines] imposed by the former act."

24. Virginia General Assembly, An Act for Suppressing Outlying Slaves (1691).

this doubt, may more carefully endeavour the propagation of christianity by permitting children, though slaves, or those of growth if capable to be admitted to that sacrament.[25]

The ruling not only upheld slavery as a legitimate institution. It also mitigated the church's moral accountability regarding the practice of enslaving Christian brothers and sisters. Questions about the extent to which enslaved people should be regarded as human beings also arose. In 1705, Act XXIII of the Commonwealth of Virginia legally declared all "negro, mullato, and Indian slaves in all courts of judicature, and other places, within this dominion, shall be held, taken, and adjudged, to be real estate (and not chattels)."[26] Defining enslaved people as real estate tethered them to the land and landowner, further negating their identity as human beings.

The Three-Fifths Compromise of 1787 reinforced such disregard for Black humanity. The Compromise grew out of a dispute between southern and northern states during the 1787 Constitutional Convention about how enslaved people should be counted in the allocation of seats to the House of Representatives. After much deliberation in the convention, James Madison proposed the Three-Fifths Compromise, counting slaves as three-fifths of a person, which resulted in increased representation and potentially greater political power for the southern states.[27] While compromise was largely a pragmatic decision, it carried broader social and ethical implications. Counting slaves as three-fifths of a person legitimized White supremacy and its valuation of enslaved Africans and all non-Whites as inferior and less human than Whites.

By the late eighteenth century, growing fervor regarding the abolition of slavery had arisen, especially in the North. And by the mid-nineteenth century, tensions between the northern and southern states about the economic and ethical viability of slavery had intensified. In 1861, during Abraham Lincoln's time in the US presidency, tensions overflowed, resulting in a war between the states, the Civil War. Chief among its causes were disputes about the abolition of slavery.[28] Eleven Southern states seceded

---

25. Virginia General Assembly, An Act for Suppressing Outylying Slaves (1691).

26 Virginia General Assembly, An act declaring the Negro, Mulatto, and Indian slaves within this dominion, to be real estate (1705). See also, Copeland, "The Nomenclature," on the implication of designating slaves as real estate rather than chattel.

27. The Southern states eventually lost that advantage because of rapid growth and significant population increases in the Northern states.

28. Northern states, whose economy was based upon manufacturing and industry, increasingly opposed slavery on economic and moral grounds. Southern and Midwestern states, whose economic viability depended upon large farms and free enslaved labor, resisted such ideas.

from the Union and formed the Confederate States of America. Notwithstanding their secession, in 1863 President Lincoln issued an executive order, the Emancipation Proclamation, abolishing slavery throughout the Union.[29] Two years later, the North having won the Civil War, Congress ratified the Thirteenth Amendment to the US Constitution (on December 18, 1865), abolishing slavery in all states and territories. The Civil War officially ended on April 9, 1865.

During the period immediately following emancipation, the Reconstruction era (1863–1877), Black Americans made significant gains. Congress passed the Fourteenth Amendment in 1868, affording all male citizens regardless of race equal protection under the law. In 1869, Congress passed the Fifteenth Amendment, granting voting rights to African American men. Congress also passed an act to establish the Bureau of Refugees, Freedmen, and Abandoned Lands (the Freedman's Bureau) on March 3, 1865, to assist freed Black people in building a new life for themselves.[30] The following year, Congress passed the Civil Rights Act of 1866, affording previously enslaved people various civil liberties, "including the right to make contracts, own and sell property and receive equal treatment under the law."[31] The racial justice and equality for which African Americans and their allies so deeply yearned was finally in sight.

From Terror Lynchings and the Great Depression to World War II

Gains in the journey toward the beloved community during the Reconstruction were short-lived. In the years following the Civil Rights Act of 1866, southern and Midwestern states enacted "black codes" restricting civil and voting rights for Black Americans. And in a society rife with White supremacist attitudes, state and local governments and individual citizens engaged in practices that terrorized Black communities. Most devastatingly, in the late nineteenth and early twentieth centuries, the race-based system of valuation that had shaped US social and religious imagination for more than 250 years gave rise to the cruel and terroristic practice of lynching.

Brian Stevenson, director of the Equal Justice Initiative (EJI), describes lynching as an act of terrorism.[32] Lynching, the lawless practice of executing Black men, women, and children, as well as allies of Black people,

---

29. United States National Archives, "The Emancipation Proclamation."
30. Howard University, "Reconstruction Era: 1866–1877."
31. Howard University, "Reconstruction Era: 1866–1877."
32. Stevenson, *Lynching*.

were "violent and public acts of torture that traumatized Black people throughout the country and were largely tolerated by state and federal officials."[33] In an extensive report documenting "terror lynchings" between the end of the Reconstruction era in 1877 and 1950, the EJI documents 4,084 racial "terror lynchings" in twelve southern states that claimed "the lives of African American men, women, and children who were forced to endure the fear, humiliation, and barbarity of this widespread phenomenon unaided."[34] They also document three hundred "terror lynchings" in other states during the same period. The practice of lynching reached its peak between 1880 and 1940.[35] Compounding the obstructive legal environment that Black people encountered as they sought to exercise their rights as US citizens, "lynching created a fearful environment where racial subordination and segregation was maintained with limited resistance for decades."[36] "Most critically," the EJI reports, "lynching reinforced a legacy of racial inequality that has never been adequately addressed in America." The practice of lynching is largely relegated to the annals of history, but systemic racial inequality persists into the present.

The Great Depression further impeded the journey toward the beloved community. In the early 1920s—the roaring twenties—the US experienced significant economic expansion, and people from all sectors of life invested in stocks. But by August of 1929 a recession was underway that eventually destabilized Wall Street, deflated the economy, and sent numerous wealthy investors and everyday people into a panic as they watched their savings dwindle, in many cases to nothing.[37] In October 1929 the stock market crashed, plunging the nation into the Great Depression. The Depression impacted everyone, especially the working class. The nation's racially hostile climate, however, made the Depression devastating for black Americans.

President Franklin D. Roosevelt's inauguration in 1933 signaled the beginning of a new day in America. Roosevelt's economic recovery plan, the New Deal, included programs to provide financial relief, improve infrastructure, and create jobs for people throughout the nation. In 1935, Congress passed the Social Security Act, which for the first time in the nation's history provided Americans with unemployment and disability insurance and pensions. But discriminatory hiring practices shut Black people out of

---

33. Stevenson, *Lynching*.
34. Stevenson, *Lynching*.
35. Stevenson, *Lynching*.
36. Stevenson, *Lynching*.

37. This period in history is colloquially referred to as the Hoover years by some, representing the presidency of Herbert Hoover (1929–1933).

the labor market, thereby limiting their access to pensions and other entitlements provided by the Social Security Act.

These challenges led the National Association for the Advancement of Colored People (NAACP), a multiracial justice organization, to turn its focus toward eradicating legalized employment discrimination.[38] In 1941, the NAACP and the Congress of Industrial Organizations (CIO) demanded the federal government "end employment discrimination in the defense industry," but President Roosevelt rejected their appeal.[39] However, when president of the Brotherhood of Sleeping Car Porters, A. Philip Randolph, "threatened a national march on Washington D.C.," Roosevelt signed Executive Order 8802, prohibiting discriminatory practices in the federal government and in the defense industry.[40] Roosevelt also created the Fair Employment Practices Commission (FEPC) to ensure compliance. In 1942, the CIO, then competitor of the American Federation of Labor (AFL), organized the Committee to Abolish Racial Discrimination, focusing on "combatting discrimination related to job assignments and promotions."[41] In 1955, the CIO and AFL merged and extended the work of the Committee to Abolish Racial Discrimination through its newly formed Civil Rights Department.[42] The organization has remained an active participant in civil rights activities for the past sixty-five years.

Youth voices also gained prominence in the journey toward racial justice and equality during the Great Depression. In "We Demand Our Rights," C. Alvin Hughes chronicles the establishment of the Southern Negro Youth

---

38. Aptheker, *A Documentary History*, 915.

39. University of Maryland, *African-Americans' Rights* (web page), "A House Divided" (section).

40. University of Maryland, *African-Americans' Rights* (web page), "A House Divided" (section); see also, United States National Archives & Record Administration et al., "Executive Order 880."

41. University of Maryland, *African-Americans' Rights* (web page), "A House Divided" (section).

42. University of Maryland, *African-Americans' Rights* (web page), "A House Divided" (section). Regarding the relationship between the AFL and CIO, curators note the AFL's decision to abandon its stance regarding discrimination against union members: "At its founding convention, the AFL required all affiliates to pledge that their member would never 'discriminate against a fellow worker or on account of color, creed, or nationality." Unfortunately, by 1895, the AFL reversed this position and allowed new affiliates to "prohibit African American members from joining their ranks." The CIO, founded in 1936, "pledged to organize workers with no distinction to race or color and opposed all forms of segregation," making them a major competitor for union members. The two organization merged in 1955 and created a Civil Rights Department "to build on the work of the Committee to Abolish Racial Discrimination."

Congress (SNYC).[43] Established in 1936 as an auxiliary of the National Negro Congress (NNC), SNYC sought to respond to the crises facing Black youth after the Great Depression.[44] SNYC's platform included economic justice, educational parity, access to municipal health facilities, recreation programs for Black youth, and increasing the number of Black teachers and representatives on local school boards. The group also proposed requiring courses in "Afro-American history" in all public schools with the goal of improving domestic race relations. Internationally, they advocated for world peace.[45] In 1937, SNYC convened a conference on "The Role of the Negro Church in Solving the Social and Economic Problems of the Negro Youth" and called upon Black ministers to respond to the "bread and butter" social, political, and economic challenges facing Black Americans.[46] However, Black southern pastors' reluctance to involve themselves in social activism precluded the Black church's participation.[47] The SNYC dissolved in 1949, but at W. E. B. Du Bois's urging during their final conference, many former members of SNYC remained active in the fight for voting and civil rights throughout the Great Depression.[48]

World War II proved instrumental in bringing the Great Depression to an end. America's decision to join forces with Britain and France in defeating Nazi Germany and its leader, Adolf Hitler, was precipitated by the bombing of Pearl Harbor by the Japanese in 1941. Involvement in the war necessitated increased production in factories and thus led to more jobs. At the conclusion of the war in 1945, approximately one million African American soldiers returned home anticipating the warm embrace of a grateful nation.[49] But instead of a national embrace, jobs, or increased opportunity, Black soldiers encountered employment discrimination and overt racial animus. Not only had Black soldiers served in segregated units during the war, but the promise of economic and racial justice also eluded them

---

43. Hughes, "We Demand Our Rights," 38. SNYC was the nation's first black direct-action youth organization.

44. Hughes, "We Demand Our Rights," 38. In 1935, Howard University convened a conference in Washington DC to address the status of the Negro, giving birth to the National Negro Congress (NNC), a civil rights organization that advocated fair labor practices and voting rights. See also Horne, "National Negro Congress."

45. Hughes, "We Demand Our Rights," 40.

46. Hughes, "We Demand Our Rights," 40.

47. Hughes, "We Demand Our Rights," 41.

48. Hughes, "We Demand Our Rights," 46.

49. Garrow, *Bearing the Cross*, 165.

afterward, leading many Black soldiers to become active in the NAACP and other racial justice organizations.[50]

During this period, the NAACP added to its antilynching and economic justice emphases initiatives to end state-mandated segregation. Its Legal Defense and Educational Fund, led by Thurgood Marshall, successfully argued *Brown v. Board of Education of Topeka, Kansas* (1954) before the Supreme Court. The ruling outlawed state-sanctioned segregation of public schools, superseding the Court's 1896 ruling in *Plessy v. Ferguson*, which had upheld the constitutionality of the Jim Crow practice of "separate but equal."[51] The *Brown* decision was foundational for future civil rights legislation, providing momentum for the journey toward the beloved commuity.

The Montgomery Bus Boycott and Freedom Rides

Despite the NAACP's victory in *Brown*, the journey toward the beloved community remained fraught by racial animus against Black Americans and all non-Whites. In 1955, a new era in the fight for racial justice and equality began, precipitated by the Montgomery bus boycott. On Thursday, December 1, 1955, in Montgomery, Alabama, Rosa Parks refused to relinquish her seat to White passengers during her city bus commute home from work.[52] When the White section of the bus filled to capacity, the bus driver moved the line separating White and Black riders to create more seating for White passengers and so requiring Black passengers either to sit farther back in the bus or to stand. Because Mrs. Parks refused to move, the police arrested her and charged her with violating chapter 6, section 11 of the Montgomery City Code. Mrs. Parks, an active member of the NAACP, was later released on bail.[53]

Immediately following Mrs. Parks's release, the Women's Political Council (founded in 1946), began circulating flyers and calling for a bus boycott on Monday, December 5, 1955, the date of her arraignment.[54] On Friday evening, December 2, Ralph D. Abernathy, pastor of Montgomey's

---

50. Cobb, "Winds of Change."

51. United States National Archives & Records Administration et al. "Brown v. Board of Education (1954)." See also United States National Archives & Records Administration et al. "Plessy v. Ferguson (1896)."

52. Garrow, *Bearing the Cross*, 11. See also "Montgomery Bus Boycott."

53. Nine months earlier, fifteen-year-old Claudette Colvin was arrested for breaking the same law, but Black leaders declined to use her actions to galvanize the protest because Ms. Colvin was pregnant and unmarried. See Garrow, *Bearing the Cross*, 15.

54. Garrow, *Bearing the Cross*, 16. The Women's Political Council (WPC) was founded in 1946 under the leadership of Jo Ann Robinson.

First Baptist Church and president of the Baptist Ministerial Alliance, convened a meeting of local pastors and community leaders at the Dexter Avenue Baptist Church where twenty-six-year-old Martin Luther King Jr. was pastor. Abernathy urged pastors to support the boycott, but his appeal fell flat due to detractors in the group. When the meeting ended, Abernathy, King (reluctantly), and twenty other leaders decided to move forward with the boycott provisioned upon community support. Following Friday's meeting, Abernathy and King "visited nightclubs to spread further news of the upcoming boycotts."[55] On Saturday, the *Alabama Journal*, a small local newspaper, advertised the boycott; this was followed by an article in the *Montgomery Advertiser's* Sunday morning edition.[56] On Sunday, December 4, pastors supportive of the effort announced the boycott in their various congregations.

Mrs. Parks's trial began on Monday, December 5, at nine a.m. before city court judge John B. Scott. Several hundred Black riders boycotted Montgomery's buses while hundreds more gathered at the courthouse.[57] In less than five minutes, Judge Scott found Mrs. Parks guilty and fined her ten dollars. On Monday afternoon, Black leaders gathered at Mount Zion AME Church to prepare for the mass meeting. Though some remained reluctant, most leaders favored continuing the boycott until city leaders agreed to ensure "courtesy [to Black riders], the hiring of black drivers, and a first-come, first-seated policy, with whites entering and filling seats from the front and African Americans from the rear."[58] At Abernathy's urging, the group also agreed to form a permanent organization, the Montgomery Improvement Association (MIA), and elected King as president.[59]

Five thousand people gathered at the Holt Street Baptist Church for Monday evening's mass meeting.[60] In his call to action, King emphasized the strategic necessity of nonviolent protest and highlighted "the right to protest for right" as a central tenet of American democracy.[61] He also appealed to his audience's commitment to the Christian faith, urging them to "keep God in the forefront" of all their actions.[62] And lest any perceive conflict between the Christian command to love and Black people's existential

---

55. Garrow, *Bearing the Cross*, 18.
56. Garrow, *Bearing the Cross*, 19.
57. Garrow, *Bearing the Cross*, 20.
58. Onion et al., "Montgomery Bus Boycott." See also Garrow, *Bearing the Cross*, 21.
59. Garrow, *Bearing the Cross*, 22.
60. Garrow, *Bearing the Cross*, 22.
61. Garrow, *Bearing the Cross*, 24.
62. Garrow, *Bearing the Cross*, 24.

demand for justice, King clarified, "Love is one of the pinnacle parts of the Christian faith. There is another side called Justice. And justice is really love in calculation."[63] Love and justice, that is, are mutually dependent practices of faith that have implications for how we exist as human community. King concluded the call to action by identifying persuasion, coercion, education, and legislation as tools of social change in Montgomery and throughout the nation. After remarks from Mrs. Parks, Abernathy presented the resolution and the people unanimously endorsed the boycott.[64]

The Montgomery bus boycott persisted 381 days. In order to support protesters' efforts to sustain the boycott, King and the MIA took several steps. They convened weekly mass meetings to hear the community's concerns, provide updates, and ensure the flow of information from movement organizers to Montgomery's Black citizenry. As a result, citizens remained resolute in the fight for racial justice and equality until they achieved the desired outcome.[65] The MIA also organized carpools as an alternative transportation system to carry riders to and from work. More than two hundred drivers volunteered, sustaining the system throughout the boycott. Importantly, despite the city's obstinate refusal to compromise, the MIA repeatedly exerted pressure upon the city's mayor and bus company executives to negotiate. MIA leaders also refused to capitulate despite escalating violence against them—bombings of church buildings and MIA leaders' homes, harassing phone calls, vandalism of personal property, and other violent acts.[66] Indeed, this violence motivated the MIA to align more closely with the NAACP's goal of completely eradicating segregation.[67]

On February 1, 1956, The NAACP, with the support of the MIA, represented five Montgomery women who sued the city of Montgomery in US district court to invalidate segregated seating on buses.[68] On June 5, the federal district court ruled racially segregated seating on public transportation a violation of the Fourteenth Amendment to the US Constitution, citing *Brown* as precedent.[69] On November 13, 1956, the US Supreme Court upheld the district court's decision.[70] Six days later, the MIA peti-

63. Garrow, *Bearing the Cross*, 24.
64. Garrow, *Bearing the Cross*, 24.
65. Garrow, *Bearing the Cross*, 27.
66. Garrow, *Bearing the Cross*, 53, 86.
67. Garrow, *Bearing the Cross*, 28, 51. NAACP president Roy Wilkins was initially reluctant about supporting the boycott. But as the MIA moved closer to the NAACP's goal of eradicating segregation, the NAACP joined the movement.
68. Garrow, *Bearing the Cross*, 61.
69. Garrow, *Bearing the Cross*, 80.
70. Garrow, *Bearing the Cross*, 80.

tioned Justice Hugo Black to make the court's order effective immediately, but the judge denied their request.

As the Black community awaited the court order's arrival, the MIA implemented a weeklong "Institute on Nonviolence and Social Change."[71] King revealed the MIA's ultimate goal in his opening address: "the end is reconciliation; the end is redemption; *the end is the creation of the beloved community*."[72] King's vision of the beloved community appeared a realizable possibility on December 17, 1956, when the Supreme Court rejected the city's final appeal.[73] The city of Montgomery received the court's order on December 20, 1956, and integrated buses the following day. King was the first passenger to board Montgomery's newly integrated buses.[74]

The Montgomery bus boycott spurred boycotts and protests across the South, necessitating coordination among organizations. The movement's expansion also required King to prioritize his commitments. In addition to his life as husband to Coretta and father to their growing family, King's leadership on multiple fronts prevented him from fully devoting himself to one organization.[75] Given these realities, King submitted his resignation as Dexter Avenue's pastor, effective January 31, 1960, and returned to Atlanta, his hometown, to serve with his father at Ebenezer Baptist Church.[76] He also relinquished his position with the MIA and supported Abernathy's election as its new president.[77]

On January 10–11, 1957, Rev. Martin Luther King Sr. hosted sixty Black leaders from ten states at Ebenezer to coordinate protest activities. This meeting gave birth to the Southern Leadership Conference on Transportation and Nonviolent Integration. Their mission was to eradicate the entire Jim/Jane Crow system through the power of the vote and nonviolent mass direct action. The organization elected Martin Luther King Jr. its president and in August 1957 adopted its current name, the Southern Christian Leadership Conference (SCLC), acknowledging the Christian religious heritage of its members.[78]

71. Garrow, *Bearing the Cross*, 81.
72. Garrow, *Bearing the Cross*, 81 (italics added).
73. Garrow, *Bearing the Cross*, 81.
74. Garrow, *Bearing the Cross*, 82.
75. At the time, King served as pastor of Dexter Avenue Baptist Church, president of the MIA, and president of the SCLC, with a rapidly increasing travel, preaching, and speaking schedule.
76. King, *The Autobiography*, 122.
77. King, *The Autobiography*, 126.
78. The executive board of directors included Dr. Martin Luther King Jr. as president; Dr. Ralph David Abernathy as financial secretary and treasurer; Rev. C. K. Steele

Youth involvement in the journey toward the beloved community also intensified after Montgomery. On February 1, 1960, four Black students from North Carolina Agricultural and Technical College, Ezell Blair Jr., David Richmond, Franklin McCain, and Joseph McNeil, staged a sit-in at Woolworth's lunch counter in downtown Greensboro.[79] The next day, the four returned with fifteen others, and by the third day more than three hundred students had joined the protests. The sit-in movement quickly spread throughout the South, motivating students to form the "Student Executive Committee for Justice to coordinate protests."[80] By the end of February 1960, students had staged sit-ins in thirty locations in seven states, and by April, more than fifty thousand students had participated.

SCLC executive director Ella Baker saw great promise in the sit-in campaigns and recognized student activists' potential for expanding the movement.[81] Over Easter weekend 1960, with an eight-hundred-dollar grant from the SCLC, Baker hosted a gathering of sit-in leaders from twelve southern states at Shaw University, in Raleigh, North Carolina, her alma mater. The 120 young activists in attendance embraced Baker's suggestion that they create their own organization, and they formed the Student Nonviolent Coordinating Committee (SNCC).[82] Over the next several years, SNCC arose as one of the most formidable civil rights organization in the nation.

In addition to the movement's expansion, post-Montgomery signaled a transitional period for the nation. Throughout the Montgomery bus boycott, President Dwight D. Eisenhower assumed a noninterventionist position to civil rights and deferred to state law on such matters.[83] As a

---

of Tallahassee, Florida, as vice president; Rev. T. J. Jemison of Baton Rouge, Louisiana, as secretary; and attorney I. M. Augustine of New Orleans, Louisiana, as general counsel. Though not initially identified as an officer, Ella Baker, who had worked as a field secretary with the NAACP, was instrumental in helping Dr. King organize the SCLC and eventually became its executive director.

79. Norris, "The Woolworth Sit-In."

80. Stanford University, *The Martin Luther King Jr. Encyclopedia*, s.v. "Sit-ins."

81. Baker left the SCLC after the Greensboro sit-ins to help students organize sit-ins throughout the South.

82. Stanford University, *The Martin Luther King Jr. Encyclopedia*, s.v. "Sit-ins." SNCC's original members, including John Lewis, Diane Nash, and Marion Barry, learned the skills and philosophy of nonviolent direct action and strategies in nonretaliation under the tutelage of James Lawson, a student at Vanderbilt Divinity School in 1959.

83. US National Archives, "Diary of President Eisenhower, 7/24/1953." Page 3 reflects Eisenhower's position regarding federal intervention in race relations: "I do not believe that prejudices, even palpably, will succumb to compulsion. Consequently, I believe that Federal law imposed unjustified prejudices upon our states in such a way as to bring conflict of the police powers of the states and of the nation, would set back

result, movement leaders were unable to convince him to fully implement the Supreme Court's ruling in *Brown* despite multiple conversations and two mass protests.[84] Eisenhower's two terms as president ended in 1961, and on January 20, 1961, John F. Kennedy was inaugurated US president. Most civil rights leaders viewed Kennedy's election favorably, as he and Attorney General Robert Kennedy appeared more sympathetic to the plight of Black Americans. This assumption would be tested in the years to come, beginning with the Freedom Rides.

From Freedom Rides to the Albany Movement

In 1961, members of SNCC, in cooperation with the Congress of Racial Equality (CORE), initiated Freedom Rides to protest segregated interstate transportation facilities. The original Freedom Riders included thirteen people, seven African Americans and six Euro-Americans. They had planned to travel from Washington, DC, to New Orleans, Louisiana, but were met with immense violence in multiple locations. As they traveled through Rock Hill, South Carolina, three Riders—seminarian John Lewis, World War II veteran Albert Bigelow, and CORE staffer Genevieve Hughes—were viciously attacked and beaten when they attempted to enter a Whites-only waiting room. Attacks in Anniston and Birmingham, Alabama, followed. In Birmingham the Ride was disrupted when on Mother's Day 1961 attackers bombed and burned the Freedom Riders' bus. Though intended to disrupt the Freedom Rides, the attacks increased national support.[85]

Anxiety intensified following the Birmingham attack. Out of an abundance of concern for the riders' safety, CORE decided to discontinue the Freedom Rides. But SNCC leader Diane Nash would not be deterred and organized ten students from Nashville to continue the rides, first from Birmingham to Montgomery and then to Jackson, Mississippi.[86] Attorney General Kennedy urged riders to desist and suggested a "cooling off period." King bluntly responded, "It's difficult to understand the position of

---

the cause of progress in race relations for a long, long time." See also Carson et al., eds., *The Papers of Martin Luther King, Jr.*; and University of Virginia, "The Struggle for Civil Rights."

84. Garrow, *Bearing the Cross*, 97. On May 17, 1957, more than twenty thousand people gathered on the steps of the Lincoln Memorial for a Prayer Pilgrimage for Freedom. In cooperation with A. Philip Randolph, on October 24, 1958, leaders also organized the Youth March for Integrated Schools at the Lincoln Memorial, in which some ten thousand college students participated.

85. Garrow, *Bearing the Cross*, 165.

86. Norris, "The Woolworth Sit-In."

THE COURAGEOUSLY AUDACIOUS PRACTICE OF HOPE   191

oppressed people. Ours is a way out—creative, moral, and nonviolent . . . It can save the soul of America . . . we've made no gains without pressure and I hope that pressure will always be moral, legal, and peaceful."[87] At each juncture, Freedom Riders met with violence and arrests, yet they persisted in desegregation efforts. On May 29, 1960, Attorney General Kennedy encouraged the Interstate Commerce Commission (ICC), an independent governmental agency, to desegregate interstate transportation facilities.[88] The ICC ordered such actions on September 22, 1961.[89]

Robert McAfee Brown highlights the order's impact. The ICC ruling "prohibit[ed] interstate busses from stopping at segregated terminals" and mandated compliance "whether the bus company operates the facilities or not."[90] Even more, the order afforded legal recourse for Black patrons, as it required facility owners to "display signs pointing out that use of all facilities 'is without regard to race, color, creed or national origin, by order of the Interstate Commerce.'"[91] The ICC ruled segregation illegal for all interstate transportation facilities. Enforcement, however, depended upon state and local governments. This led SNCC to reimagine the Freedom Rides and initiate an aggressive campaign to test state and local compliance with the ICC order, beginning with Albany, Georgia.

On November 1, 1961, SNCC organized an early morning bus ride from Atlanta to Albany. When they arrived in Albany, about a dozen police officers met them at the station with orders from Albany Police Chief Laurie Pritchett to block their access to the White waiting room.[92] SNCC staffers left peacefully but returned at three in the afternoon with nine volunteers who entered the terminal and sat in the White waiting area. When police demanded they leave, the volunteers departed without incident.

Albany quickly became the new focal point in the fight for racial justice and equality. Not only had local and state officials neglected the needs and concerns of Albany's Black community and refused to negotiate with Black leaders, but Albany Mayor Asa D. Kelley Jr., Police Chief Laurie Pritchett, and most members of the city commission sought to maintain a strict segregationist system in all aspects of Albany's public life. Regarding segregation's impact upon Albany's Black citizens, Martin Luther King Jr. wrote, "Twenty-seven thousand Negroes lived in Albany, Georgia, but

87. Garrow, *Bearing the Cross*, 159.
88. Garrow, *Bearing the Cross*, 159.
89. Garrow, *Bearing the Cross*, 167.
90. Brown, "The I.C.C."
91. Brown, "The I.C.C."
92. Garrow, *Bearing the Cross*, 175.

a hundred years of political, economic, and educational suppression had kept them hopelessly enslaved to a demonic, though sophisticated, system of segregation which sought desperately and ruthlessly to perpetuate these deprivations."[93] Despite segregationist leanings, Kelley won his reelection campaign for mayor in November 1961 against a more conservative candidate, largely due to receiving two-thirds of the Black vote. This prompted Black leaders to reassess their approach in Albany.[94]

On Friday, November 17, 1961, local and national movement leaders formed the Albany Movement, a leadership cooperative with the goal of remediating issues impacting Albany's Black community.[95] As in Montgomery, so in Albany participating organizations agreed to convene nightly mass meetings and work cooperatively to address "incidents of police brutality, the lack of employment opportunities for blacks in city government, blacks' exclusion from juries, and the meager job opportunities with private business."[96] On Saturday, December 16, the Albany Movement initiated a march from Shiloh Baptist Church to city hall resulting in the arrest of one hundred protesters, among them King and Abernathy.[97]

On Monday, December 18, the Albany Movement and the city commission reached a tentative agreement.[98] In exchange for releasing more than seven hundred demonstrators without bond, protests would cease for thirty days. The commission also agreed to "appoint an eight-member biracial committee" to facilitate desegregation efforts and to hear a presentation from Black leaders at the commission's first meeting of the new year (in 1962).[99] But soon after local leader Marion Page announced the agreement at Monday's mass meeting, the commission's duplicity became evident. When asked by reporters to confirm the agreement, Pritchett and Kelley denied its existence and insisted that Black demonstrators had posted the necessary bond for their release.[100] News reports characterized the incident a defeat for Albany's Black community.

Given the city's repeated refusal to acknowledge the agreement, Albany's Black community initiated a boycott of major stores on January 11,

---

93. Quoted in King, *The Autobiography*, 153.
94. *The Martin Luther King Research and Education Institute* (website).
95. Garrow, *Bearing the Cross*, 176.
96. Garrow, *Bearing the Cross*, 176.
97. Garrow, *Bearing the Cross*, 184.
98. Garrow, *Bearing the Cross*, 185.
99. Garrow, *Bearing the Cross*, 185.
100. Garrow, *Bearing the Cross*, 186.

1962.[101] They expanded the boycott to include city buses when on January 12, city police arrested Ola Mae Quarterman, an eighteen-year-old student who refused to move to the back of the bus.[102] The boycotts were still underway when King and Abernathy returned to Albany on February 27 and again on July 10.[103] In February, Judge A. N. Durden Sr. found King and Abernathy guilty of leading the December 1961 Albany protests. In July, he sentenced them to forty-five days in jail or $178 fine.[104] King and Abernathy chose jail, but desiring to avoid media scrutiny, Kelly ordered King and Abernathy's release after one night in jail.[105]

Following their release, King, Abernathy, and Albany Movement leaders resumed negotiations with the city. But despite extensive efforts on multiple fronts, success evaded the Albany Movement. According to King, the Albany Movement used "all the methods of nonviolence: direct action expressed through mass demonstrations; jail-ins; sit-ins; wade-ins, and kneel-ins; political action; boycotts and legal actions."[106] But Mayor Kelley, Police Chief Pritchett, and the city commission remained resolute in their opposition to desegregation. The Kennedy administration's hands-off approach to the ICC order also bolstered city officials' resolve to maintain segregation as the norm for Albany's public life.[107]

Not only had city officials and the federal government failed Albany's Black community, Black pastors in the movement also felt abandoned by White Christians. Referencing their faith in the White church, Rev. Samuel B. Wells notes, "The white church, the white community, let us down. The white community was without a heart, without a conscience."[108] The movement's faith in the White church had been misplaced. The movement's labor was not for naught, however. Reflecting upon Albany, King contends, "The people of Albany had straightened their backs" and demonstrated the fortitude and audacity necessary to continue the fight for racial justice and equality.[109] In late August 1962, the Albany Movement turned its attention to voter registration with the goal of seating a more favorable commission.

101. Garrow, *Bearing the Cross*, 190.
102. Garrow, *Bearing the Cross*, 190.
103. Garrow, *Bearing the Cross*, 195.
104. Garrow, *Bearing the Cross*, 202.
105. Garrow, *Bearing the Cross*, 203–4. According to Garrow, Pritchett falsely claimed a well-dressed black man paid their bond in cash. In actuality, Kelley ordered the release.
106. King, *The Autobiography*, 154.
107. King, *The Autobiography*, 217.
108. King, *The Autobiography*, 218.
109. King, *The Autobiography*, 168.

Birmingham, Alabama

Rather than cower in the face of defeat, movement leaders and their respective organizations reevaluated their strategy in Albany. At the conclusion of the assessment, they emerged even more determined to continue the arduous journey toward the beloved community. Soon the SCLC and other organizations set their sights on Birmingham and the SCLC's fall 1962 convention created a point of entry. Rev. Fred Shuttlesworth, pastor of Bethel Baptist Church in Birmingham and founder of the Alabama Christian Movement for Human Rights (ACMHR), proposed Birmingham as the convention site and the executive board agreed.[110]

Civil Rights efforts were already underway in Birmingham. Students from Miles College, with the support of the ACMHR, had initiated a boycott of businesses in Birmingham's downtown district in mid-March 1962.[111] They demanded "desegregation of the stores' facilities, the hiring of black sales clerks, and a general upgrading for black employees."[112] Several Birmingham business owners admitted privately their businesses were suffering, but desegregation seemed improbable without the city commission's expressed support.[113] Securing such support would be difficult, however, because most of Birmingham's city officials were avowed segregationists, especially Public Safety Commissioner Eugene "Bull" Connor.[114]

With the location of Birmingham secured for the upcoming SCLC convention, Shuttlesworth "spread the word that Birmingham would see demonstrations during the SCLC convention if concessions were not made by the merchants."[115] As a result, Birmingham's business community and Black leaders agreed upon a plan to desegregate without demonstration.[116] White merchants agreed to remove "Whites Only" signage in exchange for the cessation of public protests. Both parties honored the agreement during the September 25–28 convention.[117] However, merchants reinstated segregation in October,

---

110. Garrow, *Bearing the Cross*, 199.
111. Posey, "Civil Rights Documentary." See also Turner, "Black History."
112. Garrow, *Bearing the Cross*, 199.
113. Garrow, *Bearing the Cross*, 199.
114. Garrow, *Bearing the Cross*, 199.
115. Garrow, *Bearing the Cross*, 199.
116. Garrow, *Bearing the Cross*, 220. The agreement was secured through a series of conversations between Sidney Smyre, representing Birmingham's business leaders, and President Lucius H. Pitts of Paine College (1958–1974), representing Birmingham's black leaders.
117. Garrow, *Bearing the Cross*, 220. Garrow notes, the convention was overall peaceful until the final day when a twenty-four-year-old member of the Nazi Party attacked King during his closing address. King did not retaliate, and the man was quickly

citing Bull Connor's threats to issue building and fire code violations as the cause.[118] In response, Black leaders reinstituted the boycotts.[119]

During a December 9, 1962, visit to Birmingham, King met with Black leaders. Shortly thereafter, on December 13, a dynamite explosion shook the basement of Bethel Baptist Church, ACMHR's primary gathering space.[120] Though injuries were minor, the bombing evoked outrage among Birmingham's Black citizens and movement leaders. In the days following, King met privately with President Kennedy to urge a stronger stance in favor of civil rights. But as it had in the face of direct action for civil rights in Albany, the Kennedy administration remained hesitant to lend support.[121]

On January 3, 1963, the SCLC's executive committee met to discuss strategies for Birmingham.[122] They identified three major concerns: (1) maintaining cohesion within the Black community, (2) Connor's staunch segregationist stance, and (3) the Kennedy administration's reticence about enforcing the ICC order and advancing civil rights legislation.[123] Strategically, they sought "to precipitate a crisis situation that must open the door to negotiation," a Good Friday protest on April 12, 1963.[124] They believed Connor and the city's negative and potentially violent response would expose the crisis and invite public support for the movement. The pressure of public opinion, therefore, "would become an ally in their cause."[125]

In the weeks preceding the protest, several events transpired. City elections in Birmingham were held on March 5, 1963. Bull Connor was on the ballot for mayor against Alabama's former Lieutenant Governor Albert Boutwell and liberal candidate Tom King. Neither Connor nor his opponents received enough votes to win, necessitating a runoff between Connor and Boutwell. On April 2, Boutwell won the runoff, but Connor

---

removed from the auditorium. The following January, the same man showed up at a gathering in Chicago with five others. At King's request, the police removed the man and his companions without incident.

118. Garrow, *Bearing the Cross*, 221.

119. Garrow, *Bearing the Cross*, 236–37. Black citizens presented six demands: (1) desegregation of downtown stores (2) fair hiring practices by store managers, (3) dismissal of charges against protesters, (4) equal employment opportunities in city government, (5) desegregation of municipal recreation facilities, and (6) the establishment of a biracial committee to facilitate desegregation of all Birmingham establishments.

120. Turner, "Black History."

121. Garrow, *Bearing the Cross*, 225.

122. King, *The Autobiography*, 168.

123. Garrow, *Bearing the Cross*, 227–28.

124. Garrow, *Bearing the Cross*, 228.

125. Garrow, *Bearing the Cross*, 228.

and other segregationists challenged the election's legality and refused to relinquish their seats.[126]

Also on April 2, Students from Miles College initiated sit-ins at lunch counters in four Birmingham establishments, resulting in the arrest of twenty protesters. Additionally, Birmingham's Black community reinstituted the boycott of downtown stores.[127] During the evening's mass gathering King and Shuttlesworth stressed the necessity of continued direct mass action. Good Friday was rapidly approaching, and enthusiasm for protests was waning. Several Black leaders and White liberals "shared the hope that once a moderate administration took office, both the merchants and city government would grant some of the movement's requests without demonstrations being necessary."[128] Father Albert S. Foley, chair of the US Civil Rights Commission's Alabama advisory committee, echoed this sentiment when he "publicly criticized King's entry into Birmingham, asserting that voluntary desegregation of downtown facilities would have taken place shortly if blacks had been willing to wait."[129] Foley preferred private negotiation over public protest. But King disagreed, citing Boutwell's "polite advocacy of continued segregation" as indication that Boutwell would not willingly desegregate Birmingham.[130]

At Saturday's mass gathering on April 6, King announced plans for a Sunday march. His brother A. D., pastor of First Baptist Church in Ensley, Alabama, led the march, which became the precipitating event the SCLC had been anticipating.[131] Bull Connor dispatched canine units to arrest protesters, resulting in a shocking display of unwarranted police violence. National news reporters observed as dogs attacked marchers, in one instance pinning a man to the ground before bystanders could intervene. News of the incident made headlines, providing the movement the national coverage they desired. The movement also gained much-needed support from local leaders. Rather than deter local leaders, law enforcement's brutal response strengthened

---

126. Though Boutwell won the election, Connor and two other commissioners challenged its efficacy. The 1963 election marked a changed in Birmingham's governance from a commission-led government structure to a mayoral governmental structure. Connor and other segregationists argued their term limits were still in effect and refused to surrender control. On May 23, 1963, to the Alabama Supreme Court upheld a ruling by the lower court that Connor and his companions must vacate their seats immediately. Boutwell immediately assumed the mayorship. See United Press International, "Alabama Courts Oust."

127. Garrow, *Bearing the Cross*, 236–37.
128. Garrow, *Bearing the Cross*, 238.
129. Garrow, *Bearing the Cross*, 238.
130. Garrow, *Bearing the Cross*, 238.
131. Garrow, *Bearing the Cross*, 239.

King's appeal for continued direct action among previously reluctant Black professionals, business owners, and religious leaders.[132]

One impediment remained: Birmingham city officials' efforts to derail the march. Not only did Connor deny the ACMHR's request for a march permit. State circuit court Judge William A. Jenkins Jr. issued an injunction banning marches and protests without a permit. But King, Abernathy, and other leaders, though no fan of jail, vowed to defy the order and proceed with the march.[133]

On Good Friday, King and Abernathy and fifty others prepared to march from Sixth Avenue Zion Hill Baptist Church to city hall.[134] As expected, about four blocks into the march, Bull Connor's officers arrested fifteen protesters.[135] That evening, Wyatt Walker led the mass meeting and urged students to rally on Saturday morning. He also solicited volunteers "to 'test' segregated white churches on [Easter] Sunday."[136] SCLC leaders again appealed to President Kennedy to intervene. In response, Kennedy arranged for King and Abernathy to receive phone calls from their wives, Coretta and Juanita, who later visited them in jail.[137]

During his incarceration, King composed "Letter from a Birmingham Jail," dated April 16, 1963 and addressed to White Christian "clergymen." Endeavoring to reveal the moral inadequacy of supporting segregation, King borrows from Thomas Aquinas to elucidate the difference between a just and unjust law:

> An unjust law is a human law that is not rooted in eternal law and natural law. Any law that uplifts human personality is just. Any law that degrades human personality is unjust. All segregation statutes are unjust because segregation distorts the soul and damages the personality. It gives the segregator a false sense of superiority and the segregated a false sense of inferiority... Segregation is not only politically, economically and sociologically unsound, it is morally wrong and sinful.[138]

Segregation and all unjust laws are immoral and inimical to God's law. They distort our sense of identity and prevent us from regarding each other as

---

132. Garrow, *Bearing the Cross*, 239.
133. Garrow, *Bearing the Cross*, 242.
134. Garrow, *Bearing the Cross*, 240.
135. Garrow, *Bearing the Cross*, 242.
136. Garrow, *Bearing the Cross*, 242.
137. Garrow, *Bearing the Cross*, 245.
138. King, *The Autobiography*, 192.

imago Dei. Thereby, they stifle our ability to live as a nondestructive, nondistorting reflect of God's presence in the earth.

On Wednesday, April 24, 1963, Judge Jenkins found eleven of the fifteen defendants guilty of criminal contempt and sentenced each to five days in jail with a fifty-dollar fine.[139] The judge temporarily suspended sentences to allow for appeals, permitting King, Abernathy, and the others to attend the evening's mass gathering. Undeterred by the arrests, King called upon the Black community to continue the boycott. Following Wyatt Walker's example, King also encouraged Black "testers" to visit White churches on Sunday, April 28. Nine of thirty-eight White churches admitted Black worshipers.[140]

Despite the movement's progress, in the Black community enthusiasm for protest continued to dwindle. With the aim of sustaining the movement Wyatt Walker mobilized high school students to join the protests. On Thursday, May 2, hundreds of students left school and gathered at Sixteenth Street Baptist Church for a "pilgrimage to City Hall."[141] Their numbers permitted Walker to send them out in waves, progressively depleting Connor's forces.[142] Connor dispatched police officers with dogs, and firefighters with high-pressure hoses to drive the young protesters back and arrested more than five hundred young marchers.[143] The protest garnered national headlines, and the arrests galvanized the Black community.[144] Incensed by Connor's aggression the day before, numerous supporters gathered at Kelly Ingram Park, just across from Sixteenth Street Baptist, as youth protests resumed the next day. Onlookers yelled insults and threw bottles and rocks toward police, but the young activists remained nonviolent. Though dogs remained in their kennels, Connor again authorized police officers and firefighters to use clubs and high-pressurized hoses to disperse the crowds, garnering another national headline. Young activists remained undeterred and readied themselves for the next protest.

Out of concern for the viability of their businesses, White business leaders again considered potential points of negotiation. While they agreed to desegregate and hire Black employees, they refused to facilitate conversations between city officials and Black leaders.[145] Displeased with the response,

---

139. Garrow, *Bearing the Cross*, 246.
140. Garrow, *Bearing the Cross*, 246.
141. Garrow, *Bearing the Cross*, 246.
142. Garrow, *Bearing the Cross*, 247.
143. Garrow, *Bearing the Cross*, 247.
144. Garrow, *Bearing the Cross*, 248.
145. Garrow, *Bearing the Cross*, 251.

the SCLC, "armed with six hundred young demonstrators ready to invade downtown Birmingham," announced demonstrations would continue until an adequate settlement could be reached.[146] Young people, one might say, saved the day. On Friday, May 10, 1963, the two sides finalized an agreement, which was announced to the press that afternoon.[147] Despite Connor's and other segregationists' efforts to derail the process, a new day was on the horizon, and that was cause for celebration.

On Saturday evening, May 3, unaware the Ku Klux Klan was gathering on the outskirts of town, A. D. King welcomed the Black community to First Baptist Church in Ensley to celebrate the settlement.[148] A little before midnight on Sunday, May 11, 1963, a bomb exploded at A. D.'s home, followed by an explosion at the Gaston Motel.[149] Though no one was injured in the blasts, the bombings awakened memories of the December 9, 1962 bombing at Bethel Baptist Church, fueling outrage throughout the Black community. Thousands took to the streets, and before long a riot ensued. Alabama Governor George Wallace dispatched the state police, who in addition to responding to the violence beat numerous innocent people, including Ann Walker as she was about to enter her husband Wyatt's room at the Gaston Motel.[150]

Concerned the agreement between Birmingham's business leaders and the Black community might be at stake, Black leaders, White business leaders, and the Kennedy administration sprang into action. President Kennedy announced his intentions to "federalize the Alabama National Guard to block use of it by Governor Wallace."[151] He also positioned federal troops near Birmingham in the event that federal intervention became necessary. On Monday, May 12, business leaders held a press conference to reiterate their commitment to the agreement.[152] King and Birmingham's Black leaders visited Black establishments to promote nonviolence as the movement's guiding philosophy.[153] And, on Tuesday Attorney General Robert Kennedy "praised King's leadership and recommended that southern officials allow protests rather than suppress them."[154]

146. Garrow, *Bearing the Cross*, 253.
147. Garrow, *Bearing the Cross*, 258–59.
148. Garrow, *Bearing the Cross*, 259.
149. Garrow, *Bearing the Cross*, 260.
150. King Jr., *Autobiography*, 215.
151. Garrow, *Bearing the Cross*, 261.
152. Garrow, *Bearing the Cross*, 261.
153. Garrow, *Bearing the Cross*, 261.
154. Garrow, *Bearing the Cross*, 262.

Ratification of the agreement between White business leaders and Black leaders appeared certain. Yet Birmingham's staunch segregationists again attempted to derail the process. On Monday, May 20, Birmingham's board of education announced the expulsion or suspension of almost eleven hundred students who had participated in the protests. The NAACP Legal Defense and Education Fund appealed the decision on May 22 in federal district court, but the judge upheld the board of education's decision. Later that day, "Judge Elbert P. Tuttle, of the Fifth Circuit Court of Appeals, not only reversed the decision of the district judge but strongly condemned the Board of Education for its action."[155] Coincidentally and with the tinge of poetic justice, the Alabama Supreme Court resolved the stalemate regarding the change of leadership in Birmingham the next day, ruling in Boutwell's favor and requiring Bull Conner and his segregationist companions to relinquish their seats.[156]

Business and local Black leaders finalized the Birmingham agreement the next day, Friday, May 24, 1963.[157] Building upon the momentum of Birmingham, national civil rights leaders quickly began the process of discerning next steps. King characterizes the summer of 1963 as "a revolution because it changed the face of America."[158] The revolution had begun, I agree, but harvesting America's potential for becoming a beloved community would require perseverance.

The March on Washington for Jobs and Equality

Energized by the successful campaign in Birmingham, Martin Luther King Jr. requested a face-to-face meeting with President Kennedy to discuss civil rights legislation, but Kennedy's aide indicated the president was unavailable.[159] Disappointed by Kennedy's rebuff, Black leaders took two decisive steps. First, King renewed conversations with president of the Brotherhood of Sleeping Car Porters A. Philip Randolph about a march on Washington to pressure Kennedy into advancing civil rights legislation.[160] Randolph and his colleagues with the Negro American Labor Council (NALC) had proposed such a march in 1962 but received minimal support from other civil rights

---

155. King, *The Autobiography*, 215.
156. King, *The Autobiography*, 216.
157. King, *The Autobiography*, 216.
158. King, *The Autobiography*, 219.
159. Garrow, *Bearing the Cross*, 267.
160. Garrow, *Bearing the Cross*, 265.

organizations, even from the SCLC.[161] Nonetheless, Randolph welcomed King's interest and reached out to national civil rights organizations to ascertain their willingness to participate. The response was overwhelmingly favorable. As a second step, at a meeting with Attorney General Robert Kennedy on May 24, 1963, outspoken Black leaders and cultural representatives—among them, writer James Baldwin, psychologist Kenneth Clark, attorney Clarence Jones, and entertainer Harry Belafonte—chided the Kennedy administration for continued delays in advancing civil rights legislation.[162] In response to this and prior appeals, Robert Kennedy began work in earnest on drafting comprehensive civil rights legislation.[163]

Days later, events in Alabama and Mississippi underscored the need for such legislation. On June 11, 1963, "Alabama Governor George Wallace barred the door of the University of Alabama administration building to Deputy Attorney General Katzenbach and two black students seeking to enroll under the provision of the federal court order."[164] President Kennedy immediately federalized the Alabama National Guard, forcing Wallace to permit Katzenbach and the students to enter the building. That evening, President Kennedy announced plans to propose civil rights legislation during a televised address. The moment was shattered, however, when just hours after Kennedy's announcement, a gunman shot and killed Medgar Evers, the NAACP president in Jackson, Mississippi, outside his home in Jackson.[165]

Evers's assassination evoked outrage throughout the movement. It also strengthened movement leaders' resolve to continue the journey toward the beloved community. With the dual aim of convincing Congress to support civil rights legislation and drawing "national attention to the problem of black unemployment," planning for the March on Washington commenced.[166] On June 18, civil rights leaders from the SCLC, SNCC, CORE, NALC, ACMHR, and the Urban League met in A. Philip Randolph's New York office for the first

---

161. King, *The Autobiography*, 220. As noted earlier, Randolph also threatened a 1941 national march on Washington, DC as a means of pressuring president Franklin Roosevelt to end employment discrimination. As a result, Roosevelt signed an executive order to that end and established the Fair Employment Practice Committee. See also University of Maryland, *African-Americans' Rights* (web page), "A House Divided" (section).

162. Garrow, *Bearing the Cross*, 268.
163. Garrow, *Bearing the Cross*, 268.
164. Garrow, *Bearing the Cross*, 268.
165. Garrow, *Bearing the Cross*, 268.
166. Garrow, *Bearing the Cross*, 271.

corporate discussion about the March on Washington.[167] They later settled upon August 28 as a date, with Randolph as march director, Bayard Rustin, a longtime proponent of nonviolent direct action, as Randolph's deputy, and the remaining leaders as cochairs.[168]

Eventually, representatives from various religious fellowships, labor unions, justice movements, and nonprofit organizations joined with celebrities, dignitaries, philanthropists, and others to form one of the most diverse coalitions in American history.[169] Contributions to support the march also poured in, necessitating a process to ensure equitable distribution of funds. On June 19, at a luncheon hosted by Stephen R. Currier, president of the Taconic Foundation for Social Justice Inc., Black civil rights leaders came together and formed the Council for United Civil Rights Leaders (CUCRL), a clearinghouse to receive and distribute funds.[170]

After the Taconic meeting, Martin Luther King Jr. announced plans for the march at the ACMHR's mass meeting in Birmingham.[171] Following King's announcement, Cleveland Robinson and George Lawrence, interim march coordinators, announced the march to members of the New York press corp.[172] Over the next few weeks, the various leaders promoted the march and highlighted its rootedness in "the principle of non-violence."[173] Upon receiving news of the march, President Kennedy immediately

---

167. Garrow, *Bearing the Cross*, 270. Though initially reluctant, the NAACP later joined the effort.

168. King, *The Autobiography*, 222. See also Garrow, *Bearing the Cross*, 279. Original co-chairs included King (SCLC), Wilkins (NAACP), Young (National Urban League), and newly elected chairman John Lewis (SNCC). Later, Walther Reuther (UAW), Rev Eugene Carson Blake (Protestant Church), Rabbi Joachim Prinz (American Jewish Congress), and Mathew Ahmann (Catholic Church) also joined the planning committee. Notably, the AFL-CIO decided to forgo endorsing the march, which, according to Garrow, *Bearing the Cross*, 280, was due to a dispute between NAACP President William "George" Meany and United Auto Workers president Walter Reuther.

169. Malcolm X declined to endorse the march but was among the leaders who attended. See X, *The Autobiography*, 284. See also Brown, "Martin Luther King Jr Met Malcolm X Just Once."

170. *Opencorporates* (website), "Taconic Foundation for Social Justice, Inc." (web page).

171. Garrow, *Bearing the Cross*, 271.

172. Garrow, *Bearing the Cross*, 271.

173. Garrow, *Bearing the Cross*, 274–75. The emphasis upon nonviolence rather than civil disobedience was in contention with the views of SNCC leader Bill Mahoney. The Nation of Islam, which did not eschew the use of physical violence in response to violent attacks, also rejected the exclusive nonviolence emphasis. On the other hand, the NAACP reluctantly joined the effort because of assurances the march would not lead to violent conflict.

summoned Black leaders to the White House.[174] The march, Kennedy complained, was "ill-timed" and could jeopardize his legislation. King emphatically disagreed: "I think it will serve a purpose. It may seem ill-timed. Frankly, I have never engaged in any direct action movement which did not seem ill-timed."[175] Though sympathetic to Kennedy's concerns, the leaders continued plans for the March, which Kennedy later endorsed during a July 17 press conference.

On August 28, 1963, more than two hundred fifty thousand people converged on Washington, DC, to participate in the March on Washington for Jobs and Freedom. They gathered not simply to support President Kennedy's legislation. The ultimate goal, King emphasized, was the "untrammeled opportunity for every person to fulfil his [or her] total individual capacity," beginning with equal employment opportunities and the ability to secure housing without discrimination.[176] To that end, a multiracial, multigenerational, interreligious gathering of marchers from all sectors of American life audaciously and courageously refused to accept racial oppression as America's fated future. Among them, numerous ordinary people to whom King pays homage when he writes, "The stirring emotion came from the mass of ordinary people who stood in majestic dignity as witnesses to their single-minded determination to achieve democracy in their time."[177] The March on Washington for Jobs and Freedom captured the imagination of a nation and, over time, of the world.

The March on Washington as a signpost in the journey toward the beloved community also exposes the complex space female leaders occupied in the civil rights movement. In her article, "Where Were the Women in the March on Washington? How Men in the Civil Rights Movement Erased Women from its Ranks," Jennifer Scanlon reflects upon the March on Washington through the experience of Anna Arnold Hedgeman and other female movement leaders.[178] Describing Hedgeman's leadership in the Negro American Labor Council (NALC), Scanlon writes, "In 1944, the black press had dubbed activist Anna Arnold Hedgeman the 'young feminist' in Civil Rights leader A. Philip Randolph's circle, but nearly twenty years later, in 1963, she had made little progress in convincing him of her right, and other women's right, to exercise full leadership in the black

---

174. Garrow, *Bearing the Cross*, 271.
175. Garrow, *Bearing the Cross*, 272.
176. Garrow, *Bearing the Cross*, 280.
177. King, *The Autobiography*, 221.
178. Scanlon "Where Were the Women."

freedom movement."[179] Though women tirelessly collaborated, created, and advanced the movement's agenda, they were rarely positioned as the public face of the movement. The March on Washington was no different. While the program included speeches from each of the male movement leaders, only one woman was permitted to speak. Citing concerns about the length of the program, Randolph proposed a compromise; a "Tribute to Negro Women Fighters for Freedom," followed by greetings from one female leader.[180] The women ultimately accepted the compromise.

The march commenced at the Washington Monument and concluded at the Lincoln Memorial where throngs of protesters awaited the marchers' arrival. Male movement leaders composed the first tier of marchers. Female movement leaders, including National Council of Negro Women President Dorothy Height, Arkansas NAACP President Daisy Bates, Anna Arnold Hedgeman (NALC), Diane Nash Nevel (SNCC), Rosa Parks, Coretta Scott King, and other female activists composed a second tier alongside the wives of male leaders.[181] Upon their arrival at the Lincoln Memorial, both tiers of leaders stepped onto the dais.

After the opening reflections and introduction, A. Philip Randolph presented the tribute and introduced Daisy Bates. Bates, a newspaper publisher, NAACP director, and Little Rock Central High School desegregation leader, offered remarks on the behalf of women leaders. In an interview with author Jennifer Scanlon, Anna Arnold Hedgeman recounts her experience of the event.

> The meager "Tribute to Negro Women Fighters for Freedom" took place when Daisy Bates stepped to the microphone after an introduction by Randolph, who mistakenly announced she would be giving the women awards. Instead, she announced, "The women of this country, Mr. Randolph, pledge to you, to Martin Luther King, Roy Wilkins and all of you fighting for civil liberties, that we will join hands with you as women of this country." She continued the collective female pledge: "We will kneel-in, we will sit-in, until we can eat at any counter in the United States. We will walk until we are free, until we can walk to any school and take our children to any school in the United States. And we will sit-in and we will kneel-in and we will lie-in

---

179. Scanlon "Where Were the Women."

180. United States National Archives & Records Administration et al., "Official Program for the March on Washington."

181. Scanlon "Where Were the Women."

if necessary until every Negro in America can vote. This we pledge to the women of America.[182]

Women leaders in the civil rights movement reclaimed their time, as Congresswoman Maxine Waters asserted when a male colleague attempted to silence her during a July 29, 2017, Financial Services Committee meeting.[183] Despite attempts to relegate them to the historical margins, the women insisted upon a space on the program and made known their presence and commitment to the movement.

Following the tribute, each of the men rose to speak, culminating with a rousing speech from Rev. Dr. Martin Luther King Jr., known today as "I Have a Dream."[184] King began the speech by identifying Black people's lack of freedom in America as the context for his remarks:

> And so we've come here today to dramatize a shameful condition. In a sense, we've come to our nation's capital to cash a check. When the architects of our republic wrote the magnificent words of the Constitution and the Declaration of Independence, they were signing a promissory note to which every American was to fall heir. This note was a promise that all men, yes, black men as well as white men, would be guaranteed the unalienable rights of "Life, Liberty and the pursuit of Happiness." It is obvious today that America has defaulted on this promissory note insofar as her citizens of color are concerned . . . We refuse to believe that there are insufficient funds in the great vaults of opportunity of this nation. So we've come to cash this check, a check that will give us upon demand the riches of freedom and the security of justice.[185]

King then identified America's defaulted promissory note with Black Americans as cause for concern, necessitating an immediate response to "the fierce urgency of now." With the repetitive refrain "Now is the time," King issued an urgent call for the nation "to make real the promise of democracy," "to rise from the dark and desolate valley of segregation to the sunlit path of racial justice," "to lift our nation from the quicksands of racial injustice to the solid rock of brotherhood," "to make justice a reality for all of God's children."[186]

182. Scanlon "Where Were the Women."
183. Emba, "'Reclaiming My Time.'"
184. King, *The Autobiography*, 223. As many have noted, King's articulation of the dream was an extemporaneous add-on drawn from an earlier speech at an April mass meeting in Birmingham.
185. King, *The Autobiography*, 223.
186. King, *The Autobiography*, 223.

This urgent call demanded an active response from the U.S. government. It also served as a reminder to black America that conceding the fight was not an alternative. And, while King urged black Americans to refrain from physical violence and indiscriminate hatred, he also declared, "there will be neither rest nor tranquility in America until the Negro is granted his citizenship rights. The whirlwind of revolt will continue to shake the foundations of our nation until the bright day of justice emerges."[187]

Having explicated the contextual "Now," King speaks directly to the US government and others like Fr. Foley, who counseled patience to Black America. Responding to the rhetorical question, "When will you be satisfied?" King defiantly declares, "We can never be satisfied" until the material conditions of our lives change.

> We can never be satisfied as long as the Negro is the victim of the unspeakable horrors of police brutality. We can never be satisfied as long as our bodies, heavy with the fatigue of travel, cannot gain lodging in the motels of the highways and the hotels of the cities. We cannot be satisfied as long as the Negro's basic mobility is from a smaller ghetto to a larger one. We can never be satisfied as long as our children are stripped of their selfhood and robbed of their dignity by signs stating: "For Whites Only." We cannot be satisfied as long as a Negro in Mississippi cannot vote and a Negro in New York believes he has nothing for which to vote. No, no, we are not satisfied, and we will not be satisfied until "justice rolls down like waters, and righteousness like a mighty stream."[188]

Echoing the prophet Amos in his litany of dissatisfaction, King encourages the crowd to remain steadfastness in the fight for racial justice and equality.

As the speech concludes, King articulates his dream for the nation in two parts. The first is a comprehensive statement of possibility that dispels the myth of racial oppression's insurmountability.

> Let us not wallow in the valley of despair. I say to you today, my friends: so even though we face the difficulties of today and tomorrow, I still have a dream. It is a dream deeply rooted in the American Dream. I have a dream that one day this nation will rise up and live out the true meaning of its creed—we hold these truths to be self-evident that all men are created equal.[189]

---

187. King, *The Autobiography*, 224.
188. King, *The Autobiography*, 224–25.
189. King, *The Autobiography*, 225.

He then amplifies resonances of Hope, contextualizing the dream within the everydayness of his audience's lives.

> This is our hope. This is the faith that I go back to the South with. With this faith we will be able to hew out the mountain of despair a stone of hope. With this faith we will be able to transform the jangling discords of our nation into a beautiful symphony of brotherhood. With this faith we will be able to work together, to pray together, to go to jail together, to stand up for freedom together, knowing that we will be free one day . . .
>
> And so, let freedom ring from the prodigious hilltops of New Hampshire.
> . . . from the mighty mountains of New York.
> . . . from the heightening Alleghenies of Pennsylvania.
> . . . from the snowcapped Rockies of Colorado.
> . . . from the curvaceous slopes of California.
> . . . from Stone Mountain of Georgia
>
> But not only that. Let freedom ring from Lookout Mountain of Tennessee, from every hill and molehill of Mississippi, from every mountainside, let freedom ring.
>
> And when this happens, when we allow freedom [to] ring . . . we will be able to speed up that day when all of God's children, black men and white men, Jews and Gentiles, Protestants and Catholics, will be able to join hands and sing in the words of the old Negro spiritual, "Free at last, free at last, Thank God Almighty, we are free at last."[190]

King's dream is an invitation to imagine a world in which people with radically different histories and social realities will work together to secure freedom as our shared inheritance. A poignant reminder that freedom becomes possible when we all participate in its actualization.

The March on Washington and President Kennedy's decision to pursue civil right legislation evinced significant progress in the journey toward the beloved community. Yet, even as the eradication of legalized racial oppression was in view, White racial animus toward Black Americans persisted. The deadly potential of racial hatred was on shocking display on Sunday, September 15, 1963. At 10:22 a.m., a bomb stunned worshipers at Birmingham's Sixteenth Street Baptist Church, injuring several and killing four schoolgirls who were attending Sunday school in the church's basement—Addie Mae Collins, Denise McNair, Carole Robertson, and Cynthia Wesley.[191] Outraged by the bombing, hundreds of people flooded the streets resulting in violent

---

190. King, *The Autobiography*, 226.
191. King, *The Autobiography*, 229.

and in one instance deadly confrontations between police officers and Black citizens. Violent racial clashes sparked throughout the city. On September 19, 1963, King and other movement leaders met with President Kennedy. They left, writes King, "with an almost audacious faith that, finally, something positive, something definitive, something real would be done by the leadership of this nation to redeem the community in which horror had come to make its home."[192] But, their faith was again misplaced, as the administration's promised response never materialized.[193]

Two month later, on November 22, 1963, President Kennedy was assassinated while riding in a motorcade through Dealey Plaza in downtown Dallas, Texas.[194] Shots rang out at 12:30 p.m., striking Kennedy in the neck and head.[195] The Secret Service rushed Kennedy to Parkland Memorial Hospital where he was pronounced dead at 1:00 p.m. Vice President Lyndon B. Johnson took the oath of office at 2:38 p.m. and was sworn in as president by US district court judge Sarah Hughes.[196]

Following President Kennedy's assassination, civil rights leaders, allies in Congress, and newly inaugurated president Lyndon B. Johnson united in support of Kennedy's civil rights legislation. On February 10, 1964, the House passed H.R. 7152, which outlawed discrimination on the basis of race, color, religion, sex, or national origin.[197] After extensive debate, the Senate passed the bill on June 19, 1964, and President Johnson signed the bill into law on July 2, 1964.[198] Among attenders at the signing were civil rights leaders Martin Luther King Jr, Dorothy Height, Roy Wilkins, and John Lewis.

---

192. King, *The Autobiography*, 233.

193. The FBI reportedly possessed information about the bombing in 1965, which then FBI Director J. Edgar Hoover stifled. The FBI refutes this claim. In 1977, Alabama Attorney General Bob Baxley brought Ku Klux Klan leader Robert E. Chambliss to trial and a jury subsequently convicted Chambliss of murder. Chambliss died in prison in 1985 still maintaining his innocence. See United States Federal Bureau of Investigation, "Baptist Street Church Bombing."

194. The John F. Kennedy Presidential Library and Museum, "November 22, 1963."

195. The John F. Kennedy Presidential Library and Museum, "November 22, 1963." First Lady Jacqueline Kennedy was in the car with the president but was not injured. Texas governor John Connally was shot in the back and later recovered.

196. The John F. Kennedy Presidential Library and Museum, "November 22, 1963."

197. United States National Archives & Records Administration et al., "The Civil Rights Act of 1964."

198. United States National Archives & Records Administration et al., "The Civil Rights Act of 1964."

Selma, Alabama

Though the Civil Rights Act of 1964 represented significant progress in the journey toward the beloved community, Black Americans still faced large-scale disenfranchisement due to a lack of legal protections for the vote. Naturally, securing the vote became the movement's next milestone, beginning in Selma, Alabama. At the invitation of Dallas County Voter League President Frederick D. Reese, a local pastor and public school teacher, the SCLC initiated plans in December 1964 for a voter registration campaign in Selma.[199] As in Montgomery, Albany, and Birmingham, leaders soon realized no one group would find success by acting alone and agreed to consolidate their efforts under the auspices of the Alabama Project with the SCLC as the project's clearinghouse.[200]

On January 2, 1965, the Alabama Project convened its first mass gathering at Brown Chapel AME Church in Selma to announce the project's voter registration initiative.[201] Protest efforts in Selma began on January 22 when "over one hundred black Selma teachers, led by Voters League President Reese, marched to the courthouse to protest the unfair voter registration system that had denied many of them the ballot."[202] Simultaneously, project lawyers petitioned the courts to restrain city and county officials from obstructing the vote. On January 23, US district court Judge Daniel H. Thomas "issued a temporary restraining order barring Selma and Dallas County officials from hindering voter registration applicants."[203] But Dallas County Sheriff James D. Clark, determined to deny Black citizens the vote, defied the order and persisted in obstructing the registration process. On February 1, Clark arrested 260 protesters as they marched toward the courthouse, among them King and Abernathy, drawing national attention to the movement.[204] On Thursday February 4, Judge Thomas imposed further restrictions, which Clark and other city officials similarly defied.[205]

---

199. King, *The Autobiography*, 272.

200. Garrow, *Bearing the Cross*, 360. In previous years, SNCC, CORE, and the MFDP had initiated voter registration and desegregation campaigns to support Selma's fifty-percent Black population, but success was minimal.

201. Garrow, *Bearing the Cross*, 371.

202. Garrow, *Bearing the Cross*, 381.

203. Garrow, *Bearing the Cross*, 381.

204. Garrow, *Bearing the Cross*, 382.

205. Garrow, *Bearing the Cross*, 385. The second order "instructed the Dallas County registrar to stop using Alabama's difficult registration test, to not reject applicants because of minor errors on the forms, and to process at least one hundred applications each day the registrars met."

King and Abernathy were released from jail on Friday evening. During their brief incarceration, Malcolm X visited Selma in support of the movement and addressed the mass gathering. Mrs. King welcomed Malcolm's support and thought "he seemed sincere," but Martin was less enthusiastic about the visit, noting their philosophical differences.[206] Malcolm X was assassinated a few days later on February 21, 1965 while speaking at the Audubon Ballroom in Harlem, New York. Though King and Malcom never reconciled their differences, King characterized the assassination "an unfortunate tragedy."[207] Indeed, Malcolm X's death was tragic and his voice a great loss to the continual journey toward racial justice and equality.

As the city continued to defy Judge Thomas's orders, the Alabama Project proceeded with plans for a march from Selma to Montgomery on March 7. In anticipation of the march, King announced to a group of registrants at the Dallas County courthouse during a March 1 visit, "We are going to bring a voting bill into being in the streets of Selma."[208] On Sunday, March 7, march coordinators Hosea Williams and James Bevel (SCLC staffers) and John Lewis (SNCC chairperson) led six hundred protesters in double file from Brown Chapel through the streets of Selma.[209] The marchers quietly and carefully wound their way toward the Edmund Pettus Bridge. As they "reached the crest of the bridge, they could see the blue-uniformed state troopers deployed across the four-lane width of U.S. 80 about three hundred yards ahead of them."[210] Trooper commander Major John Cloud ordered the marchers to stop and disperse within two minutes. Lewis and Williams halted the march and stood their ground.[211] After approximately one minute state troopers advanced on Cloud's order, dispensing teargas and viciously beating the protesters. Bruised and battered, the marchers retreated. Television cameras captured the assault, and by Sunday night the troopers' violent attack on peaceful protesters aired on national television. The American public was appalled as they observed the dastardly events of what became known as Bloody Sunday unfold in graphic detail.

The next day, with the nation watching, protesters attempted to cross the bridge again, this time with King leading the march. Determined to avoid a repeat of the previous day's violence, LeRoy Collins director of a new federal agency, the Community Relations Service, and mediator A.

---

206. Garrow, *Bearing the Cross*, 392.
207. Garrow, *Bearing the Cross*, 392.
208. Garrow, *Bearing the Cross*, 393.
209. Garrow, *Bearing the Cross*, 397.
210. Garrow, *Bearing the Cross*, 397.
211. Garrow, *Bearing the Cross*, 397.

M. Secrest reportedly brokered an agreement between King, Sheriff Clark, and state trooper commander Colonel Al Lingo.[212] In exchange for restraint from law enforcement, the marchers would cross the Edmund Pettus Bridge, conduct a ceremony, and return to Brown Chapel.

When King and two-thousand marchers walked across the Edmund Pettus Bridge, they could see the troopers' blockade ahead.

> King led the procession to within fifty yards of the blockade ... King brought the marchers to a halt. He informed the lawmen that his followers would conduct prayers, and different notables came forward to recite homilies as a tense LeRoy Collins watched from the roadside. Then after singing "We Shall Overcome," King and those immediately behind him turned and began to lead the column in a narrow loop back toward Pettus Bridge. Just as they turned, however, the line of troopers that had been blocking the highway suddenly withdrew to the side of the road, leaving it wide open. As newsmen and nervous federal officials looked on, however, each successive rank of marchers followed those in front and turned back across the bridge.[213]

Contrary to Garrow's account, King contends the marchers "did not disengage until they [Clark and Lingo] made it clear they were going to use force."[214] Whatever his reason, the decision to turn back garnered criticism from within the ranks of the Alabama Project and from without, requiring King to do damage control on multiple fronts.[215]

The next few days included a complex series of events. On the evening of the march, White vigilantes attacked three ministers from Massachusetts in downtown Selma, evoking outrage from national leaders and everyday citizens.[216] People sympathetic to the movement organized protests in Chicago, New York, Detroit, Boston, and Washington, DC. In the nation's capital, six hundred people "appeared at the White House to call for federal intervention," and "fifty members of Congress denounced the attack."[217] To curtail civil unrest, law enforcement cordoned off the neighborhood around Brown Chapel and blocked all attempts to march. Movement supporters held vigils and awaited word regarding the three men's health. And, in a public statement, President Johnson called upon

---

212. Garrow, *Bearing the Cross*, 401.
213. Garrow, *Bearing the Cross*, 402.
214. King, *The Autobiography*, 281.
215. King, *The Autobiography*, 281.
216. Garrow, *Bearing the Cross*, 404.
217. Garrow, *Bearing the Cross*, 405.

the nation to join him in denouncing the attacks and announced his intent to advance voting rights legislation.[218]

Following his public statements, Johnson met with Alabama Governor George Wallace to impress upon Wallace the necessity of voting rights for Black Americans. Following the meeting, Johnson invited Wallace to accompany him to a press conference in the White House rose garden.[219] With reporters and civil rights activists present, Johnson asserted, "It is wrong to do violence to peaceful citizens in the streets of their town. It is wrong to deny Americans the right to vote. It is wrong to deny any person full equality because of the color of their skin."[220] He then divulged to all his directive that Wallace support voting rights in Alabama. Wallace offered no public response. On Monday, March 15, Johnson again urged the nation to support the movement: "Their cause must be our cause too. Because, it is not just Negroes, but really it is all of us, who must overcome the crippling legacy of bigotry and injustice."[221] Johnson called upon the nation to live true to its founding ideal of liberty and justice for all.

On Sunday, March 21, 1965, the SCLC initiated its third march from Selma to Montgomery. More than three thousand marchers convened at Brown Chapel AME Church in Selma and made their way to the Edmund Pettus Bridge. Though state troopers were present, the marchers crossed the bridge without incident and commenced upon a five-day walking journey from Selma to Montgomery, their numbers swelling daily. On Thursday, March 25, more than twenty-five thousand mostly Black protesters and a growing number of allies converged on the Alabama state capital to stand against the disenfranchisement of Black citizens throughout the nation.[222] The 1965 Voting Rights Act was signed into law on August 6, 1965, prohibiting voter disenfranchisement.[223] The act outlawed literacy tests and

---

218. Garrow, *Bearing the Cross*, 405.
219. Garrow, *Bearing the Cross*, 405.
220. Garrow, *Bearing the Cross*, 407.
221. "President Johnson's Special Message to the Congress."
222. Garrow, *Bearing the Cross*, 411–12. Sadly, the excitement over the march's success was muted the next day when Viola Gregg Liuzzo's murder became public. Liuzzo, a white Detroit "housewife" was shot and killed by Klan night riders as she and a young black SCLC volunteer traveled to Montgomery through Lowndes County to help ferry marchers back to Selma. Liuzzo's suspected killer, Klansman Collie Leroy Wilkins, evaded conviction when a Lowndes County jury deadlocked at his trial despite eyewitness testimony from an FBI informant.
223. The Voting Rights Act was amended and reauthorized in 1970, 1975, 1982, 2006. The House again voted to reauthorize the Act in 2019. However, as of October 2020, the most recent reauthorization had not been taken up by the Senate.

provided federal oversight of voting regulations in counties resistant to securing Black citizens' right to vote.[224]

Tragically, on April 4, 1968, while in Memphis, Tennessee, to support a sanitation workers' strike, Dr. King was assassinated as he stood on the balcony of the Lorraine Motel. King's sermon the night prior at the Mason Temple Church appeared to foreshadow his untimely death. Highlighting parallels between his and the biblical deliverer Moses's experience, King assured his audience that though he may not get to the land of freedom and equality with them, God had allowed him to "go up to the mountain" and see "the promised land."[225] On April 9, 1968, family, friends, movement leaders, activists, and a grateful nation bade farewell to this monumental figure and architect of freedom.

The civil rights movement did not end with King's death. In 1965, the Coordinating Council of Community Organizations invited the SCLC and other civil rights organizations to join their campaign against housing discrimination, which gave birth to the Chicago Campaign. The NAACP, the National Association of Real Estate Brokers, the GI Forum, and the National Committee against Discrimination in Housing lobbied Congress to adopt fair housing legislation prohibiting housing discrimination against African Americans, Hispanics, and other minoritized groups, including veterans of the Vietnam War and their families.[226] On April 4, 1968, the day of King's assassination, the Senate passed Title VIII of the Civil Rights Act, the Fair Housing Act, prohibiting discrimination in renting, selling, or financing a house based upon race, religion, national origin, or sex. The House of Represaentatives passed the bill on April 10, and President Johnson signed the Fair Housing Act into law the next day.[227]

Since 1968 a wide range of local, national, and international organizations have joined the journey toward a more loving, just, and life-affirming existence for all creation. Among those groups most closely identified with the civil rights movement of the 1950s to 1960s are Marian Wright Edelman's Children's Defense Fund (founded in 1973), Rev. Al Sharpton's National Action Network (founded in 1991), the Samuel Dewitt Proctor Conference (begun in 2003), and Rev. Dr. William Barber II's Repairers

---

224. Garrow, *Bearing the Cross*, 406.

225. Garrow, *Bearing the Cross*, 621. Many scholars, including this writer, advocate new metaphors for the journey toward justice and equality, as the biblical image of "promised land" predicates the promise of one group upon the displacement and destruction of another.

226. United States Department of Housing and Urban Development "History of Fair Housing."

227. United States Department of Justice, Fair Housing Act.

of the Breach movement, and Poor People's Campaign: A Call for Moral Revival (begun in 2015).[228] Grassroots organizations also arose in response to the pressing concerns of the day. These groups include organization that have blossomed into international movements, such as Black Lives Matter (begun in 2013) and the Women's March (begun in 2016); and political action efforts such as Fair Fight (begun in 2019); and small, local community-action organizations such as the Greater Duval Neighborhood Association in my hometown of Gainesville, Florida.[229] Numerous international efforts also joined the journey, including Bring Back Our Girls in response to the abduction of Chibok schoolgirls in Nigeria; the Mothers of Plaza de Mayo March in response to disappeared children in Buenos Aires, Argentina; and *Akashingo*, meaning "the Brave Ones" in Shona, Zimbabwe, a group of female rangers dedicated to protecting elephants and other wildlife from poachers.[230] These organizations all share in common an imaginative abundance that provokes purposeful, Hope-filled action indicative of Hope's assurance and call. They in no wise represent a comprehensive list of communal and individual efforts toward living with Hope; the numbers are immense. Nor do their efforts exhaust the human capacity to imagine possibilities or our ability to live true to our identity as *imago Dei*. For as quiet as it is kept amid the clanging noise of despair, many have answered yes to Hope's assurance and call.

Wisdom from the Journey

The African American journey toward justice and equality, viewed through the lens of the beloved community, is a case study in the courageously audacious practice of living with Hope. It is an example of sustained multigenerational communal responsiveness to Hope's assurance and call under adverse and oftentimes deadly conditions. In this respect, insights from this journey provide faithful proclaimers wisdom for enabling those with whom we preach to sense and respond to Hope's assurance and call. The first insight highlights the necessity for an image of possibility sufficient enough to sustain us in the present and toward the future. In Chapter 4, we described Jesus's proclamation of the good news of the kin(g)dom of God as such an image, as the archetypal reservoir from which Hope's anticipatory

---

228. See websites (listed in the bibliography) for the Children's Defense Fund, the Samuel Dewitt Proctor Conference, and Repairers of the Breach.

229. See the websites (listed in the bibliography) for Black Lives Matter, the Women's March, Fair Fight, and the Greater Duval Neighborhood Association.

230. See the website (listed in the bibliography) for Bring Back Our Girls; and also Nuwer, "Meet the 'Brave Ones.'"

language flows. In Chapter 5, we proposed the use of "thick description" to enhance the gospel's accessibility and intelligibility for modern-day worshipers, especially as regards the use of "kingdom" language. Whether one chooses the biblical language (the expressions "kingdom of God" or "kingdom of heaven") or terms such as "kin-dom of God," "kinship community," "reign of God," or "beloved community," thick description can enhance our ability to make the gospel accessible, intelligible, and inspirational enough to power imaginative abundance and purposeful, Hope-filled action. Martin Luther King Jr.'s use of thick description is evident in his explication of the beloved community. He describes and makes accessible a theologically grounded, contextually significant vision of possibility that reflects in microcosm the ethical demands of the kin(g)dom of God. When proclaiming the good news of the kin(g)dom of God, preachers today might likewise thicken our descriptive language and choose contextualized images that embody the ethical thought and practice necessary to live as citizens of God's still-emerging community.

The journey also highlights the necessity of acknowledging humanity's inherent identity as *imago Dei*. To acknowledge is to claim for ourselves and for others the dignity and respect due all people. And it is to surrender to the soulish desire for loving and just relationship with God, self, and others. Surrender of this sort can empower us to repudiate systemic and individual acts of violation, oppression, and dehumanization, no matter where they exist or by whose authority they persist. Black people's assiduous rejection of past acts of overt racial animus and of the various microaggressions and systemically racist practices today is rooted in soulish awareness of their inherent identity as *imago Dei* and our value as human beings. "Black lives matter!" in this sense, is more than a rallying cry. It is a prophetic declaration and proclamation of truth in and to a society that throughout its history has perpetuated the notion that Black life is both insignificant and expandable.

Preaching that acknowledges humanity's inherent identity as *imago Dei* amplifies Hope's resonance within in two respects. First, it makes known the inherent value of all people and particularly of those individuals and communities who bear the sting of oppression and devaluation as a daily reality. This aspect of acknowledgment reminds us and the communities with whom we preach about our call to partnership with God. We are not called to dominate, exploit, oppress, take, displace, destroy, or otherwise negate or dishonor any aspect of God's creation. God calls us to manifest, to *bring to light* or *prove by our actions,* God's expansive love for all people and all creation. Second, preaching that acknowledges the *imago Dei* within humanity gives meaning to the troubling in our souls, to the *something within* that will not permit us to become or remain comfortable with attitudes, practices, and institutional arrangements that negate and dehumanize. It authorizes and invites expressions of righteous discontent and holy indignation in opposition to injustice, inequality, and maltreatment in any form.[231] And it conjures within us the courage and audacity to exclaim, as Fannie Lou Hamer did, "I'm sick and tired of being sick and tired."[232] This sentiment enlivens imaginative abundance and powers purposeful, Hope-filled action even when life's circumstances suggest futility.

The necessity of sustained imaginative abundance and purposeful, Hope-filled action grows naturally out of the previous insights. For four hundred years, Black leaders, activists, and everyday people, enslaved and free, imagined the possibility of wholeness, health, and prosperity for themselves and future generations as a tangible, realizable destination for the journey toward justice and equality. Efforts to forestall the vision, however, have made for a long and arduous journey with more death-dealing, heart-breaking, dignity-denying obstacles than we care to enumerate. These realities necessitate, in addition to an ultimate vision of possibility, contextually significant intermediating images to sustain imaginative abundance in each historical era. During the era of enslavement, Black people imagined themselves free from the dehumanizing gaze of a slaveholding nation; free from chains, toils, violence, and violation, and free for life more abundantly. During the Reconstruction era, with the sweet taste of freedom in their mouths, Black people imagined themselves free for the full benefits of US citizenship. But the nation's defaulted promise of citizenship during the Jim/Jane Crow era necessitated reconstitution of the dream with visions of freedom from racialized violence and oppression once again. During the civil rights era, Black people again imagined themselves free for full citizenship, an imagining that undergirded their unequivocal demand for civil and voting rights, equal housing and employment opportunities, and equal protection under the law. With those freedoms legally secured, Black people today imagine themselves free for the rights afforded to all US citizens: the Declaration's guarantee of equality and its acknowledgment of life, liberty, and the pursuit of happiness without discrimination, violence, or marginalization based upon phenotype or any other distinguishing factor. When

---

231. See Higginbotham, *Righteous Discontent*; Parker, *Trouble Don't Last Always*; Crawford, *Hope in the Holler*; Townes, *Breaking the Fine Rain of Death*; and Brown, *Can a Sistah*. These authors and others affirm expressions of discontent as theological praxis.

232. Hamer, *The Speeches*, 62. According to the epigraph, "Hamer delivered this speech with Malcolm X at a rally at the Williams Institutional CME Church, Harlem, New York, that was organized to support the Mississippi Freedom Democratic Party's Congressional Challenge."

preachers, teachers, activists, and everyday folk make the vision plain, they also enhance each era's intermediating image's potential to transform life in the present and nurture imaginative abundance for the future.

Intermediating images power sustained imaginative abundance by augmenting our ultimate vision of possibility, contextualizing it for the present and catalyzing purposeful, Hope-filled action. Incorporating intermediating images in preaching can likewise enhance our ability to contextualize the gospel for the (local, national, and global) moment in which we stand so that we and the people with whom we preach can live responsive to Hope's assurance and call. While we continue to live in anticipation of God's kin(g)dom fully realized, intermediating images enable preachers to make known the implications of Jesus's gospel proclamation for life in the present. The kin(g)dom of God *continues* to come near, inviting faithful proclaimers to preach the gospel, not only in the thin sense of its eschatological trajectory, but also in the thick sense of its significance for the quality of our relationships with God, self, and others and for our ability to navigate the contextual realities and dynamics we encounter as we daily perform our lives. Incorporating intermediating images of possibility enable us to make sociopolitical and ecclesial maladies even the more evident in our preaching by drawing them out of abstraction so that we can name, resist, remediate, and transform them. Through the use of intermediating images in preaching, in other words, we make the vision plain, which enables the people with whom we preach, and ourselves, to discern and embrace new patterns of perceiving, thinking, imagining, and behaving—patterns grounded in the ethic to which the gospel invites us.

As faithful gospel proclaimers, we are called to the courageous and audacious task of making the vision plain. This is no small matter in a world in which visions of division, destruction, and discord predominate. Yet God invites us to amplify Hope's assurance and call by taking up as our own Jesus's gospel proclamation and the ethic to which it invites us. God invites us to live in right relationship with God, self, and others, even when righting relationship entails crossing boundaries too ideologically entrenched to imagine, or severing negating and destructive bonds for the sake of others' well-being, our own well-being, or both. God urges us to name the disordered state of our existence and discern possibilities for its remediation and transformation, even when we and the structures to which we are attached are the ones in need of transformation. God calls us to envisage our world through the prism of God's *shalom* and to live as if that reality were already discernible in our midst—to acknowledge humanity's inherent identity as *imago Dei* and our vocational call to live as a nondistorting, nondestructive reflection of God's presence in the earth.

God invites us to say yes to God's yes for creation and for our own lives, and no to the deceptive language of despair's invitation to acquiesce. God calls us to courageously and audaciously proclaim, demonstrate, and advocate the gospel in word and deed so that we—these faithful proclaimers and the communities with whom we preach—might steadfastly live toward a more loving, just, and God-infused existence for all creation.

—— EPILOGUE ——

Contemplating Embodied Hope

I CONCLUDE THIS BOOK by reflecting upon our conversation thus far and wondering what I want readers to take away from our journey together—what insight, vision of possibility, or nugget of truth. I begin, therefore, with my most elemental claim, that Hope is an ontological necessity—necessary for life, for survival, for vocation, for a qualitatively better state of existence, which I describe as a more loving, just, and God-infused existence for humanity, the earth, and all the earth's inhabitants. Throughout our conversation, we have described embodied Hope as a conceptual metaphor for that which creates within human beings yearning for wholeness and well-being. Hope, we've said, is the always-speaking voice of God's Spirit assuring us of God's presence, power, and faithfulness, and calling us to participate in God's loving, just, and restorative work in the world. Equally important are my contentions regarding theological anthropology: We are beings created in God's likeness, vivified by divine *ruach* (the Hebrew word for "breath" or "wind"), and called to live as a nondistorting, nondestructive reflection of God's presence in the earth, as fitting partners in God's redemptive work in the world.

Faithful proclaimers and the people with whom we preach share in common our inherent identity as *imago Dei*. Hope's presence within is an aspect of that identity and at least one of the means by which the Spirit invites us to link our hearts with the heart of God for the sake of our own well-being and the well-being of creation.[1] We sense Hope's presence as a yearning within, as a *something within* us that when perceived will not permit us to remain comfortable with the disordered state of our existence. It seems important, therefore, to reiterate the role of preaching in nurturing our ability to live with Hope. Faithful proclaimers seek to amplify Hope's resonance, to

---

1. Though not the focus of the current research, I am convinced Love and Faith are also sensibilities by which the Spirit makes her presence within us known.

strengthen our sensitivity to Hope's assurance and call as well as to our own deep yearning for wholeness and well-being. Preaching also acknowledges the dialectical tension in which we live—the dissonance between the world we know and the world to which Hope invites us. But rather than endorse acquiescence to the way things are as the only possibility for life, preaching invites and emboldens us to reimagine or reenvision our world and our participation in it through the prism of God's *shalom* as revealed in Jesus's gospel proclamation. Our practices of proclaiming, demonstrating, and advocating the gospel in word and deed bear witness to the radical possibility of a different kind of world and invite all with whom we preach to live as though that world were already coming to fruition. We also endeavor to make known, as did the apostle Paul in his Letter to the Romans (12:1), that lending our hands to God's redemptive work is our "reasonable" (KJV) or logical service as *imago Dei* and as Christian people of faith.

The capacity to imagine or dream is among humanity's greatest gifts, a third insight I wish to highlight. Echoing Patricia Williams, we can change our world for better or worse by way of imagination. Evil imaginings, when systemically and socially sanctioned, diminish well-being and legitimize dehumanization of myriad forms—from enslavement to internment to genocide to ethnic cleansing to physical and psychic abuse to indiscriminate violence, murderous impulses, the infliction of pain and suffering, violation, exploitation, oppression, suppression, and numerous other heinous acts impacting individuals and communities across the globe. Indifference and apathy fuel and are fueled by evil imaginings, making those of us who surrender to such impulses unwitting accomplices in dehumanization's deep entrenchment in our world today. Evil imaginings rob us of the ability to live true to our vocational call.

Hope, on the other hand, calls us to a life of vocation, invites us to say yes to God's yes for creation and for our lives by adopting God's vision of *shalom* as our own. Hope's resonance within enables us to imagine the day when all will be well, and no one will be relegated to the margins or to a life of dearth; to envisage a time when our shared inheritance of wholeness, health, and prosperity will become a tangible reality; a day when the inadequacies of the present will give way to new life. We make such Hope-filled dreams tangible, not by wishful thinking or blind faith in a social system, theology, or ideology, but through concrete acts of justice, love, and peace grounded in ethical and moral imperatives that arc us toward the good for all. Hope-filled imaginings engender life, and that life more abundantly, which becomes possible when people of faith and good conscience live into our vocational call.

Many Christian people of faith experience our call to vocation through Jesus's gospel proclamation: the good news of the kin(g)dom of God. We have described Jesus's gospel proclamation as the archetypal reservoir through which Hope's anticipatory language flows. The gospel echoes Hope's assurance and call and invites a human response, as Jesus demonstrates throughout his preaching, teaching, healing, and delivering ministry. Responding to Hope's assurance and call today involves the courageously audacious act of living with Hope, of adopting patterns of imagining, perceiving, thinking, and behaving indicative of the ethical thought and practice to which the gospel invites us. Living with Hope entails attending to the quality of our relationship with God, self, and others; living with Hope entails seeking each day to exemplify in word and deed our immense love for God, for neighbor, and for all that God has created. Living with Hope, in other words, is more expansive and expressive than words alone. Living with Hope involves attending to the numerous ways we articulate our lives, including our religious sensibilities, communal engagement, and civic deportment.

Thus far, our conversation has privileged communal responses to Hope's assurance and call. Therefore, it seems important in these concluding comments to note in a more pronounced manner the significance of living with Hope for our individual sense of well-being. If Jesus's gospel proclamation is indeed the reservoir through which Hope's anticipatory language flows, as I have claimed, where does our personal need for wholeness, health, and prosperity enter this conversation? Many of us overlook or minimize the final two words of Jesus's response to the lawyer's question about the greatest commandment in Matt 22:39: "And the second is like it: 'You shall love your neighbor *as yourself.*'" Jesus unambiguously appropriates Lev 19:18, omitting only the final clause: "I am the LORD." I wish to reappropriate this final clause, as it adds gravity to God's injunction against exploiting the neighbor and reveals God's positive valuation of self-love as the foundation upon which neighbor love rests. Viewed through this theological lens, self-love is also a practice of Hope. We live with Hope, in other words, when we tend our own emotional, physical, and spiritual well-being.

Self-love as a practice of Hope includes but is not limited to permitting ourselves to give and receive love; to pray, meditate, and connect with others; to eat well, exercise, laugh, play, study, and work; and to build, create, imagine, and explore. Practicing self-love involves acknowledging our inherent identity as *imago Dei,* recognizing the *Godness* within, and knowing ourselves as deserving recipients of the inheritance of wholeness, health, and prosperity we share with all creation. Hope's assurance and call afford us the right to speak and stand in prohibited spaces, to transgress boundaries erected to isolate or exclude, to know more than others think is good for us, to live interdependently with others who also desire our well-being, and to do so without facing harassment, violence, or violation in any form. Hope's resonance within, the troubling in our souls, beckons us to not only respond to the needs of others but also acknowledge and seek to remediate the brokenness in our own lives; to name violence, suffering, oppression, and other forms of dehumanization as such, no matter their source or by whose authority they are sanctioned. Self-love as a practice of Hope involves the refusal to acquiesce to the notion that unhealthy, life-denying, sorrow-inducing life circumstances are natural, normal, acceptable, and inevitable for our lives and to acknowledge ourselves as subjects of God's vision of *shalom* with all creation.

I am compelled by Thomas Hayden's assertion: "The existence of evil requires the consciousness of good." The consciousness of good entails more than the acknowledgment that evil exists. It also entails cognizance, wokeness, intentional awareness of that which promotes the good. This includes awareness of our ability to live toward the well-being of creation—our own, others', and the earth's as our shared home. The good, at its most basic level, is that which promotes a loving, just, and life-affirming existence for all. As faithful gospel proclaimers, we pray that our sermons will indeed awaken the people with whom we preach as ourselves to that which promotes the good. And we pray that our sermons will embolden individuals and communities to envision and work toward a qualitatively better state of existence for all creation as made evident in Jesus's gospel proclamation of the kin(g)dom of God. For God knows, "the world would be worse off if no one did"![2] May we lend our hearts and hands to the actualization of a more loving, just, and God-infused existence for all creation.

---

2. Hayden, *Irish on the Inside*, 67.

— APPENDIX —

A Critical Analysis for Preaching (ACAP)

Exposing Distortions and Amplifying Hope's Assurance and Call

Identify Congregation (name and brief description):

Reference Biblical Text

A. Exposing Distortion

1. Describe the problem to which the sermon responds. By what tangible or observable means does this problem reveal itself?

2. If required to describe the problem to which this sermon responds to a group of ten-year-olds and a group of sixty-year-olds together, how would I describe it?

3. When in history does this problem arise? What has contributed to its persistence over time? In what stories, tales, or images do we experience it? Is it embodied in colloquial sayings, common practices, or myths? If so, how? (*This would be a great time to consider the role of negating images, myths, ideologies, and theologies in perpetuating the problem. Also consider how ecclesial and cultural mores, attitudes, practices, beliefs, assumptions, biases, isms, and other harmful dispositions enable the problem's persistence.*)

4. What have I or has my congregation seen, heard, or experienced that reinforces the idea that this malady is unchangeable? That it is beyond remediation? How does my worship community or the church contribute to the view that this malady is unchangeable? How does

my society contribute to the view that this malady or problem is unchangeable? To what extent do I believe this malady is unchangeable?

5. In what way, if any, has Christian theology or the church's history of biblical interpretation perpetuated the problem?

6. How does Jesus's gospel proclamation shed light on the dangers of this problem?

B. Analyzing the Impact

7. Who benefits most from the continuation of this problem? In what ways do I or the people with whom I preach benefit from the problem's continuation? Describe these benefits and their significance for the congregation, its members, or my own well-being.

8. How does this problem impact people's quality of life in my community—physical, spiritual, emotional, relational?

9. In what ways is the problem I have identified compelling or enticing for people I know? How does it hinder our ability to image alternative possibilities reflective of God's desire for *shalom*? In what ways does the problem thwart our ability to practice empathy tempered with compassion?

10. Who is harmed by the continuation of this problem? Describe the harm. What danger does the identified harm pose for vulnerable people throughout the world and in this particular congregation? How does the harm impact other living beings and the natural world? What implications does this harmful impact hold for the life of this congregation or for the well-being of its members?

11. What risks might I incur as a result of exposing the mechanistic rootedness of this problem and its implications for people within and without the congregation with whom I preach? How do those risks impact my ability to live into my vocation as faithful proclaimer, congregational leader, or both?

C. Inviting a Faithful Response

12. To what faithful response does this inquiry invite me and the congregation with whom I preach?

13. In what way is this response affirmed by Scripture, experiences, theology, reason, and Jesus's ministerial vision of the kin(g)dom of God?

14. What risk might the congregation incur by embracing this response? Is negating the malady worth the risk? If so, why?

15. Given the range of biblical, exegetical, theological, rhetorical, demonstrative, ecclesial, sociocultural, and other such resources available to me as a preacher and coworshiper with the congregation, how will the sermon enhance the congregation's ability to live with Hope? That is, how will it heighten the congregation's sensitivity to Hope's assurance of God's power, faithfulness, and redemptive presence, and call to colabor with God in actualizing God's vision of *shalom* as a realizable possibility?

Bibliography

Aaron, Charles L. "Exegetical Perspective: Matthew 3:1–6." In *Feasting on the Gospels: Matthew*. Vol. 1, *Chapters 1–13*. Edited by Cynthia A. Jarvis and E. Elizabeth Johnson. 2 vols. Louisville: Westminster John Knox, 2013, Kindle.

Act XII, *Laws of Virginia*, December 1662. In *Statutes at Large*, edited by W. W. Henning, 2:170.

Acts of the Commonwealth of Virginia, 1667 and 1705, *Acts of the Commonwealth of Virginia, 1642–43, December 1662, October 1705*, cited in *The Statutes At Large; Being A Collection of all the Laws of Virginia, from the First Session of The Legislature In The Year 1619*, vols I and II, edited by William Waller Henning. New York: Bartow, 1823. https://www.thirteen.org/wnet/slavery/experience/legal/docs1.html/.

Addleshaw, G. W. O. *The High Church Tradition: A Study in the Liturgical Thought of the Seventeenth Century*. London: Faber & Faber, 1941.

Ahmed, Saeed, and Ralph Ellis. "Mass Shooting at Inland Regional Center: What We Know." *CNN*, updated December 5, 2015. https://www.cnn.com/2015/12/03/us/what-we-know-san-bernardino-mass-shooting/index.html/.

Allen, Donna. *Toward a Womanist Homiletic: Katie Cannon, Alice Walker, and Emancipatory Proclamation*. Martin Luther King Jr. Memorial Studies in Religion, Culture, and Social Development 13. New York: Lang, 2013.

Allen, George N. "Must Jesus Bear the Cross Alone?" (1852). In *Baptist Standard Hymnal with Responsive Readings*, edited by Mrs. A. M. Townsend, hymn 404. Nashville: Sunday School Publishing Board, National Baptist Convention, U.S.A., 1961.

Alves, Rubem A. *A Theology of Human Hope*. Washington, DC: Corpus, 1969.

Allyn, Bobby. "Ex-Dallas Officer Who Killed Man In His Own Apartment Is Found Guilty of Murder." *National Public Radio*, Oct. 1, 2019. https://www.npr.org/2019/10/01/765788338/ex-dallas-officer-who-killed-neighbor-in-upstairs-apartment-found-guilty-of-murd/.

Anderson, E. Byron. "Liturgical Catechesis: Congregational Practice as Formation." *Religious Education* 92 (1997) 349–62.

Aptheker, Herbert. *A Documentary History of the Negro in the United States*. Vol. 2, *From the Reconstruction to 1910*. New York: Citadel, 1951.

Baker-Fletcher, Karen. "The Strength of My Life." In *Embracing the Spirit: Womanist Perspectives on Hope, Salvation, and Transformation,* edited by Emilie M. Townes, 122–39. Bishop Henry McNeal Turner/Sojourner Truth Series in Black Religion 13. Maryknoll, NY: Orbis, 1997.

Baldwin, Lewis V., and Victor Anderson. "The Promptings of Some Beneficent Force: Dimensions of the 'Spiritual' in the Life and Language of Martin Luther King Jr." In *Revives My Soul Again: The Spirituality of Martin Luther King Jr*. Minneapolis: Fortress, 2018, Kindle ed.

Bauer, Walter. *A Greek-English Lexicon of the New Testament and Other Early Christian Literature.* Edited by F. William Gingrich and Frederick W. Danker. 2nd rev. ed. Chicago: University of Chicago Press, 1979.

Bedford, Nancy E. "Theological Perspective: Matthew 4:12–17." In *Feasting on the Gospels: Matthew.* Vol. 1, *Chapters 1–13,* edited by Cynthia A. Jarvis and E. Elizabeth Johnson. 2 vols. Louisville: Westminster John Knox, 2013, Kindle.

Berkes, Howard. "New Studies Confirm a Surge in Coal Miners' Disease." *National Public Radio,* May 22, 2018. https://www.npr.org/2018/05/22/613400710/new-studies-confirm-a-surge-in-coal-miners-disease/.

Black Lives Matter (website). https://blacklivesmatter.com/.

Bogel-Burroughs, Nicholas. "8 Minutes, 46 Seconds Became a Symbol in George Floyd's Death: The Exact Time Is Less Clear." *New York Times,* updated June 20, 2020. https://www.nytimes.com/2020/06/18/us/george-floyd-timing.html/.

Booth, Amy. "Mothers of Argentina's Disappeared March Against G20." *Aljazeera,* Nov. 29, 2018. https://www.aljazeera.com/news/2018/11/29/mothers-of-argentinas-disappeared-march-against-g20/.

Bring Back Our Girls (website). https://bringbackourgirls.ng/.

Brown, DeNeen L. "Martin Luther King Jr. Met Malcolm X Just Once: The Photo Still Haunts Us with What Was Lost." Retropolis. *Washington Post,* Jan. 14, 2018. https://www.washingtonpost.com/news/retropolis/wp/2018/01/14/martin-luther-king-jr-met-malcolm-x-just-once-the-photo-still-haunts-us-with-what-was-lost/.

Brown, Robert McAffee. "The I.C.C. and Integration." *Christianity and Crisis* 21/17 (1961) 170.

Brown, Teresa L. Fry. *Can a Sistah Get a Little Help? Encouragement for Black Women in Ministry.* Cleveland: Pilgrim, 2008.

———. *God Don't Like Ugly: African American Women Handing on Spiritual Values.* Nashville: Abingdon, 2000.

———. *Weary Throats and New Songs: Black Women Proclaiming God's Word.* Nashville: Abingdon, 2003.

Bruckner, James K. "A Theological Description of Human Wholeness in Deuteronomy 6." *Ex Auditu* 21 (2005) 1–19.

Brueggemann, Walter. "The Costly Loss of Lament." *Journal for the Study of the Old Testament* 36 (1986) 57–71.

———. "The Formfulness of Grief." *Interpretation* 31 (1977) 263–75.

———. *Hope within History.* Atlanta: John Knox, 1987.

———. *The Prophetic Imagination.* 2nd ed. Minneapolis: Fortress, 2001.

Buechner, Frederick. *Wishful Thinking: A Seeker's ABC.* Rev. and exp. ed. San Francisco: HarperSanFrancisco, 1993.

Bullard, Robert D. "Anatomy of Environmental Racism and the Environmental Justice Movement." In *Confronting Environmental Racism: Voices from the Grassroots,* edited by Robert D. Bullard and Benjamin Chavis Jr., 15–40. Boston: South End, 1999.

———. "Introduction." In *Confronting Environmental Racism: Voices from the Grassroots*, edited by Robert D. Bullard and Benjamin Chavis Jr., 7–14. Boston: South End, 1999.

Campbell, Lucie Eddie. "Something Within." In *The New National Baptist Hymnal*, hymn 275. Nashville: National Baptist Publishing Board, 1977.

Carmichael, Calum M. "The Sabbatical/Jubilee Cycle and the Seven-Year Famine in Egypt." *Biblica* 80 (1999) 224–39.

Carr, Joi. "The Paraphernalia of Suffering: Chris Rock's Good Hair, Still Playing in the Dark." *Black Camera* 5/1(2013) 56–71.

Carson, Clayborne, et al., eds. *The Papers of Martin Luther King, Jr*. Vol. 3, *Birth of a New Age, December 1955—December 1956*. 7 vols. Berkeley: University of California Press, 1997.

Children's Defense Fund (website). https://www.childrensdefense.org/.

Cobb, Charles. "Winds of Change." *SNCC Digital Gateway*, SNCC Legacy Project and Duke University. https://snccdigital.org/inside-sncc/the-story-of-sncc/winds-of-change/.

Collins, Patricia Hill. *Black Feminist Thought: Knowledge, Consciousness and the Politics of Empowerment*. Rev. 10th anniv. ed. New York: Routledge, 2000.

Collins, Raymond F. *First Corinthians*. Sacra Pagina 7. Collegeville, MN: Liturgical, 1999.

Collins, Sheila D. *A Different Heaven and Earth*. Valley Forge, PA: Judson, 1974.

Cone, James H. *God of the Oppressed*. San Francisco: Harper & Row, 1975.

———. *The Spirituals and the Blues: An Interpretation*. Maryknoll, NY: Orbis, 1992.

Conzelmann, Hans. *First Corinthians: A Commentary on the First Epistle to the Corinthians*. Translated by James W. Leitch et al. Hermeneia. Philadelphia: Fortress, 1975.

Copeland, M. Shawn. *Enfleshing Freedom: Body, Race, and Being*. Innovations. Minneapolis: Fortress, 2010.

Copeland, Roy W. "The Nomenclature of Enslaved Africans as Real Property or Chattels Personal: Legal Fiction, Judicial Interpretation, Legislative Designation, or Was a Slave a Slave by Any Other Name." *Journal of Black Studies* 40 (2010) 946–59.

Crawford, A. Elaine Brown. *Hope in the Holler: a Womanist Theology*. Louisville: Westminster John Knox, 2002.

Cross, F. L. ed. *The Oxford Dictionary of the Christian Church*. London: Oxford University Press, 1957.

Crowder, Stephanie Buckhanon. "Exegetical Perspective: Matthew 4:12–17." In *Feasting on the Gospels: Matthew*. Vol. 1, *Chapters 1–13*. Edited by Cynthis A. Jarvis and E. Elizabeth Johnson. 2 vols. Louisville: Westminster John Knox, 2013, Kindle.

Cummings, Elijah E. "Child Separation by the Trump Administration." Staff Report, Committee on Oversight and Reform, U.S. House of Representatives, July 2019. https://oversight.house.gov/sites/democrats.oversight.house.gov/files/2019-07-2019.%20Immigrant%20Child%20Separations-%20Staff%20Report.pdf.

Davis, Angela Y. "Afro Images: Politics, Fashion, and Nostalgia." *Critical Inquiry* 21/1 (1994) 37–45.

Deane-Drummond, Celia. "Empathy and the Evolution of Compassion: From Deep History to Infused Virtue." *Zygon* 52 (2017) 258–78.

Dines, Gail, and Jean M. Humez, eds. *Gender, Race and Class in Media: A Critical Reader*. 3rd ed. London: Sage, 2011.

Domonoske, Camila. "Minnesota Gov. Calls Traffic Stop Shooting 'Absolutely Appalling at All Levels.'" *The Two-Way* (blog), National Public Radio, July 7, 2016. http://www.npr.org/sections/thetwo-way/2016/07/07/485066807/police-stop-ends-in-black-mans-death-aftermath-is-livestreamed-online-video/.

Doniger, Wendy. *The Implied Spider: Politics and Theology in Myth*. American Lectures on the History of Religions 16. New York: Columbia University Press, 1998.

Dorsey, Thomas A. "The Lord Will Make a Way Somehow." Los Angeles: Hill and Range Songs, Inc., 1943. In *The New National Baptist Hymnal*, hymn 286. Nashville: National Baptist Publishing Board, Triad Publications, 1977.

Dowler, Kenneth. "Media Consumption and Public Attitudes toward Crime and Justice: The Relationship between Fear of Crime, Punitive Attitudes, and Perceived Police Effectiveness." *Journal of Criminal Justice and Popular Culture* 10 (2003) 109–26.

Downing, John, and Charles Husband. *Representing 'Race': Racism, Ethnicities and Media*. London: Sage, 2005.

Du Bois, W. E. B. *The Souls of Black Folk*. 1903. Reprint, Dover Thrift Editions. New York: Dover, 1994.

Dulik, Matthew C., et al. "Mitochondrial DNA and Y Chromosome Variation Provides Evidence for a Recent Common Ancestry between Native Americans and Indigenous Altaians." *American Journal of Human Genetics* 90 (2012) 229–46.

Ellis, Ralph, et al. "Orlando Shooting: 49 Killed, Shooter Pledged ISIS Allegiance." *CNN*, updated June 13, 2016. https://www.cnn.com/2016/06/12/us/orlando-nightclub-shooting/.

Emba, Christine. "'Reclaiming My Time' Is Bigger Than Maxine Waters." Opinion. Post Partisan. *Washington Post*, Aug. 1, 2017. https://www.washingtonpost.com/blogs/post-partisan/wp/2017/08/01/reclaiming-my-time-is-bigger-than-maxine-waters/.

Equal Employment Opportunity Commission vs. Catastrophe Management Solutions, Case: 14–13482, D.C. Docket No. 1:13-cv-00476-CB-M, 12/05/2017/.

Faber, Riemer. "The Apostle and the Poet: Paul and Aratus." *Clarion* 42/13 (1993). http://spindleworks.com/library/rfaber/aratus.htm/.

Fair Fight (website). https://fairfight.com/.

Fausset, Richard. "Two Weapons, a Chase, a Killing, and No Charges." *New York Times*, updated May 17, 2020. https://www.nytimes.com/2020/04/26/us/ahmed-arbery-shooting-georgia.html/.

Fee, Gordon D. *The First Epistle to the Corinthians*. New International Commentary on the New Testament. Grand Rapids: Eerdmans, 1987.

Fowler, James W. *Becoming Adult, Becoming Christian: Adult Development and Christian Faith*. San Francisco: HarperCollins, 1984.

Freire, Paulo. *Pedagogy of the Oppressed*. Translated by Myra Bergman Ramos. New, revised 20th anniv. ed. Reprint, New York: Continuum, 1999.

Gadamer, Hans-Georg. *Truth and Method*. Translation revised by Joel Weinsheimer and Donald G. Marshall. 2nd rev. ed. New York: Continuum, 2006.

Garcia, Alma M., ed. *Contested Images: Women of Color in Popular Culture*. Lanham, MD: AltaMira, 2012.

Garland, David E. *1 Corinthians*. Baker Exegetical Commentary on the New Testament. Grand Rapids: Baker Academic, 2003.

BIBLIOGRAPHY

Garrow, David J. *Bearing the Cross: Martin Luther King, Jr. and the Southern Christian Leadership Conference*. Reprint, New York: Open Road Integrated Media, 2015. Kindle ed.

Geertz, Clifford. *The Interpretation of Cultures*. New York: Basic Books, 1973.

Gerbner, George, and Larry Gross. "Living with Television: The Violence Profile." In *Television: The Critical View*, edited by Horace Newcomb, 363–93. 2nd ed. New York: Oxford University Press, 1979.

Gilman, Sander L. "Black Bodies, White Bodies: Toward an Iconography of Female Sexuality in Late Nineteenth-Century Art, Medicine, and Literature." *Critical Inquiry* 12 (1985) 204–42.

Girard, Rene. *The Girard Reader*. Edited by James G. Williams. New York: Crossroad, 2000.

Giroux, Henry. *On Critical Pedagogy*. Critical Pedagogy Today. New York: Continuum, 2011.

González, Justo L. *The Story of Christianity*. Vol. 1, *The Early Church to the Dawn of the Reformation*. 2 vols. San Francisco: HarperSanFrancisco, 1984.

Goudzwaard, Bob, and Harry de Lange. *Beyond Poverty and Affluence: Towards a Canadian Economy of Care*. 3rd ed. Toronto: University of Toronto Press, 1995.

Grant, Jacquelyn. *White Women's Christ and Black Women's Jesus: Feminist Christology and Womanist Response*. American Academy of Religion Academy Series 64. Atlanta: Scholars, 1989.

Greater Duval Neighborhood Association (website). https://www.greaterduval.org/.

Greene, Maxine. *The Dialectic of Freedom*. The John Dewey Lecture. New York: Teacher College Press, 1987.

Griffen, Wendell L. *The Fierce Urgency of Prophetic Hope*. Valley Forge, PA: Judson, 2017.

Griffin, Chanté. "How Natural Black Hair at Work Became a Civil Rights Issue." *JSTOR Daily*, updated July 3, 2019. https://daily.jstor.org/how-natural-black-hair-at-work-became-a-civil-rights-issue/.

Guenther, Eileen Morris. *In Their Own Words: Slave Life and the Power of Spirituals*. St. Louis: Morningstar Music, 2016.

Gutiérrez, Gustavo. *A Theology of Liberation: History, Politics, and Salvation*. Translated and edited by Sister Caridad Inda and John Eagleson. Rev. ed. Maryknoll NY: Orbis, 1988.

Haines, Errin. "Breonna Taylor: Family Seeks Answers in Fatal Police Shooting of Louisville Woman in Her Apartment." *Washington Post*, updated May 11, 2020. https://www.washingtonpost.com/.

Hall, Stuart, and Sut Jhally. *Representation & the Media*. San Francisco: Kanopy Streaming, 1997.

Hamer, Fannie Lou. *The Speeches of Fannie Lou Hamer: To Tell It Like It Is*. Edited by Maegan Parker Brooks and Davis W. Houck. Margaret Walker Alexander Series in African American Studies. Jackson: University Press of Mississippi, 2011.

Harris, Maria. *Teaching and Religious Imagination*. 1987. Reprint, Eugene, OR: Wipf & Stock, 2001.

Hawkins, Tramaine, vocalist. "The Potter's House." Written by Varn Michael McKay. *All My Best to You*. Sparrow Records SPD1429 1994, compact disc.

Hayden, Thomas. *Irish on the Inside: In Search of the Soul of Irish America*. Brooklyn: Verso, 2001.

Hayes, Diana L. "A Great Cloud of Witnesses: Martin Luther King Jr.'s Roots in the African American Religious and Spiritual Traditions." In *Revives My Soul Again: The Spirituality of Martin Luther King Jr.*, edited by Lewis V. Baldwin and Victor Anderson, chapter 2. Minneapolis: Fortress, 2018, Kindle.

Hein, David. "The High Church Origins of the American Boarding School." *Journal of Ecclesiastical History* 42 (1991) 577–95.

Henderson, J. Frank. "Justice and the Jubilee Year." *Liturgical Ministry* 7 (1998) 190–95.

Hendricks, Obery M., Jr. *The Politics of Jesus: Rediscovering the True Revolutionary Nature of Jesus' Teaching and How They Have Been Corrupted.* London: Three Leaves, 2007.

Herzog, William R., II. "Exegetical Perspective: Matthew 3:1–12." In *Feasting on the Word: Year A.* Vol. 1, *Advent through Transfiguration*, edited by David L. Bartlett and Barbara Brown Taylor, 44–49. Louisville: Westminster John Knox, 2010.

Hess, Carol Lakey. *Caretakers of Our Common House: Women's Development in Communities of Faith.* Nashville: Abingdon, 1997.

Hiers, Richard H. "The Problem of the Delay of the Parousia in Luke-Acts." *New Testament Studies* 20 (1974) 145–55.

Higginbotham, Evelyn Brooks. *Righteous Discontent: The Women's Movement in the Black Baptist Church, 1880–1920.* Cambridge: Harvard University Press, 1993.

hooks, bell. *Black Looks: Race and Representation.* Boston: South End, 1992.

———. *Teaching to Transgress: Education as the Practice of Freedom.* New York: Routledge, 1994.

Hopkins, Dwight N. "Holistic Health & Healing: Environment Racism & Ecological Justice." *Currents in Theology and Mission* 36 (2009) 5–19.

Horne, Gerald. "National Negro Congress." In *Encyclopedia of Negro Culture and History*, 1996. https://www.encyclopedia.com/history/encyclopedias-almanacs-transcripts-and-maps/national-negro-congress/.

Howard University. Howard University Library System. "Reconstruction Era: 1866–1877." https://www.howard.edu/library/reference/guides/reconstructionera/#:~:text=The%20period%20after%20the%20Civil,huge%20areas%20of%20the%20South/.

Hudley, Cynthia. "Education and Urban Schools." *The SES Indicator*, May 2013. American Psychological Association. https://www.apa.org/pi/ses/resources/indicator/2013/05/urban-schools/.

Hughes, C. Alvin. "We Demand Our Rights: The Southern Negro Youth Congress, 1927–1949." *Phylon* 48 (1987) 38–50.

Izadi, Elahe, and Peter Holley. "Video Shows Cleveland Officer Shooting 12-Year-Old Tamir Rice within Seconds." *Washington Post*, November 26, 2014. https://www.washingtonpost.com/news/post-nation/wp/2014/11/26/officials-release-video-names-in-fatal-police-shooting-of-12-year-old-cleveland-boy/.

James, William. *The Varieties of Religious Experience.* 1902. Reprint, A Touchstone Book. New York: Simon & Schuster, 1997.

Jobe, Margaret M. "Native Americans and the U.S. Census: A Brief Historical Survey." *Journal of Government Information* 30 (Jan. 2001) 66–80.

The John F. Kennedy Presidential Library and Museum (website). "November 22,1963: Death of the President." https://www.jfklibrary.org/learnabout-jfk/jfk-in-history/november-22-1963-death-of-the-president/.

Johnson, Elizabeth A. *Ask the Beasts: Darwin and the God of Love*. London: Bloomsbury, 2015.

Johnson, Luke Timothy. *The Writings of the New Testament: An Interpretation*. With the assistance of Todd C. Penner. Rev. ed. Minneapolis: Fortress, 1999.

Johnson, Lyndon B. "President Johnson's Special Message to the Congress: The American Promise." Public Papers of the Presidents of the United States: Lyndon B. Johnson, 1965. Volume 1, entry 107, 281–87. Washington, DC: Government Printing Office, 1966. http://www.lbjlibrary.org/lyndon-baines-johnson/speeches-films/president-johnsons-special-message-to-the-congress-the-american-promise/.

Jones, Serene. *Feminist Theory and Christian Theology: Cartographies of Grace*. Guides to Theological Inquiry. Minneapolis: Fortress, 2000.

King. Martin Luther, Jr. *The Autobiography of Martin Luther King, Jr*. Edited by Clayborne Carson. New York: Intellectual Properties Management in association with Grand Central Publishing, 1998.

———. "Letter from Birmingham Jail (1963)." In *King Remembered*, by Flip Schulke and Penelope Ortner McPhee, 276–84. New York: Pocket Books, 1986.

———. "Remaining Awake through a Great Revolution." Sermon delivered at the National Cathedral in Washington, DC, on March 31, 1968. In *A Testament of Hope: The Essential Writings and Speeches of Martin Luther King Jr.*, edited by James Melvin Washington, 268–78. New York: HarperOne, 1991.

Ladd, George E. "Pondering the Parousia." *Christian Century* 78/37 (September 1961) 1072–73.

Lambrecht, Jan. "Paul's Christological Use of Scripture in 1 Cor 15:20–28." *New Testament Studies* 28/4 (1982) 502–27.

Leary, Joy DeGruy. *Post Traumatic Slave Syndrome: America's Legacy of Enduring Injury and Healing*. Milwaukie, OR: Uptone, 2005.

Lee, Charles. "Beyond Toxic Wastes and Race." In *Confronting Environmental Racism: Voices from the Grassroots*, edited by Robert D. Bullard and Benjamin Chavis Jr., 41–52. Boston: South End, 1999.

Lester, Julius. "God and Social Change." *Cross Currents* 56 (2006) 303–11.

Lischer, Richard. *The Preacher King: Martin Luther King Jr. and the Word That Moved America*. New York: Oxford University Press, 1995.

Little, Nadra. "It's Still Legal to Ban Dreadlocks in the Workplace." *Racked*, May 18, 2018. https://www.racked.com/2018/5/18/17366610/dreadlocks-ban-supreme-court-case-chastity-jones/.

Long, Thomas G. *Preaching from Memory to Hope*. Louisville: Westminster John Knox, 2010.

———. "When Half Spent Was the Night: Preaching Hope in the New Millennium." *Journal for Preachers*, 22/3 (1999) 11–20.

Lowery, Wesley. "'I Can't Breathe': Five Years after Eric Garner Died in Struggle with New York Police, Resolution Still Elusive." *Washington Post*, updated June 13, 2019. https://www.washingtonpost.com/.

Lundblad, Barbara K. *Transforming the Stone: Preaching through Resistance to Change*. Nashville, Abingdon, 2001.

MacKinnon, Catherine A. *Feminism Unmodified: Discourses on Life and Law*. Cambridge: Harvard University Press, 1987.

Mahan, Brian. *Forgetting Ourselves on Purpose: Vocation and the Ethics of Ambition*. San Francisco: Jossey-Bass, 2010.

McKay, Varn Michael. *The Potter's House*. Performed by Tramaine Hawkins, Capital Christian Music Group. Hollywood: Capital Records, 1990.

Miles, Margaret R. *Image as Insight: Visual Understanding in Western Christianity and Secular Culture*. Boston: Beacon, 1985.

———. *Image as Insight: Visual Understanding in Western Christianity and Secular Culture*. 1985. Reprint, Eugene, OR: Wipf & Stock, 2006.

———. "Vision: The Eye of the Body and the Eye of the Mind in Augustine's *De Trinitate* and Other Works." *Journal of Religion* 63 (1983) 125–42.

Minear, Paul S. *Eyes of Faith: A Study in the Biblical Point of View*. Philadelphia: Westminster, 1946.

Mitchell, Henry H. *Celebration and Experience in Preaching*. Abingdon, 1990.

Moltmann, Jürgen. *Theology of Hope: On the Ground and the Implications of a Christian Eschatology*. Translated by James W. Leitch. 1st Fortress Press ed. Minneapolis: Fortress, 1993.

Montgomery, David. "The Death of Sandra Bland: Is There Anything Left to Investigate?" *New York Times*, May 8, 2019. https://www.nytimes.com/2019/05/08/us/sandra-bland-texas-death.html/.

Moss, Otis, III. *Blue Note Preaching in a Post-Soul World: Finding Hope in an Age of Despair*. Louisville: Westminster John Knox, 2015.

National Action Network (website). https://nationalactionnetwork.net/.

New York Times. "US Deaths Near 100,000, an Incalculable Loss." *New York Times*, updated May 24, 2020. https://static01.nyt.com/images/2020/05/24/nytfrontpage/scan.pdf/.

Niebuhr, H. Richard. *Christ and Culture*. New York: Harper & Row, 1951.

Nilsen, Sarah, and Sarah E. Turner, eds. *The Colorblind Screen: Television in Post-Racial America*. Edited by Sarah Nilsen. New York: New York University Press, 2014.

Norris, Michele. "The Woolworth Sit-In That Launched a Movement." *All Things Considered*, National Public Radio, Feb. 1, 2008. https://www.npr.org/templates/story/story.php?storyId=18615556/.

Nussbaum, Martha C. *Upheavals of Thought: The Intelligence of Emotions*. Cambridge: Cambridge University Press, 2003.

Nuwer, Rachel. "Meet the 'Brave Ones': The Women Saving Africa's Wildlife." *BBC Future*, updated September 27, 2018. https://www.bbc.com/future/article/20180926-akashinga-all-women-rangers-in-africa-fighting-poaching/.

Onion, Amanda, et al. "Montgomery Bus Boycott." *History.com* (website). Updated February. 10, 2020. https://www.history.com/topics/black-history/montgomery-bus-boycott/.

Opencorporates: The Open Database of the Corporate World (website)."Taconic Foundation for Social Justice, Inc." (web page). Last updated February 22, 2020. https://opencorporates.com/companies/us_de/523525/.

Parker, Evelyn L. *Trouble Don't Last Always: Emancipatory Hope among African American Adolescents*. Cleveland: Pilgrim, 2003.

Parker, Theodore. "Of Justice and Conscience." In *Ten Sermons of Religion*. Boston: Crosby, Nichols, 1853.

Patton, Tracey Owens. "Hey Girl, Am I More than My Hair? African American Women and Their Struggles with Beauty, Body Image, and Hair." *NWSA Journal* 18/2 (2006) 24–51.

Peterson, Gregory R. "Is My Feeling Your Pain Bad for Others?: Empathy as Virtue versus Empathy as Fixed Trait." *Zygon* 52 (2017) 232–57.
Pinn, Anthony B. "Of God, Money, and Earth: The Black Church on Economics and Environmental Racism." *Journal of Religious Thought*, 56/2–57/1 (Spring-Fall 2000–2001) 43–61.
Posey, Melanie. "Civil Rights Documentary Focuses on Campaign Led by Miles College Students." *6 WBRC* (website of WBRC-TV), Feb. 4, 2014, updated Aug. 28, 2014. https://www.wbrc.com/story/24633804/civil-rights-documentary-focuses-on-campaign-led-by-miles-college-students/.
Powery, Emerson B. "The Groans of 'Brother Saul': An Exploratory Reading of Romans 8 for 'Survival.'" *Word & World* 26 (2004) 315–22.
Powery, Luke. *Dem Dry Bones: Preaching, Death, and Hope*. Minneapolis: Fortress, 2012.
Randle, Brenda A. "I Am not My Hair: African American Women and Their Struggles with Embracing Natural Hair!" *Race, Gender & Class* 22 (2015) 114–21.
Rasmussen, Larry L. "Environmental Racism and Environmental Justice: Moral Theory in the Making?" *Journal of the Society of Christian Ethics* 24 (2004) 3–28.
———. "Jesus and Power." Lecture given at Union Theological Seminary in New York in 1986.
Repairers of the Breach (organization). *Repairers of the Breach* (website). https://www.breachrepairers.org/.
Rivers, Prince Raney. "The God Who Will Not Give Up." Sermon delivered at United Metropolitan Missionary Baptist Church, July 10, 2016. http://www.unitedmetropolitan.org/resources/media/media-item/159/the-god-who-will-not-give-up/.
Ricœur, Paul. *History and Truth*. Translated, with an introduction by Charles A. Kelbley. Northwestern University Studies in Phenomenology & Existential Philosophy Evanston, IL: Northwestern University Press, 1965.
Riggans, Walter. "The Parousia: Getting Our Terms Right." *Themelios* 21/1 (1995) 14–16.
Riggs, Marlon T., dir. and prod. *Ethnic Notions*. 57 min. Berkeley: California Newsreel, 1986. Videocassette.
Rosette, Ashleigh Shelby, and Tracy L. Dumas. "The Hair Dilemma: Conform to Mainstream Expectations or Emphasize Racial Identity." *Duke Journal of Gender, Law, and Policy* 14/407 (2007) 407–21.
Rossi, Phillip J., and Paul A. Soukup, eds. *Mass Media and the Moral Imagination*. Communication, Culture & Theology. Kansas City, MO: Sheed & Ward, 1994.
Samuel Dewitt Proctor Conference (website). https://sdpconference.info/.
Scanlon, Jennifer. "Where Were the Women in the March on Washington? How Men in the Civil Rights Movement Erased Women from Its Ranks." *New Republic*, updated March 16, 2016. https://newrepublic.com/article/131587/women-march-washington/.
Schade, Leah D. *Creation-Crisis Preaching: Ecology, Theology, and the Pulpit*. St. Louis: Chalice, 2015.
Schaeffer, Katherine. "6 Facts about Economic Inequality in the U.S." *Pew Research Center*, February 7, 2020. https://www.pewresearch.org/fact-tank/2020/02/07/6-facts-about-economic-inequality-in-the-u-s/.

Sixteenth Street Baptist Church, Birmingham, Alabama. *Sixteenth Street Baptist Church* (website). https://16thstreetbaptist.org/.

Smith, Allen. "'Lock Her Up:' Anti-Whitmer Coronavirus Lockdown Protesters Swarm Michigan Capitol." *NBC News,* updated April 15, 2020. https://www.nbcnews.com/politics/politics-news/lock-her-anti-whitmer-coronavirus-lockdown-protestors-swarm-michigan-capitol-n1184426/.

Smith, Yolanda. *Reclaiming the Spirituals: New Possibilities for African American Christian Education.* 2004. Reprint, Eugene, OR: Wipf & Stock, 2010.

Soelle, Dorothee. *The Silent Cry: Mysticism and Resistance.* Translated by Barbara and Martin Rumscheidt. Minneapolis: Fortress, 2001.

———. *Suffering.* Translated by Everett R. Kalin. Philadelphia: Fortress, 1975.

Spears, Arthur K. *Race and Ideology: Language, Symbolism, and Popular Culture.* African American Life Series. Detroit: Wayne State University Press, 1999.

Stevenson, Brian. *Lynching in America: Confronting The Legacy of Racial Terror.* 3rd ed. The Equal Justice Initiative, 2017. https://lynchinginamerica.eji.org/report/#back-to-brutality/.

Stanford University: The Martin Luther King Jr. Research and Education Institute. *The Martin Luther King Jr. Encyclopedia.* https://kinginstitute.stanford.edu/encyclopedia/.

———. *The Martin Luther King Jr. Encyclopedia,* s.v. "Sit-ins." https://kinginstitute.stanford.edu/encyclopedia/sit-ins/.

———. *The Martin Luther King Jr. Research and Education Institute* (website). https://kinginstitute.stanford.edu/.

Stewart, Alexander E. "The Temporary Messianic Kingdom in Second Temple Judaism and the Delay of the Parousia: Psalms 110:1 and the Development of Early Christian Inaugurated Eschatology." *Journal of the Evangelical Theological Society* 59 (2016) 255–70.

Stewart, Dianne. *Three Eyes for the Journey: African Dimensions of the Jamaican Religious Experience.* New York: Oxford University Press, 2005.

Strauss, Valerie. "Columbus Day Is Still a U.S. Federal Holiday. But Why?" *Washington Post,* Oct. 10, 2016. https://www.washingtonpost.com/news/answer-sheet/wp/2016/10/10/columbus-day-is-still-a-u-s-federal-holiday-but-why/.

Taylor, Barbara Brown. Baccalaureate address given at Wake Forest University, May 14, 2006.

———. *The Preaching Life.* Cambridge, MA: Cowley, 1993.

Thiselton, Anthony C. *The First Epistle to the Corinthians.* New International Commentary on the New Testament. Grand Rapids: Eerdmans, 2006.

Thompson, Lisa L. *Ingenuity: Preaching as an Outsider.* Nashville: Abingdon, 2018.

Thomas Aquinas. *Summa Theologiæ.* Vol. 33. Edited and translated by William J. Hill. 60 vols. London: Eyre & Spottiswoode, 1966.

Thomas, Frank A. *How to Preach a Dangerous Sermon.* Nashville: Abingdon, 2018.

Thurman, Howard. *Deep River: Reflections on the Religious Insight of Certain of the Negro Spirituals.* Illustrated by Elizabeth Orton Jones. Rev. and enlarged ed. New York: Harper, 1955.

Tisdale, Leonora Tubbs. *Preaching as Local Theology and Folk Art.* Fortress Resources for Preaching. Minneapolis: Fortress, 1997.

Townes, Emilie M. *Breaking the Fine Rain of Death: African American Health Issues and a Womanist Ethic of Care.* New York: Continuum, 1998.

———, ed. *Embracing the Spirit: Womanist Perspectives on Hope, Salvation, and Transformation*. The Bishop Henry McNeal Turner/Sojourner Truth Series in Black Religion 13. Maryknoll, NY: Orbis, 1997.

———. "Introduction: Creating Ruminations of the Spirit." In *Embracing the Spirit: Womanist Perspectives on Hope, Salvation, and Transformation*, xi–xix. The Bishop Henry McNeal Turner/Sojourner Truth Series in Black Religion 13. Maryknoll, NY: Orbis, 1997.

———, ed., *A Troubling in My Soul: Womanist Perspectives on Evil and Suffering*. The Bishop Henry McNeal Turner Studies in North American Black Religion 8. Maryknoll, NY: Orbis, 1999.

Tutu, Desmond. "Reflections on Wholeness." In *An African Prayer Book*, 110–13. New York: Doubleday, 1995.

Turner, Nathan, Jr. "Black History: Bethel Baptist Church in Birmingham Played Key Role in Civil Rights Movement." *Birmingham Times*, update February 2, 2017. https://www.birminghamtimes.com/2017/02/despite-bombings-bethel-baptist-church-never-missed-a-service-and-played-pivotal-role-in-history/.

Turpin, Katherine. *Branded: Adolescents Converting from Consumer Faith*. Cleveland: Pilgrim, 2006.

United Press International. "Alabama Courts Oust 'Bull' Connor, Mayor." May 23, 1963. https://www.upi.com/Archives/1963/05/23/Alabama-court-ousts-Bull-Connor-Mayor/5349805152894/.

US Center for Disease Control and Prevention. "CDC COVID Data Tracker." *The Center for Disease Control* (website), updated November 28, 2020. https://covid.cdc.gov/covid-data-tracker/#cases_casesper100klast7days/.

US Department of Housing and Urban Development. "History of Fair Housing." https://www.hud.gov/program_offices/fair_housing_equal_opp/aboutfheo/history/.

US Department of Justice. Fair Housing Act. https://www.justice.gov/crt/fair-housing-act-2/.

US Federal Bureau of Investigation."Baptist Street Church Bombing." *Federal Bureau of Investigation: History, Famous Cases & Criminals* (website). https://www.fbi.gov/history/famous-cases/baptist-street-church-bombing/.

US National Archives. "The Emancipation Proclamation." https://www.archives.gov/exhibits/featured-documents/emancipation-proclamation#:~:text=President%20Abraham%20Lincoln%20issued%20the,and%20henceforward%20shall%20be%20free.%22/.

US National Archives. "Diary of President Eisenhower, 7/24/1953, page 3." In *Eisenhower, Dwight D.: Papers as President of the United States, 1953–1961*, National Archives Catalog, https://catalog.archives.gov/id/186481/.

US National Archives & Records Administration et al. "Brown v. Board of Education (1954)." On *Our Documents* (website).Updated August 24, 2020. http://www.ourdocuments.gov/doc.php?doc=87/.

US National Archives & Records Administration et al. "The Civil Rights Act of 1964." On *Our Documents* (website). https://www.ourdocuments.gov/doc.php?flash=false&doc=97/.

US National Archives & Records Administration et al. "Executive Order 8802: Prohibition of Discrimination in the Defense Industry (1941)." June 25, 1941. General Records of the United States Government; Record Group 11. On *Our Documents* (website). https://www.ourdocuments.gov/doc.php?flash=true&doc=72/.

US National Archives & Records Administration et al. "Official Program for the March on Washington, August 28, 1963." Found among the Bayard Rustin Papers at the John F. Kennedy Presidential Library and Museum. On *Our Documents* (website). https://www.ourdocuments.gov/doc.php?flash=false&doc=96#/.

US National Archives & Records Administration et al. "Plessy v. Ferguson (1896)." On *Our Documents* (website). Updated August 24, 2020. https://www.ourdocuments.gov/doc.php?flash=false&doc=52/.

University of Maryland. University of Maryland Libraries. University Archives and Special Collections. *African-Americans' Rights* (web page). "A House Divided: African American Workers Struggle against Segregation" (section). Web page content prepared by Benjamin Blake et al. https://www.lib.umd.edu/unions/social/african-americans-rights/.

University of Virginia. The Miller Center at the University of Virginia. "The Struggle for Civil Rights" (web page). *The Age of Eisenhower* (website). *The Presidency* (series of websites): https://millercenter.org/the-presidency/educational-resources/age-of-eisenhower/struggle-civil-rights/.

Virginia General Assembly. Act XII, In *Laws of Virginia, December 1662*. In *The Statutes at Large*, edited by William Waller Hening, 2:170. 13 vols. New York: Bartow, 1823. For the full text of Act XII, see *Encyclopedia Virginia* (website): https://encyclopediavirginia.org/entries/negro-womens-children-to-serve-according-to-the-condition-of-the-mother-1662/.

———. An act declaring the Negro, Mulatto, and Indian slaves within this dominion, to be real estate (1705). In *The Statutes at Large*, edited by William Waller Hening, vol. 3. 13 vols. New York: Bartow, 1823. For the full text of the Act, see *Thirteen.org/* (website): https://www.thirteen.org/wnet/slavery/experience/legal/docs1.html/.

———. An Act for Suppressing Outlying Slaves (1691). In *The Statutes at Large*, edited by William Waller Hening, 3:86–88. 13 vols. New York: Bartow, 1823. For the full text of An Act for Suppressing Outlying Slaves see *Encyclopedia Virginia* (website): https://encyclopediavirginia.org/entries/an-act-for-suppressing-outlying-slaves-1691/.

Vreeland, Derek . "A Christian Memory of 9/11." *Missio Alliance,* 2016. https://www.missioalliance.org/christian-memory-911/.

Warren, Michael. *Seeing through the Media: A Religious View of Communications and Cultural Analysis*. Harrisburg, PA: Trinity, 1997.

Weil, Simone. "The Love of God in Affliction." In *Awaiting God: A New Translation of "Attente de Dieu" and "Lettre a un Religieux,"* 31–46. Translated by Bradley Jersak. Introduction by Sylvia Weil. Abbotsford, BC: Fresh Wind, 2012.

Westfield, N. Lynne. *Dear Sisters: A Womanist Practice of Hospitality*. Religion, Race, and Ethnicity. Cleveland: Pilgrim, 2001.

———. "'Mama Why'?'—A Womanist Epistemology of Hope." In *Deeper Shades of Putrple: Womanism in Religion and Society,* edited by Stacey M. Floyd-Thomas, 128–41. Religion, Race, and Ethnicity. New York: New York University Press, 2006.

———. "Toward a Womanist Approach to Pedagogy." *Religious Education* 98 (2003) 521–34.

Wesley Theological Seminary. "The Community Engagement Institute" (web page). https://www.wesleyseminary.edu/ice/about-us/overview-2/.

Williams, Delores S. *Sisters in the Wilderness: The Challenge of Womanist God-Talk.* Maryknoll, NY: Orbis, 2001.

Williams, Patricia J. *Seeing a Color-Blind Future: The Paradox of Race.* The 1997 BBC Reith Lectures. New York: Noonday, 1997.

Williams, Raymond. *The Sociology of Culture.* With a new foreword by Bruce Robbins. Fontana New Sociology. Chicago: University of Chicago Press, 1981.

Wimberly, Anne Streaty. *Soul Stories: African American Christian Education.* Nashville: Abingdon, 1994.

The Women's March. *The Women's March* (website). https://womensmarch.com/.

Wood, Frances E. "'Take My Yoke upon You': The Role of the Church in the Oppression of African-American Women." In *A Troubling in My Soul: Womanist Perspectives on Evil and Suffering,* edited by Emilie M. Townes, 37–47. The Bishop Henry McNeal Turner Studies in North American Black Religion 8. Maryknoll, NY: Orbis, 1999, .

World Health Organization. "Weekly Epidemiological Update—22 December 2020." https://www.who.int/publications/m/item/weekly-epidemiological-update---22-december-2020/.

Wykes, Maggie, and Barrie Gunter. *The Media and Body Image: If Looks Could Kill.* London: Sage, 2014.

X, Malcolm. *The Autobiography of Malcolm X.* With the assistance of Alex Haley. 1965. Reprint, New York: Ishi, 2015.

Young, Iris Marion. "Five Faces of Oppression." In *Justice and the Politics of Difference,* 39–65. Paperback reissue, with a new foreword by Danielle Allen. Princeton: Princeton University Press, 2011.

Yudkin, Marjorie. "The Shalom Ideal." *Judaism* 33 (1984) 85–90.

Index

Aaron, Charles, 118n14
Abernathy, Ralph D., 185–88, 188–89n78, 192–93, 197–98, 209–10
abundance. *See* imaginative abundance
action, purposeful. *See* Hope-filled action
Acts 2, 145
Acts 9, 147
Acts 10, 96
Acts 11, 97, 149
Acts 15, 149
Acts 17:16–18, 23
Adhemar, 107
African Americans
  and Black hair, 48–49, 48–49n31
  and chattel slavery, 178
  distrust for law enforcement, 1
  emphasis on community, 176
  imagining equality, 216
  impacts of the New Deal on, 182–83
  journey toward racial justice, as an example of audacious Hope, 175, 214
  lynching, terrorism against, 182
  negative stereotyping, 34n2, 49–50, 78–79, 84–85, 178
  singing as an example of Hope, 167–68
  sources of courage and Hope, 13
  Ubuntu (full humanity) concept, 176–77
  youth activists, 183–84

See also chattel slavery; civil rights movement; enslaved people
agency, conversion and, 143–44
Alabama Christian Movement for Human Rights (ACMHR), 194–97, 201
Alabama Project, 209–11
Albany, GA, activism in, 191–93
Alves, Rubem, 6, 116, 116n7
American Federation of Labor (AFL), 183, 183n42, 202n168
Amos
  call for justice, 35
  efforts to energize/inspire, 67
  litany of dissatisfaction, 118–19, 206
Anderson, Victor, 176, 179
Antioch, capture of, 107–8
apathy, sources of, 18, 45–46, 138, 220. *See also* deceptive language of despair
Apostles' Creed, 106n130
Areopagite Council, 23–24
ascetic imagination, 68
Ask the Beasts: Darwin and the God of Love (Johnson), 81–82
Aubery, Ahmaud, 2

Baker, Ella, 188–89n78, 189, 189n181
Baker-Fletcher, Karen, 120
Baldwin, James, 201
Baldwin, Lewis V., 176, 179
baptism, 117–20, 119n15, 179–80
Barber, William II, 213–14

Bates, Daisy, 204
Baxley, Bob, 208n193
"Bearing the Cross" sermon, 168–70
becauseness, 124–25
Bedford, Nancy E., 110, 122, 132n40
Belafonte, Harry, 201
beloved community. *See* civil rights movement; King, Martin Luther Jr.
Bevel, James, 210
Bigelow, Albert, 190
binary/bifurcated world views
    dangers of, 83–85
    and dehumanizing others, 178–79
    vs. the idea of *shalom*, 21
    and *imago Dei*, 83, 148–50
    and inequality, 49–50, 153–54
    media imagery as reinforcing, 73–74
    and negating concepts and ideologies, 43, 82–83, 86
    role of constituent cultural elements in reinforcing, 52–53
    See also despair
Birmingham, AL. *See* civil right movement
"Black Bodies, White Bodies" (Gilman), 83–85
"Black Lives Matter," 1–2, 133, 214–15
Black Looks: Race and Representation (hooks), 61, 76
Black women
    expressions of Hope, 133
    sexualizing of, 84–85, 85n68
    and surrogacy oppression, 144n18
Bland, Sandra, 2
Bourdieu, Pierre, 16–17
Boutwell, Albert, 195–96, 196n126
Branded: Adolescents Converting from Consumer Faith (Turpin), 140
breath (*ruach*) of God
    and breathing with Spirit, 115
    and God the Creator, 23–25
    and *imago Dei*, 32, 173, 219
    vivifying nature of, 15, 69, 115
"brood of vipers" metaphor, 119, 119n16
Brown, Michael, 1
Brown, Robert McAfee, 191

Brown Chapel AME Church, Selma, AL, 209–12
Brown v. Board of Education of Topeka Kansas (1954), 185
Bruckner, James S., 26
Brueggemann, Walter, 6, 57–58, 125–26
Byzantine Empire, 104

Campbell, Lucie Eddie, 19
Capernaum, Galilee, 122, 122n21, 125
caring for self and others, 25–26, 111, 123–24, 127. *See also* empathy/compassion
Carmichael, Calum M., 129, 129n36
Castile, Philando, 1
Celebration and Experience in Preaching (Mitchell), 45
Chambliss, Robert E., 208n193
Charlemagne, 105–6
chattel slavery
    American colonists' embrace of, 178
    and baptism, 179–80
    and dehumanization/stereotyping, 178–79
    and imagining freedom, 216
    and slaves as real estate, 180, 180n26
    Virginia definition of, 1662, 179–80, 179n23
    See also enslaved people
Christian church, early Christians
    abandonment of circumcision, 97
    communal characteristics, 98
    and creating a distinct identity, 95–96, 98–99
    distancing from Judaism, 97
    early conflicts with Muslims, 105
    Edict of Milan, 101
    militarism/imperialism, 102, 107–9
    patriarchal hierarchy, 103
    persecutions of, 92n74, 95–96, 99–100
    sanctioned theology, 103
    status in the Roman Empire, 97–98
    third century martyrs, 100n96
    and the welcoming of Gentiles, 96–97, 96n85
    Western and Eastern churches, 106–7, 106n130

See also communities of faith; parousia, delay of; preaching
civil rights movement
  Albany GA, 191–93
  Birmingham, AL, 190, 194–96, 194n116, 195n119, 198–200, 207, 208n193
  campaign against housing discrimination, 213
  Civil Rights Act of 1866, 181
  community organizing and, 214
  following King's assassination, 213–14
  Freedom Rides, 190
  international efforts, 214
  male domination, 203–4
  March on Washington for Jobs and Equity, 202
  Selma, AL, 209–12, 209n200, 209n205
  student activism, 189–91, 194, 196, 197–98, 200
  violent responses to, transforming, 208
  voter registration efforts, 210–11
Civil War, US, 180–81, 181nn27–28
Clark, James D., 209, 211
Clark, Kenneth, 201
coal miners, Appalachian, black lung disease, 55–56
Cohen, Robert, 55–56
Collins, LeRoy, 210–11
Collins, Patricia Hill
  on binary thinking and judgment, 62
  on controlling imagery, 5, 34n2, 43
  on culturally induced despair, 82–83
  on cultural "norms" as basis for despair, 34
  use of the term "other," 83n62
colloquial/idiomatic expressions of culturally induced despair, 43–46
Colvin, Claudette, 185n53
communication
  and the deceptive language of despair, 39–46
  and dehumanizing messages, 33–34
  of despair, underlying dangers, 12–13
  and language as a metaphor, 12
  See also dehumanizing messages and communications
communion (*koinōnia*), living in, 25–27, 29
communities of faith
  and call to fulfillment/transformation, 150
  and communal well-being, 25–26, 89–91, 122
  complex responses to tragedies associated with police and Vigilante violence, 9
  failure to address incidents of suffering and oppression, 27
  and focus on love of God, 123
  as Hope-filled bodies, 90, 112
  King's beloved community, 13, 132, 166, 176–77, 203
  opening to outsiders, the Other, 91
  participation in God's redemptive work, 220
  as source of courage and action, 13
  See also Christian church, early Christians; preaching
Cone, James H., 6, 32, 32n45
Congress of Industrial Organizations (CIO), 183, 183n42, 202n168
Connor, Eugene "Bull," 194–98
Constantine, 101–3
constituent cultural elements, 50–51, 56
consumption, unrestrained, 80, 109, 140
controlling images, 34n2
conversion, 143, 147–48, 150–51
Copeland, M. Shawn
  embodied theology concept, 7, 16
  on *imago Dei*, 26
  theological anthropology, 22–23, 23n20
1 Cor 15:23–28, 94–95
2 Cor 6:11–12, 79
CORE (Congress of Racial Equality), Freedom Rides, 190
Cornelius, encounter with Simon Peter, 96, 145–46

Council for United Civil Rights Leaders (CUCRL), 202
courage
    and creating imaginative abundance, 174
    and loving God, self, and others, 86–91, 123–24, 142, 174
    and manifesting audacious Hope, 27–28, 120n19, 172–75
    sources of, 13
COVID-19 pandemic, 140–42, 152–53
Crawford, A. Elaine Brown, 133
creative imagination, 68
A Critical Analysis for Preaching (ACAP) tool, 158–59, 223–25
critical thought, 70–71
Crowder, Stephanie B., 122
Crusades, the, 107–9
culturally induced despair
    and apathy, 45–46
    contributions of colloquial and idiomatic expressions to, 43–45
    dehumanizing messages and communications, 33–35, 39–42
    as the enemy of embodied Hope, 12
    and fatalism, 35–36
    and "high" vs. "low" emotions, 33, 45–46
    and inertia, 42
    insidiousness of, 28
    and irresponsibility, 36
    language that sustains, 43–46
    and normalizing injustice and inaction, 37, 56–58
    origins and sources, 31–32
    and presumed shared social conventions, 48
    as the result of exhaustion, pragmatism, 36
    See also binary/bifurcated world views
culture, characteristics and impacts, 40–41
Currier, Stephen R., 202
Cuvier, George, 85n68

"Dare to Dream" sermon, 159–61
Deane-Drummond, Celia, 151

dearth, imaginative, and despair, 64–65, 109, 111–12
deceptive language of despair. *See* despair
dehumanization
    controlling images, 34n2
    examples, 34–35
    language of, 43–45
    language that promotes, 43–45
    and normalizing injustice, 35–36, 56
    and obscuring/denying racism, 51–52
    turning away from, 123
despair
    acquiescing to, 36, 52–53, 56
    Brueggemann on, 57–58
    countering through Hope, 28, 132, 157–58, 168
    as culturally induced, 39–42, 48, 50–51
    culturally induced, 50–51, 69–72, 76
    dehumanizing nature of, 43–45
    and focus on survival vs. flourishing, 56–57, 117
    and incorporating negative stereotypes, 44–45
    Job's, 35–36n4
    King's rejection of, 206
    as mortal sin, Aquinas's view, 29–30, 30n31, 33
    and negating ideologies and myths, 83–86
    and normalizing inaction, 52–53, 56–57
    and normalizing suffering, 31–32
    and normalizing violence, 39–42
    and preoccupation with barriers and obstacles, 112
    recognizing characteristics of, 47
    and selfishness, 56
    and theological and ecclesiastic distortion, 86
    as a theological concept, 28–30, 29n32
    transmission and reproduction, 42
    and viewing Christian love as "too hard," 109
    See also imaginative dearth

Deut 6:4–5, 87
The Dialectic of Freedom (Greene), 69
Diocletian, 100–101
Doniger, Wendy, 80–81
Dorsey, Thomas A., 4
"Down by the Riverside" (song), 167
Dumas, Tracy L., 49
Durden, A. N. Sr., 193

Edelman, Marian Wright, 213
Eden, departure from, 16
Edict of Milan, 101
Edmund Pettus Bridge, Selma, AL, march over, 210–11
Eisenhower, Dwight D., 189–90, 189–90n83
Embracing the Spirit: Womanist Perspectives on Hope, Salvation and Transformation (Townes), 4
emotions, "high" vs. "low," 45–46
empathy/compassion (*compassio*)
    and ascetic imagination, 68
    as a Christian concept, 151–57
    and embracing the well-being of all, 21
    and experiential touchstones, 156–57
    framing scriptural text to reflect, 155–56
    and living in unity with and empathy for the God-created, 27
    and love of God, self, and neighbor, 99, 123
    and preaching practice, 138
    for the vulnerable, proofing of by compassion, 151–55
enslavement
    Christian support for, 86
    and Levitical law, 129, 129n36
    See also African Americans; chattel slavery
environmental racism/classism, 54–55
Equal Employment Opportunity Commission (EEOC), 48
equality
    African American journey towards, 13, 175, 183, 214–16
    finding new metaphors for, 213n225
    working towards, 41
    See also civil rights movement; justice
Equal Justice Initiative (EJI), 181–82
eschatology
    as the doctrine of Christian Hope, 6–7
    and the gift of anticipatory Hope, 91, 96
    See also kin(g)dom of God, kin(g)dom of heaven; parousia, delay of
Ethnic Notions (film, Riggs), 62, 78–79
Eusebius, 103

Fair Employment Practices Commission (FEPC), 183
Fair Fight organization, 214
Fair Housing Act, 213
faith. *See* communities of faith; kin(g)dom of God, kin(g)dom of heaven
First Crusade, 107–8
Flint, MI, water crises, 55
Floyd, George, 2
Foley, Albert S., 196, 206
Fourteenth and Fifteenth Amendments, 181
Fowler, James, 143, 143n15
Freedman's Bureau, 181
Freedom Rides, 190–91
Freire, Paulo, 5, 70–71, 70n29, 143

Galarius, 100–101
Garner, Eric, 2
γάρ (*gar*; "for" or "becauseness"), 124
Gen 1–3, 16, 24–26, 81
Gentiles, welcoming into the early church, 96–97
Gerbner, George, 60, 77–78
Gilman, Sander L., 83–85, 85n68
Girard, René, 74
"Girl Call the Midwife, I'm About to Give Birth" sermon, 162–64
God
    desire for *shalom* and human well-being, 11, 20
    and the diversity of humankind, 23

God *(continued)*
   enduring love for all creation, 111, 128–29, 147–49, 162
   and the fundamental goodness of creation, 11–12
   and God's presence within, 19
   Hope as a gift from, 15, 29
   human partnership with, 11, 24–27, 59–60, 137
   impartiality of, 96–97, 96n85
   law of, vs. unjust human laws, 197–98
   loving God as act of courage, 86–91, 123–24, 142, 174
   as "the Other," 83n62
   redemptive work of, 24, 111, 113, 161–62
   restorative presence of, 3, 115
   See also Holy Spirit; *imago Dei*; Jesus Christ; *shalom* (peace) of God
"God is Waiting for Us!" service, 8–12
"The God Who Will Not Give Up" sermon (Rivers), 10–11
González, Justo
   on the Crusades and Crusaders, 107
   on the dissociation of humans from nature, 100n96
   on the early church and the Roman Empire, 97
   on Roman persecution of Christians and Jews, 99
   on tensions between the Western and Eastern Christian Churches, 106n130
gospel proclamation
   and call to fulfillment/transformation, 150–51
   challenges to hearers, 141
   disruptive potential, 136–37
   genuine vs. wrong obstacles, 170–71n49
   making accessible through thick description, 215
   message of, presenting without distortion, 157–61
   proclaiming with intentionality, 139
   and qualitative betterment as goal of ministry, 173
   testing through preaching, 137
   See also Jesus Christ; kin(g)dom of God, kin(g)dom of heaven
Great Depression, 182
Greenberg, Irving, 120n19
Greene, Maxine, 69–70, 134
Gross, Larry, 60, 77–78
Gutiérrez, Gustavo, 80, 133, 173

habitus (perception)/*habitat* (shared experience over time), 16–18
"The Hair Dilemma: Conform to Mainstream Expectations or Emphasize Racial Identity" (Rosette and Dumas), 49
Hamer, Fannie Lou, 216
Harris, Maria, 5, 61, 63, 68
Hayden, Thomas, 172, 175, 222
Hayes, Diana L., 175–76
Heb 1:13, 93
Heb 3:1, 95n82
Heb 4:14, 95n82
Heb 10:23–25, 93
Hebrew people
   anticipation of a Messiah, 92–93, 96
   return from exile, 58–59n56
Hedgeman, Anna Arnold, 203–4
Henderson, J. Frank, 128–29
Hendricks, Obery M., 98, 102
Hiers, Richard H., 92n74, 93n77
"high church," 43
History and Truth (Ricoeur), 17, 66
"Holistic Health and Healing: Environmental Racism and Ecological Justice" (Hopkins), 54–55
Holler, the, 133
Holy Roman Empire, 106–8
Holy Spirit
   assured presence of, 113–14, 219
   as God's gift to humans, 149
   and God's vivifying breath (*ruach*), 115
   as groaning within, 116–17, 116n6
   as the power behind faith, 114
homiletical values
   ad empathy proofed by compassion, 151–57

INDEX

and amplifying Hope's assurance
and call, 5, 160–61
for approaching sermon
preparation, 150–51
and cultivating imaginative
abundance, 165–71
eliminating distortion, 157–61
and womanist scholars, 5
hooks, bell, 61, 76
Hope
actions associated with, 7
anticipatory language of, 92–93,
110–11, 132–35, 138
as antidote to despair, 13, 32
call of, amplifying when preaching,
4–5, 160–65, 177
characteristics, 7, 19, 221
courage involved in responding to,
27–28, 172–75
and the desire for wholeness and
well-being, 112, 115–16, 219,
221
as an expression of God's presence,
15–16
as God's voice within, 6–7, 15, 19,
117, 170
handling doubt about, 47, 109
healing nature of, 3
and Hope-filled action, 5, 36–37,
157–58, 165–71, 206–7, 214,
215–16
and imaginative abundance, 18, 24,
63, 67, 165–70
and living with purpose, 7–8, 19–20,
28, 56–57, 115, 131–32, 134–35
necessity of, 4–5, 12, 219
and relating to others, 27
and repentance, 121
role of Christian praxis, 5–6, 22–23,
137–38
and trusting in God's love, 21
See also civil rights movement;
imago Dei; kin(g)dom of God;
kin(g)dom of heaven; the Holy
Spirit; *shalom*
Hope in the Holler (Crawford), 133
Hope Within History (Brueggemann),
125–26

Hopkins, Dwight N., 54–55
Hos 11:1–10, 10–11
Hudley, Cynthia, 53–54
Hughes, C. Alvin, 183–84
Hughes, Genevieve, 190
humans
accepting identity as *imago Dei*, 14,
19, 27, 111, 144
and culturally induced despair, 28,
31–32, 40–41
desire for wholeness and well-being,
15, 19
diversity of, 23
and embodied revelation, 22–23
ethical/moral responsibility, 11, 20,
117n9, 127, 132, 174
as fallen, inherently damaged, 16,
123–24
focus on afterlife, 14
focus on survival, 56
God's purpose in creating, 4, 24–26
impatience, 6
as mimetic, 74
partnership with God, 11, 24–27,
59–60, 220
preoccupation with the material,
6–7
relational identity of, 27

icons/iconic images
formative power of, 74–75
and ideology, 82–86
media images as, 73–74
and perpetuation of violence, 77–79
and religious imagery, 74
repetitive exposure to, and
stereotyping, 75
and responsibility, 79–80
See also media images
"I Have a Dream" (King), 166, 205–7
imaginative abundance
and the anticipatory language of
Hope, 134
capacity for, importance, 220
challenges of, 62–64
and conversion, 144
gospel as underlying, 140
and *imago Dei*, 110

INDEX

imaginative abundance *(continued)*
    in King's "I Have a Dream" speech, 166, 206–7
    nurturing, through preaching, 132, 138–39, 157, 165–71
    and restorative possibilities, 66–69, 216–17
    in spirituals, 167–68
    sustaining image of, 216
imaginative dearth, 62–65, 69–72.
    See also deceptive language of despair
imago Dei
    and concept of *nepesh* (soul), 26
    and consciousness of good, 222
    and dwelling together with others, 23
    and early Christian faith communities, 91–92
    and the embodied theology of hope, 7–8, 11, 15–16, 18–19, 20, 29, 47
    embracing, 170
    and embracing empathy and compassion, 154–55
    and frailty, 173
    and God's presence within, 19, 26–27
    and human agency/responsibility, 11, 16, 25, 83, 144
    and imaginative abundance, 168
    inability of humans to recognize within selves, 14
    ministry as channel for fostering understanding of, 138
    recognizing shared identity as, 60–61, 132, 219
    and repentance, 124
    and self-love, 221
    and valuing diversity, 50, 215.
    See also God; imaginative abundance; *shalom* (peace) of God
The Implied Spider: Politics and Theology in Myth (Doniger), 81
inaction, complacency, 39–41, 43–45
Indigenous peoples, colonizing of, 177–78
inequality
    binary/bifurcated world views, 49–50, 153–54
    as a distortion of God's intent, 25–26
    and environmental racism, 54–55
    role of negating iconic images, 77–78
Inland Regional Center, San Bernadino, CA, 2
Interstate Commerce Commission (ICC), 191
Isaiah
    warnings about God's judgment, 118–19
    and the Year of Jubilee, 129
Isa 40:3, 117–18
Isa 61:1–2, 138
Islam, 105–6

James, Epistle of, 174
James, teachings, 89–91
Jean, Botham, 2
Jenkins, William A. Jr., 197–98
Jer 2:18, 58–59n56
Jer 31:15, 3
Jessica's story ("Mercy Suits Our Case" sermon), 155–56
Jesus Christ
    approach to preaching, 138
    baptism of, 119
    calls for humans to love God, 86–89
    demonstrations and parables, 71–72
    focus on theological and sociopolitical transformation, 122–23
    as God incarnate, 15–16
    gospel proclamation as central message of, 72, 120, 122, 125–27, 220, 221
    life of, making visible, 47
    as Messiah, 92–93, 96
    ministry of love and well-being, 7, 21–22, 71, 102–4, 119–20, 122
    redefinition of family and relationships, 22
    suffering with, as path to redemption, 113–14, 152
Jim Crow practices, 79, 182, 185
Job, 35–36n4

1 John 4:11–21, 90
1 John 7:53–8:11, 155–56
Johnson, Elizabeth A., 25n25, 81–82
Johnson, Kimberly, 5
Johnson, Luke Timothy, 161
Johnson, Lyndon B., 208, 211–13
Johnson, Micah Xavier, 2
John the Baptist, 117–20, 118n13, 119n15
Jones, Chastity, 48
Jones, Clarence, 201
Jones, Serene, 33, 58
Judaism
   efforts of early Christian to distinguish selves from, 95–97
   and persecution of Jews, 100n96, 107
justice
   actualizing, 69
   and communal well-being, 21
   and dismantling dehumanizing systems, 28
   and God's law, 19, 197–98
   racial, African Americans' journey toward, 175, 214
   See also civil rights movement

Kelley, Asa D., 191–93, 193n105
Kennedy, John F., 190, 196–97, 199, 201–3, 208
Kennedy, Robert, 191, 199, 201
King, A. D., 196
King, Martin Luther Jr.
   in Albany, GA, 191–92, 193
   assassination, 213
   beloved community, 13, 132, 166, 176–77, 203
   in Birmingham, AL, 194–95n117, 197
   "I Have a Dream" speech, 205–7
   the March on Washington, 200–201, 202–3
   in Montgomery, AL, 186–87
   nonviolence as reflection of faith, 176, 186–89, 191
   in Selma, AL, 211
   Selma-Montgomery March, 210
   use of thick description, 166, 215

   See also civil rights movement
kin(g)dom of God, kin(g)dom of heaven
   anticipatory Hope, 18–19
   and blessedness, beatitude, 29, 29n34
   as core theme in each Synoptic Gospel, 126
   discomfort associated with proclamation of, 125
   as a divine promise, 117, 128
   ethical foundations, 127–28, 127n33, 132
   fulfillment of, necessary conditions for, 124, 126–32, 126n31
   and God's reign on earth, 122
   and God's retributive justice, prophecies of, 118, 118n14
   imagining, anticipating, 66, 120, 124, 173
   as a metaphor for Hope, 7–8, 13, 21–22, 113, 125–26, 214–15
   and monarchical societies, 165
   and the need for justice and equality, 176–77
   and nonviolent resistance, 176
   and partnership with God, 11
   proclaiming, as a goal of preaching, 145, 171
   as a term, 8n17
   See also Jesus Christ; parousia, delay of; preaching
koinōnia. *See* communion (*koinōnia*)

language as metaphor, 12
Lawrence, George, 202
Lawson, James, 189n82
Leary, Joy DeGruy, 178
Leo I (Leo "the Great"), 104n122
Leo III, 105
"Letter from a Birmingham Jail" (King), 197
Lev 19:18, 88
Lev 25, 128–29
Levine, Lawrence, 78–79
Lewis, John, 189n82, 190, 210
LGBTQAI rights, 65, 133
Liuzzo, Viola Gregg, 212n222

"Living with Television: The Violence Profile" (Gerbner and Gross), 77–78
Long, Thomas G., 6, 111
love
  as basis for God-ordained ethical domain, 132
  expressions of, as core of preaching with moral imagination, 174
  as focus of Jesus and early Christians, 123–24
  and good works, as response to delay in parousia in Hebrews, 92–93
  and the importance of self-love, 221
  King's emphasis on, 186–87
  practicing, and imagining an unseen world, 111
  upholding Jesus's teachings on, 86–91, 102–4, 108–10, 142, 221
Luke, Gospel of
  and the delay of the parousia, 92n74
  emphasis on God's love, 88
  gospel proclamation as central message of, 127–30
  Simon Peter's visionary experience, 145–47
Luke 4, 138
Luke 4:14–15, 120n18
Lundblad, Barbara K., 22
lynching, 181–82

MacKinnon, Catherine A., 77
Malcolm X, 210
maleness (gendered masculinity), 83
March on Washington for Jobs and Equity, 200–207
Mark, Gospel of
  announcement of the kin(g)dom of heaven, 117–18, 118n13, 120, 126
  and the call for humans to love God and neighbors, 88–89
Mark 1:15, 7, 150
Mark 8:31–36, 168–69
Marshall, Thurgood, 185
Martin, Trayvon, 1
Matthew, Gospel of
  announcement of the kin(g)dom of heaven, 117–18, 118n13, 120, 122, 127
  on loving God, self, and others, 89
  Mary and Joseph's escape to Egypt, 58–59n56
  reference to Capernaum, 122–23
Matt 4:17, 7, 150
Matt 19:16–30, 137
Matt 22:39, 89, 221
McKay, V. Michael, 10
media images
  formative power of, 61, 84
  negative, 78–79
  ubiquity of, 72
  viewing critically, 72–73
Melchizedek, 92–93
"Mercy Suits Our Case" (sermon), 155–56
Mic 3:5, 53
Mic 6:6–8, 159–61
midwife metaphor, 162–64
ministry. *See* preaching
Missionary Baptist Church, 176
Mitchell, Henry H., 45
Mohammed, 105
Moltmann, Jürgen, 6, 116n6
Montgomery, AL, 185–88
moral imagination, 172, 174–75
mortal sin, definition, 30n41
Mother Emmanuel African Methodist Episcopal (AME) Church, Charleston, SC, 2
myths
  characteristics and function, 80–83
  formative power of, 16

National Association for the Advancement of Colored People (NAACP)
  and Birmingham student protests, 200
  Brown v. Board of Education of Topeka Kansas, 185
  challenges to employment discrimination, 183
  challenges to housing discrimination, 213

INDEX

March on Washington, 202,
    202n168, 202n173, 204
    and the Montgomery bus boycott,
        187, 187n67
    shooting of Evers, 201
National Negro Congress (NNC),
    184n44
Nazareth, Jesus's sermon in, 129
Negro American Labor Council
    (NALC) had, 200
Nero, 99
New Deal, 182
Nicene Creed, 106n130
Niebuhr, H. Richard, 9
9/11 terrorist attacks, 37–39
nonviolence
    King's commitment to, 176, 186–89,
        191
    and the Montgomery, AL, bus
        boycott, 185
    and the sit-in movement, 189
    and SNCC, 189, 189n82
    Southern Christian Leadership
        Conference (SCLC), 188
    as theologically ethical, 176
    See also civil rights movement

objectifying language, 43–44
oppression
    actively opposing, 20, 27–28, 131,
        136, 203, 215–16
    as cultural habit, 16–17, 31
    exposing and countering, 67, 70–71,
        110, 122–23
    human perpetuation of through
        habit, 17
    and love for self and others, 222
    and selfishness, 56
    surrogacy oppression, 144–45n18
    tolerating as normal, 13, 39–42,
        44–45, 51–52, 57–60, 69, 121,
        142, 159, 220
    and unequal power systems, 153
    See also culturally induced despair

Page, Marion, 192
Parks, Rosa, 185–87
parousia, delay of
    acceptance of by Eusebius, 103
    and the "day" of the Lord, scriptural
        references, 93–94n78
    early church responses to, 92–95
    early expectations, 91–92
    and impacts on early Christian
        communities, 95–96
    and loss of Hope, 6
    responses to, 91–94, 93–94n78
    as topic in the New Testament, 92
    See also kin(g)dom of God, kin(g)
        dom of heaven
patriarchy, ideologies supporting, 80
Paul
    circumcision of the heart, 97, 97n86
    on the delay of parousia, 95
    encouragement of early Christians,
        112–13
    goals, 45
    on God's existence in the human
        form, 23–24
    on God's redemptive work, 220
    on making Jesus's life visible, 47
    on the power of Spirit, 115
    on the salvic efficacy of Hope,
        161–62
    on suffering with Christ and
        redemption, 113–14
Pedagogy of the Oppressed (Freire), 70
People's Crusade, 107
Peter, visionary experience, 96–97,
    96n85, 145–50
Peter the Hermit, 107
Pickney, Clementa, 2
Plessy v. Ferguson (1896), 185
pneumatology, functional, 114
polarities, dualisms. *See* binary/
    bifurcated world views
The Politics of Jesus (Henricks), 98
Post Traumatic Slave Syndrome (Leary),
    178
"The Potters House" (McKay), 10
poverty
    accepting as natural, 34n2, 45, 47,
        54
    and environmental racism, 54–55
    vs. individual prosperity, 46
    and resource distributions, 53–54

poverty *(continued)*
   as sin, reinforcement of through iconic imagery, 75
   viewing as "sin," 75
Powery, Emerson, 114
Prayer Pilgrimage for Freedom, 190n84
preaching
   applying contemplative imagination, 68
   and call to fulfillment/transformation, 150–51
   central task, 139, 142
   and communicating embodied Hope, 8, 13, 162–64
   and communicating transformative values, 138
   and the context of the congregation, 165
   and countering consumerism, 140–41
   disruptive and energizing nature of, 144–46, 220
   and eliminating distortions, 138
   and emotive consciousness, 45
   and empathy, 151–55
   and esteem given to pastors, 79–80
   and living the gospel, 144
   and making *shalom* plain, 217–18
   and manifesting *imago Dei*, 215–16, 219, 222
   and moral imagination, 157–58, 172, 174–75
   power and potential of, 4–5
   and proclaiming Jesus's ministerial vision, 79–80, 145, 171, 173
   realistic/inclusive focus, 139–40
   scholarship related to Hope, 5–6
   sermon preparation, 150–51, 157–61
   and testing the gospel, 137
   and "thick description," 166, 215
   ultimate goal, 144
Pritchett, Laurie, 191–93, 193n105
property, rules governing in Scripture, 128–29
Prophetic Words in Modern Times sermon series, 10
Ps 110, 93n77

Ps 110:4, 92–93, 93n76
Pulse Nightclub, Orlando, FL, 2

Quarterman, Ola Mae, 193

Rachel, 3
racism
   and controlling imagery/myths, 34n2, 82
   entrenchment in US culture, 45, 51–52, 142, 152
   environmental racism, 54–56
   and imagining equality, 64
Randolph, A. Philip, 180n84, 200–204, 201n161
Rasmussen, Larry, 120, 120n19
Reconstruction, 181
redemption
   and the avoidance of sociopolitical responsibility, 9
   human participation in, 111
   and imagination, 67
   Jesus's ministerial vision, 22
   and King's beloved community, 188
   living in anticipation of, 115
   and suffering with Christ, 113–14
   yearning for, 161–64, 169, 173
   See also kin(g)dom of God, kin(g)dom of heaven; parousia, delay of
Reese, Frederick D., 209
relationships
   and dwelling together as *imago Dei*, 23
   and the dynamics of power and privilege, 40–41
   impact of embodied Hope, 20
   life-affirming, as reflection of God within, 24, 28
   limited, impact of habits/habitus on, 18
religious imagination, 68–69
repentance
   as available to all, 97
   and baptism, 117–19
   and care for the good of all, 123
   as the embracing of a new spiritual practice, 121

as manifestation of Hope, 111
misunderstanding of as punitive, 123–24
need for, 121, 124, 146
overcoming obstacles to, 155
as spiritual practice, 122–23
resilience, 56–57
Revives Our Souls Again (Hayes), 175–76
Reynolds, Diamond, 1
Rice, Tamir, 2
Ricoeur, Paul, 17, 66–67, 69
Riggs, Marlon T., 62, 78–79
Rivers, Prince Raney, 10–11
Robinson, Cleveland, 202
Robinson, Jo Ann, 185n54
Roman Empire
    benefits and challenges for early Christians, 97, 99–100
    church and state relationship, 104
Romans, Paul's letter to the
    participating in God's redemptive work, 220
    and the salvic efficacy of Hope, 161–62
Rom 2:29, 97, 97n86
Rom 8, 112–15, 162
Roof, Dylan, 2
Roosevelt, Franklin D., 182–83, 201n161
Rosette, Ashleigh Shelby, 49
royal law, 89–90
Rustin, Bayard, 202

Sabbatical laws, 128–29
sacramental imagination, 68–69
salvation. *See* parousia, delay of; redemption
Samuel Dewitt Proctor Conference, 213
Scanlon, Jennifer, 203
SCLC. *See* Southern Christian Leadership Conference (SCLC)
Scott, John B., 186
Secrest, A. M., 211
Seeing a Color-Blind Future (Williams), 51, 80
Seeing through the Media (Warren), 61, 72–73

Selma, AL, 209, 209n200, 209n205, 210–12
sermons
    "Bearing the Cross" sermon, 168–70
    A Critical Analysis for Preaching (ACAP) tool, 157–61
    "Dare to Dream" sermon, 159–61
    experiential touchstones, 156–57
    "Girl Call the Midwife, I'm About to Give Birth" sermon, 162–64
    "The God Who Will Not Give Up" sermon (Rivers), 10–11
    homiletical values, 150–51
    Jesus's at Nazareth, 129
    "Mercy Suits Our Case" (sermon), 155–56
    preparing, attending to homiletical values, 150–51
    See also preaching
shalom (peace) of God
    and the anticipatory language of Hope, 132–33
    characteristics, 21
    and the desire for wholeness and well-being, 20–21, 116
    and embodied Hope, 112, 132
    global scope of, importance, 36–37
    handling doubt about, 18, 37–39, 47, 52
    importance of imagination, 65, 110–11
    and interconnection with all creation, 222
    and Jesus's ministerial vision, 21, 220
    making plain, through preaching, 217–18
    and valuing diversity, 50
    See also God; *imago Dei*
Sharpton, Al, 213
Shuttlesworth, Fred, 194, 196
Simon Peter. *See* Peter, visionary experience
sin
    and despair, Aquinas on, 29–30, 29n32, 30n39
    mortal sin, 30n41
Sister in the Wilderness (Williams), 126

SNCC. *See* Student Nonviolent Coordinating Committee (SNCC)
Soelle, Dorothee, 45–46, 152, 152n26
"Something Within" (Campbell), 19
soul (*nepesh*), 26
Southern Christian Leadership Conference (SCLC), 188–89, 188–89n78, 212–13
Southern Negro Youth Congress (SNYC), 183–84
spiritual practice
  among African Americans, 176
  and God's vision of *shalom*, 111–12
  and the quality of the relationship with God, 121–22
  repentance as, 122–23
  Ubuntu (full humanity) concept, 176–77
stereotyping
  negative, 34n2, 49–50, 84–85, 178
  role of iconic imagery in reinforcing, 73–75, 78–79
Stevenson, Brian, 181
Stewart, Alexander E., 91, 94–95
"Student Executive Committee for Justice," 189
Student Nonviolent Coordinating Committee (SNCC), 189–91, 189n82
suffering
  and apathy, 45–46
  and culturally induced despair, 31–32
  embodied Hope as counter to, 20
  human perpetuation of through habit, 17
  with Jesus, and *compassio*, 152–53
  normalizing, 39–42, 43–45, 153–54
Suffering (Soelle), 45–46

Taylor, Breonna, 2
Teaching and Religious Imagination (Harris), 68
theology
  and anthropocentric views of creation, 81–82
  of Hope, embodiment of, 7–8, 11, 15–16, 20, 29, 47
  theological/ecclesial distortions, 17–18, 86
  theological virtues, 113n3
  See also communities of faith; *imago Dei*; preaching; *shalom* (peace) of God
Theology of Hope (Moltmann), 6
thick description, 166, 215
At This Time, In This Place: The Spirit Embodied in the Local Assembly (Warren), 16–17
Thomas, Daniel H., 209, 210n205
Thomas, Frank, 172, 174
Thomas Aquinas, 6, 28–30, 29n32, 29n34, 197
Three-Fifths Compromise of 1787, 180
Tillich, Paul, 170–71n49
Tisdale, Leonora Tubbs, 136, 142, 170–71n49
Townes, Emilie, 4, 6, 123, 173
Trump, Donald, 86, 141
Turpin, Katherine, 140, 143–44
Tutu, Desmond, 133

Ubuntu (full humanity) concept, 176–77
United Metropolitan Missionary Baptist Church, Winston-Salem, NC, 2–4, 8–10
Urban II, 107

violence, normalizing, 39–42, 43–45, 123
Virey, J. J., 85n68
Virginia General Assembly
  definition of slavery, 1662, 179–80, 179n23
  determination related to baptism and slave status, 86
  redefining slaves as real estate, 1705, 180, 180n26
Voting Rights Act, 1965, 212, 212n223
Vreeland, Derek, 38

Walker, Wyatt, 197–98
Wallace, George, 199, 201, 212
Warren, Michael

on the mimetic nature of icons/
  media, 40, 74, 74n40, 84
on the relationship of habitat and
  habitus, 16–17
on viewing media critically, 61,
  72–73
"We Demand Our Rights" (Hughes),
  183–84
Weil, Simone, 35–36n4
Wells, Samuel B., 193
Wesley Theological Seminary
  "Bearing the Cross" sermon, 168–71
  Community Engagement Fellows
    Seminar, 46–47
  "Dare to Dream" sermon, 159–61
Westfield, Nancy Lynn, 5, 56–57
white privilege
  constituent cultural elements that
    reinforce, 51–53
  and dehumanizing images of
    African Americans, 78–79
  role of iconic imagery in reinforcing,
    75–76
White privilege/supremacy
  and empathy for the vulnerable and
    deluded, 153–54
  and gospel-opposing norms, 141–42
  ideologies supporting, 80
  and Jim Crow practices, 79, 182, 185
  and non-whites as inferior others,
    83
  policies developed to reinforce,
    181–82
  and the White Christian church, 193
Wilkins, Collie Leroy, 212n222
Wilkins, Roy, 187n67

Williams, Delores S.
  on Jesus's ministerial vision, 21–22,
    144–45n18
  on the kin(g)dom of God as
    metaphor for Hope, 21–22, 112,
    125–26
  on survival as living with Hope,
    56–57
Williams, Hosea, 210
Williams, Patricia J., 16–17, 51, 80, 220
Williams, Raymond, 40
Wimberly, Anne, 115
womanist epistemology/theology, 5–6,
  144–45n18
women
  Black, sexualizing of, 84–85, 85n68
  expressions of Hope, 133
  negative stereotyping, 34n2, 48–50,
    75, 83–85
  ordination of, 65
  and surrogacy oppression, 144n18
Women's March, 214
Women's Political Council, 185–86
Wood, Francis E., 58
World War II, 184

Year of Jubilee, 128–29
Youth March for Integrated Schools,
  180n84
Yudkin, Marjorie, 20–21

Zebulun and Napthali, territories of,
  122, 122n21
Zimmerman, George, 1

Made in the USA
Columbia, SC
07 February 2022